PERU AND PERUVIAN TALES

broadview editions
series editor: L.W. Conolly

Helen Maria Williams, 1792. Stipple etching by Joseph Singleton, after a miniature by Ozias Humphry. © Trustees of the British Museum, London.

PERU AND PERUVIAN TALES

Helen Maria Williams

edited by Paula R. Feldman

Associate Editors:
Catherine England
John Higgins
Glenn Jellenik
Shelley Jones
Clayton Tarr
Carrie Young

broadview editions

Library and Archives Canada Cataloguing in Publication

Williams, Helen Maria, 1762-1827
[Poems. Selections]
    Peru and Peruvian tales / Helen Maria Williams ; edited by Paula R. Feldman ;
associate editors: Catherine England, John Higgins, Glenn Jellenik, Shelley Jones,
Clayton Tarr, Carrie Young.

(Broadview editions)
Includes bibliographical references.
ISBN 978-1-55481-128-1 (pbk.)

    1. Peru—Poetry. I. Feldman, Paula R., editor II. Title. III. Title: Peruvian tales.
IV. Series: Broadview editions

PR3765.W54A6 2014   821'.6   C2014-905996-5

Broadview Editions

The Broadview Editions series represents the ever-changing canon of literature in English by bringing together texts long regarded as classics with valuable lesser-known works.

Advisory editor for this volume: Juliet Sutcliffe

Broadview Press is an independent, international publishing house, incorporated in 1985.

We welcome comments and suggestions regarding any aspect of our publications—please feel free to contact us at the addresses below or at broadview@broadviewpress.com.

North America
PO Box 1243, Peterborough, Ontario K9J 7H5, Canada
555 Riverwalk Parkway, Tonawanda, NY 14150, USA
Tel: (705) 743-8990; Fax: (705) 743-8353
email: customerservice@broadviewpress.com

UK, Europe, Central Asia, Middle East, Africa, India, and Southeast Asia
Eurospan Group, 3 Henrietta St., London WC2E 8LU, United Kingdom
Tel: 44 (0) 1767 604972; Fax: 44 (0) 1767 601640
email: eurospan@turpin-distribution.com

Australia and New Zealand
NewSouth Books
c/o TL Distribution, 15-23 Helles Ave., Moorebank, NSW 2170, Australia
Tel: (02) 8778 9999; Fax: (02) 8778 9944
email: orders@tldistribution.com.au

www.broadviewpress.com

Broadview Press acknowledges the financial support of the Government of Canada through the Canada Book Fund for our publishing activities.

Typesetting and assembly: True to Type Inc., Claremont, Canada.

PRINTED IN CANADA

Contents

Illustrations

Acknowledgements

We would like to express our warm thanks to Jessica Damián, Joel Myerson, David Shields, and Laura Walls—scholars who assisted us, not just through their published works but through their advice and conversation. Their generosity and knowledge have made this a better book than it might otherwise have been. We are grateful, as well, to Peter Mugglestone, the creator of software which aided us in our collaboration.

Our sincere thanks also go to William Rivers, Mary Anne Fitzpatrick, and Tim Mousseau, who believed in this project and made possible the crucial financial support it received from the Department of English and the College of Arts and Sciences at the University of South Carolina. We are grateful to the staffs of the British Library, Cornell University Library, and the Thomas Cooper Library, University of South Carolina. For permission to publish the portrait of Helen Maria Williams engraved by Ozias Humphrey in 1792, we are grateful to the Trustees of the British Museum, London. For all other illustrations, we wish to thank a private collector, who wishes to remain anonymous. Cathy Jellenik kindly translated for us passages in French by de Graffigny. Thanks also go to Ellen Brightwell, and to our summer research assistant, Matthew Starke. Finally, it has been a pleasure to work with the editors and staff at Broadview Press, including Marjorie Mather, Tara Lowes, Juliet Sutcliffe, and Leonard Conolly.

Introduction

Helen Maria Williams's epic poem *Peru*, first published in 1784, movingly recounts the story of Pizarro's brutal conquest and exploitation of the Incas and their subsequent revolt against Spain. Williams has long been recognized by historians as the most important contemporary British chronicler of the French Revolution, but it is less well known that she was a major poet, who saw *Peru* as a centerpiece of her career. Like William Wordsworth, who revised *The Prelude* over the course of his life, Williams revisited her epic several times within almost four decades, transforming it with each revision. It began as an ambitious poetic blueprint for revolution—in terms of politics, gender, religion, and genre. By the time it appeared in 1823, under the title "Peruvian Tales" in her last collection, *Poems on Various Subjects*, Williams's voice had become more moderate, more restrained; in her words, her muse had become "timid," reflecting the cultural shift that had taken place in England since the poem's earliest publication. This present volume is the first scholarly edition of Williams's landmark epic; its textual history documents the birth and evolution of Romanticism.

Peru is a virtuoso performance, still extremely readable today. Williams constructs an exotic, lush landscape with a serene native people, as she cinematically pans from jungle scenes to battle fields to the heights of the frozen Andes. When Pizarro and his Spanish forces arrive, motivated by greed for gold and religious fanaticism, they shatter an idyllic community in harmony with the natural world, plunging the Incas from their prelapsarian innocence into a chaos of conflict and bloodshed. The Inca leader, Ataliba,[1] nobly faces the onslaught of Pizarro and his overwhelming colonial forces, while lovers, parents, and brothers struggle against the unthinkable destruction of an entire culture and way of life. In six vignette-style cantos, Williams structures the action through a series of ill-fated love stories that explore the limits of spiritual and bodily passion. *Peru* is a captivating and tragic narrative that portrays violent clashes between true faith

---

1   Williams loosely bases the character of Ataliba on the historical figure of Atahuallpa (1502-33). See p. 53, note 2.

and zealotry; charity and materialistic greed; and new-world American and old-world European ideals.

The poem relies on contemporary histories, particularly William Robertson's popular *History of America* (1777) and Abbé Raynal's *Histoire philosophique et politique* (1770), as well as on fictional accounts, including Françoise de Graffigny's *Lettres d'une Péruvienne* (1747) and Jean-François Marmontel's *Les Incas* (1777),[1] to draw a sharp contrast between the public sphere of history and the private sphere of what Williams calls the "romantic story."[2] *Peru* offers an extended meditation on the human and moral costs of the colonial venture, one that amounts to a scathing, and surprisingly early, post-colonial critique. Williams focuses her historical/poetic narrative on a set of marginal characters—the women and poets of lost Peruvia. In the process of revising her poem over the course of her poetic career, she transformed it from an ambitious epic to a collection of proto-feminist tales. Williams explored the narrative possibilities of a poetic history, and reading *Peru* in its successive stages complicates our understanding of eighteenth-century notions of colonialism, gender politics, war, religion, and the public/private sphere.

Written in elegant and seemingly effortless heroic couplets, our 1786 copy text is the work of a poet at the height of her powers. This ambitious and yet unusually accessible epic poem conjures a vision of an Edenic landscape and civilization in the mode of *Paradise Lost*. Yet Williams's work is original—and unprecedented—in its seamless blending of historical narrative with an imaginative and self-reflective verse. Haunted throughout by death and inevitability, by prophecy and foreboding, the epic includes a chorus of passionate soliloquies by compelling, multidimensional female characters. It draws readers into a poetic space "Where fancy glows with all her native fire" (V: 7).

Williams's major revisions between her epic's 1784 and 1786 publications—the heightening of language, finer modulation of emotion, and tightening of syntax and rhythm—reflect a poet in full command of her craft. Yet the poem's power lies beyond mere technical proficiency. As she writes in her 1786 "Advertisement," *Peru* dramatizes "the unparalleled sufferings of an innocent and

---

1 Short extracts from each of these works are printed in Appendix B, pp. 179-212.

2 See the "Advertisement" to *Poems* (1786), p. 49 in this edition.

amiable people, [which] form the most affecting subjects of true pathos." Indeed, the poem's transformative and inspirational power comes from sustained dramatic tension, for the Incas, ennobled by fine feeling, are painfully aware of the apocalyptic tragedy that is befalling them. Williams's *tour de force* remains as stirring a call for freedom today as it was in its own time.

The poem's aesthetic and political shifts reflect the fact that the nearly forty-year span between Williams's first and final versions of *Peru* witnessed fundamental changes not only in genre but also in the economics of publication. Williams originally published the poem by subscription, during a period that saw the last vestiges of literary patronage disappearing. By 1823, the dynamics of the literary marketplace had largely done away with subscription publishing in favor of the modern model of commercial publication, with publishers functioning as venture capitalists. This poem offers an intriguing case study, for the author's revisions give readers a glimpse not only into the changing mind of the poet but also into the process of poetic composition as it responds to an altered literary marketplace and the demands of a popular audience. Moreover, the history of this single text serves as a history of Romanticism itself. Readers can trace the aesthetic—and, by extension, philosophical and cultural—arc of the period. The poem depicts a world shaken by earthquake and revolution. In its very instability, this text maneuvers through the radical period of the late eighteenth century into a more cautious and conservative nineteenth century. *Peru* reveals the dilemmas of an ever-broadening world, just as we hope this edition will help readers today rethink the borders of Romanticism.

Helen Maria Williams in Her Time

Williams was a highly respected figure at the center of literary and social culture in both England and France.[1] Indeed, the subscription list for the 1786 volume that contained the revised text of *Peru* reads like a *Who's Who* of late eighteenth-century writers and

---

1 Williams is now commanding increased attention. Of particular importance are Deborah Kennedy's valuable monograph, *Helen Maria Williams and the Age of Revolution* (Bucknell Studies in Eighteenth-Century Literature and Culture, 2002), which informs this biographical sketch, and Neil Fraistat's and Susan Lanser's paperback edition of her *Letters Written in France* (Broadview Literary Texts, 2001).

Letter (c. 1791) in the hand of Helen Maria Williams to Robin Lawless, chief assistant to her publisher, Thomas Cadell, concerning the distribution of *Poems* and *A Farewell, for Two Years, to England*. Private collection.

thinkers, and includes, among many others, Elizabeth Montagu, Horace Walpole, Samuel Richardson, David Hume, William Hayley, Charlotte Smith, Joanna Baillie, and the Duke and Duchess of Devonshire. In much the same way as Williams's *Letters from France* served as a bridge across the English Channel, her Paris salons brought together influential expatriates from across the globe. William Wordsworth's first published poem was a tribute to her: "Sonnet, on Seeing Miss Helen Maria Williams Weep at a Tale of Distress."[1] In 1791, when he traveled to Paris, he carried a letter of introduction to Williams written by Charlotte Smith. But he did not actually meet her for three decades—in the early fall of 1820. When she republished "To Hope" in 1823,

1 He published it under the pen name "Axiologus" in *The European Magazine, and London Review* in 1787 (see Appendix C6, p. 218). The description was purely imaginary, for the young Wordsworth had not yet met Williams.

Williams proudly reported in a note that Wordsworth had recited the sonnet to her "from memory, after a lapse of many years."[1]

Like Wordsworth, Williams's origins were middle class, and her childhood was deeply affected by the loss of a parent. The author of *Peru* was born in London on 17 June 1761 to Charles and Helen Williams. Just over a year later, her father died and her mother moved the family north to Berwick-upon-Tweed. There Williams spent most of her childhood, absorbing the culture of the Anglo-Scottish border. She was better read than she later admitted, for her mother had the economic resources to educate her children and to provide them with a practical library.

The family moved back to London in 1781, where Williams, now a young woman, got to know Andrew Kippis, Anna Letitia Barbauld, Hester Lynch Piozzi, William Godwin, and others among the city's intellectual elite. Williams lived with her family at the first house in Southampton Row, Bloomsbury, not far from where Virginia Woolf would reside more than a century later.[2]

By 1782, Williams had met William Hayley (later William Blake's patron), Thomas Warton (named Poet Laureate in 1785), and Warton's older brother, Joseph. The latter wrote two short poems, "The Revenge of America" and "The Dying Indian," both of which probably contributed to Williams's interest in the Spanish conquest of Peru.[3] But Williams's friendship with Hayley may have proved most influential to her formal conception of *Peru*.

Williams began writing *Peru* no later than 1782—just months after moving back to London. She was only twenty-one. Although she gained attention from her earlier poetic works, *Edwin and Eltruda* (1782) and *An Ode on the Peace* (1783), Williams's celebrity was confirmed when *Peru* was published by Thomas Cadell.[4]

---

1 *Poems on Various Subjects* (1823), p. 203.
2 Clayden 68.
3 Williams would later include a translation of "Dulce Domum" at the request of Joseph Warton in her *Poems on Various Subjects* (1823). John Dryden's play *The Indian Queen* (1664), written in collaboration with Sir Robert Howard, is another possible influence. The play concerns the courts of Mexico and Peru just before the Spanish invasion.
4 In his advertisement of 19 volumes "lately published," tipped into the Bodleian Library copy of Elizabeth Keir's *Interesting Memoirs* (1785), Thomas Cadell lists *Peru* (1784) second, just behind William Hayley's six-volume *Poems and Plays*. When the firm published Charlotte Smith's *Ethelinde, or the Recluse of the Lake* (1789), an advertisement for both Williams's *Poems* (1786) and *Peru* appeared immediately following three works by Hannah More.

Reviews were enthusiastic.[1] *The Critical Review* said that *Peru* displayed "that warmth of imagination, that harmony of numbers, and that energy of expression, which distinguish the genuine poet from the mere coupler of rhymes."[2] *The New Annual Register* described Williams as "a truly poetic genius."[3] A laudatory poem signed "Eliza" and titled "To Miss Helen Maria Williams: On her Poem of *Peru*" appeared in *The Gentleman's Magazine* for July 1784,[4] and Anna Seward's "Sonnet to Miss Williams on her Epic Poem, *Peru*" appeared in the *Gentleman's Magazine* in August 1784.[5]

At the pinnacle of her London celebrity, Williams left England for France, where she became a respected translator and the best known British chronicler of the French Revolution. She would eventually publish eight volumes of letters, today known collectively as *Letters from France* (1790-96).[6] As in London, her salon in Paris became the meeting place of the city's intelligentsia. She entertained such visitors as Thomas Paine, Maria Edgeworth, Robert Southey, Amelia Opie, and Mary Wollstonecraft, who wrote of her first meeting with Williams in Paris:

> Miss Williams has behaved very civilly to me and I shall visit her frequently, because I *rather* like her, and I meet French company at her house. Her manners are affected, yet the *simple* goodness of her heart continually breaks through the varnish, so that one would be more inclined, at least I should, to love than admire her.—Authorship is a heavy weight for female shoulders especially in the sunshine of prosperity.[7]

In Paris, Williams met the Venezuelan, Francisco de Miranda (1750-1816), a political leader of freedom movements in Latin

---

1 A range of reviews are printed in Appendix D, pp. 219-35.

2 See Appendix D2, p. 221.

3 See Appendix D1, pp. 219-21.

4 See Appendix C2, pp. 214-15.

5 See Appendix C1, pp. 213-14. Williams revised *Peru* and included it in her 1786 collection, which contains a stunning list of more than 1500 subscribers.

6 For more information about the publication history, see Neil Fraistat's and Susan S. Lanser's edition.

7 To her sister, Everina Wollstonecraft, dated 24 December 1792 (Wardle 225-26). Godwin states in Wollstonecraft's *Memoirs* that she shared a "sincere friendship" with Williams, whom he calls the author of "poems of uncommon merit" (102).

America and a participant in the American and French Revolutions. Williams admired Miranda for his talents as a general, orator, and literary critic and defended him against charges of conspiracy against the French government.[1]

In the midst of the Terror, Williams and her family were imprisoned for six weeks, during which time she worked on her translation of Bernardin de Saint-Pierre's *Paul et Virginie*, incorporating into the narrative eight exquisite sonnets of her own. After her release in late 1793, she traveled to Switzerland, accompanied by the recently divorced British radical political reformer John Hurford Stone. Rumors that they were lovers, along with her continued defense of revolutionary ideals, caused derision in England. Hester Lynch Piozzi cattily quipped: "The Rival Wits say that Helena Williams is turned to *Stone*."[2] Two years later, Piozzi reported: "Helen Williams is given up here by her most steady Adherents."[3]

Williams and Stone ran a small publishing house for almost ten years until they were forced to declare bankruptcy, which, as Nigel Leask argues, was "induced by the exorbitant costs" of publishing Alexander von Humboldt's works; these they brought out first in French and later Williams translated them into English.[4] Humboldt admired Williams's "eloquent pen."[5]

Stone died in 1818. In 1823, after a hiatus of almost twenty years, Williams published a substantially altered version of *Peru* entitled "Peruvian Tales." Her last publication was *Souvenirs de la*

---

1 See Robertson *Life*, I: 1, 136; II: 238-39. Although Miranda was acquitted in 1793, Robespierre's hatred of him eventually landed him in jail (I: 136, 142). Soon after his imprisonment in 1795, he was allowed to visit Williams on the condition that he remain under police surveillance, a favor that Williams thought indicative of their strong friendship (I: 154). Unfortunately, by the end of the evening, the friendship was over. While gendarmes knocked on Williams's door after dinner, Miranda slipped out of the house through a back entrance, leaving his hostess embarrassed and without explanation for his conduct (Racine 133). Subsequent to this event, Williams's house was under surveillance for weeks, an imposition that she could not forgive Miranda for having caused (Thorning 132).

2 Dated 17 February 1795 (Piozzi II: 239-40).

3 Dated 26 April 1797 (Piozzi II: 422).

4 Leask 221.

5 Kennedy 185. For more on Humboldt, see Laura Dassow Walls, *The Passage to Cosmos*; for more on Williams, Humboldt, and the influence of Humboldt's *Personal Narrative* on Charles Darwin, see Kennedy 184-87.

Helen Maria Williams, 1816. Stipple engraving, published 1 February 1816 by Dean & Munday, after an unknown artist. Private collection.

Révolution Française (1827), translated by her nephew, Charles Coquerel. Williams died in Paris on 15 December 1827 and was buried next to her mother and John Hurford Stone in Père Lachaise Cemetery.

Genre

Peru is a grand narrative that defines a nation and includes such traditional, epic elements as battles, warriors, moving speeches, dangerous journeys, and supernatural interventions. The quality and cultural importance of *Peru* calls into question the assumption that *Paradise Lost* is the last, great English epic.[1] In *An Essay on Epic Poetry* (1782), William Hayley called for writers to return to the epic, a call that Williams answered, even though many of her most ambitious contemporaries failed to do so.[2] While there was a popular tradition of writing mock-epics in the years after the publication of *Paradise Lost*, Williams succeeded at the epic without resorting either to slavish imitation of Milton or to comic parody of ancient conventions.[3]

From the first lines of her epic, written in six cantos of heroic couplets, rather than Milton's twelve books of blank verse, Williams situates "lost Peruvia" in relation to Milton's Eden (I: 3) and alludes to *Paradise Lost* when comparing Valverde's "impious crest" to that of Milton's Satan (III: 123; *PL* IV: 988-89 and VI: 188). Peruvians are not driven by God out of their Paradise after having sinned but, rather, are innocents expelled by the greedy Spanish. In the eleventh book of *Paradise Lost*, Adam sits upon a high hill and catalogues the world's kingdoms, but he sees Peru only "in spirit perhaps" (*PL* XI: 406). Indeed, he gazes upon "Cusco in Peru, the richer seat / Of Atabalipa, and yet unspoil'd" (XI: 408-09). Williams takes up Milton's tentative vision, expanding and dramatizing the happenings on the other side of the globe.

Not only does *Peru* build upon the legacy of Milton, but it also engages with classical epics. In its concerns with warfare and imperialism, it bears similarities to Homer's *Iliad* and Virgil's *Aeneid*. Homer occasionally allows the focus to turn from martial adventures and masculine exploits to the domestic and the feminine; Williams creates domestic scenes that evoke her Greek predecessor but are far more intimate. Manco Cápac's farewell to his wife Cora and their son in Canto IV of *Peru* directly parallels Hector's bidding farewell to Andromache and their son Astyanax. In both, the men anticipate death upon the battlefield, and the mothers fear their sons will not live until adulthood. While it is Andromache who cries and clings to Hector (VI: 425-26), Cápac's and Cora's tears are "mutual" (IV: 78). Unlike Andromache, who

---

1   Herbert F. Tucker also questions this notion by arguing that the Romantic and Victorian periods consistently produced works of epic scope (1).

2   See Dustin Griffin's "Milton and the Decline of the Epic in the Eighteenth Century" for a discussion of why poets wrote fewer epics in Milton's wake.

3   The best known of the mock epics include Pope's *Rape of the Lock* (1714) and Lord Byron's *Don Juan* (1819-24).

only feels the pain of parting, Williams's Cora asks to share in Cápac's misery:

Still let me feel the pressure of thy chain,
Still share the fetters which my love detain;
Those piercing irons to my soul are dear,
....
This breast can bear the pain thy dangers give
(IV; 81-83, 86)

Williams stresses Cora's strength and her willingness to participate in the misery of her warrior husband—and, through him, the nation. For Williams, women experience the pain of warfare not only through post-war enslavement, which is Andromache's fate, but also during and throughout the conquest, because their concerns are inextricably linked to the nation's welfare.

Alan Richardson calls *Peru* a "domestic revision of epic heroism," which he sees as a response to the imperial focus of the Virgilian epic. In fact, Williams's revision is both domestic and intensely feminine in its resistance to the aggressive imperialism of the *Aeneid*. Suicidal Incas have more in common with "the archetypal epic loser" Dido than Aeneas, and Williams's constant focus on the misery caused by conquest prevents any romanticizing of imperial violence.[1] Her epic envisions a more humane focus for the ancient, and often bloodthirsty, genre.

By the time Williams published her last revision of *Peru* in 1823, the most popular genre in Britain had become the tale. Retitled "Peruvian Tales," the poem appeared in a volume published by the commercial firm of G. and W.B. Whittaker, without the support of subscribers. The generic category of "tale" was, at this period, applied to many disparate sorts of texts, and Williams took advantage of this generic flexibility and exploited current literary tastes when she transformed *Peru* from an epic into a collection of tales.[2]

---

1 Richardson 269, 266, 270, 271.
2 In the "Introduction" to *Poems on Various Subjects* (1823), Williams asserts that the title of her epic, *Peru*, "seemed to promise far more than it performed" and that she thought it more appropriate to change the poem's form to that of a collection of tales, which she chooses not to "dignify ... with the appellation of historical, although they are chiefly composed of facts taken from Robertson's History" (x). The cantos, newly realized as tales, have been "corrected with care" and shortened.

Her proto-feminist tales endow female characters with greater prominence than they had in her earlier narrative. Indeed, each of the tales is named after a heroic woman: Alzira, Zilia, Cora, and Aciloe. Yet the poetry within each tale does not emphasize the titular heroine any more than had the cantos of her epic. In Williams's generic shift, despite her newly re-titled cantos, the six tales function no more independently than they had in their earlier incarnations.

Additionally, her more moderate, restrained voice suited a British reading public that had cooled toward revolution. Herbert F. Tucker writes of a "sadder but wiser phase of Romanticism" that is interested in how the epic "might be revised and made good"; following Walter Scott's example, tales during this period attempted to treat the culture's chronic conditions, rather than resolve its troubles definitively.[1]

Having witnessed over the course of her life the restoration of the House of Bourbon to the French throne as well as Peru's halting march toward liberation, Williams tamed the ambitious claims of her early revolutionary spirit and excised important passages concerning the function of the poet in society, all while continuing to foreground the role of women and the impact of political events on the domestic sphere. Williams's choice to rewrite *Peru* as "Peruvian Tales" reveals her marketing savvy and adaptability to a changing literary and political landscape.

Historical and Literary Sources

Williams cites two hugely popular works of history in her notes to *Peru*: Abbé Raynal's *A Philosophical and Political History of the Settlements and Trade of the Europeans in the East and West Indies* (1777) and William Robertson's *The History of America* (1777). These works provided her with more than simply a chronicle of events within which to set her epic. They offered philosophical frameworks that challenged intellectual and political power structures with their revolutionary humanism. Within their pages,

---

Notable tales by other authors from this period include Mary Robinson's *Lyrical Tales* (1800), Robert Southey's *Thalaba* (1801), Lord Byron's *Oriental Tales* (1813-18), Thomas Moore's *Lalla Rookh* (1815), and the immensely popular *Tales of Terror* published in the 1820s in *Blackwood's Edinburgh Magazine*. For more on the genre of the tale, see Anthony Jarrells.

1 Tucker 11.

Peru became a case study in civilization, empire, commerce, class, and freedom.

Originally published in 1770 as *L'Histoire philosophique et politique des établissements et du commerce des Européens dans les deux Indes*, Raynal's book ultimately saw thirty-eight editions in French, eighteen in English, and five in other languages.[1] Abolitionist and democratic, the work was deeply critical of the Catholic Church and of imperialism, advocating for revolution against all forms of tyranny. It was not only widely read, but was a major influence on such authors as William Robertson and Edward Gibbon. The book was banned in France in 1779 and burned in public displays.

Raynal championed Jean-Jacques Rousseau's "noble savage," an idealized notion of perfection enjoyed by uncivilized peoples living in harmony with nature. William Womack argues that Raynal "consistently depicts the European explorer-conqueror as a satan arriving unexpected and unwanted in the noble savage's paradise."[2] Raynal portrays pre-conquest Peruvians as largely determined by the languid climate of the torrid zone; they live in peace and harmony, existing in a state of freedom and enjoying equality. Raynal's depiction influenced Williams's portrayal of the Edenic bliss of Peru disrupted by Christianity.

Raynal's discussion of Peru ranges far beyond history, including more about the natural history of the country than about its conquest. Williams drew heavily upon Raynal's natural and cultural histories (in the universalizing impulse of Romantic-era science that would see its fullest realization in Alexander von Humboldt's 1845-47 *Cosmos*), footnoting passages from Raynal to document her portrayal of local festivals and llamas.[3] She also drew heavily from his descriptions of the Peruvian countryside and natural events, especially earthquakes. She sympathized both with Raynal's philosophical ideals of freedom and revolution and with his idealization of the "artless" and "innocent" Indians of Peru, children of nature whose nobility is crushed by the fanaticism and greed of "civilized" Europe.

Williams drew her history from the Scottish author, William Robertson, who offers a detailed account of the conquest of Peru. Less well known than fellow Scottish Enlightenment historians Edward Gibbon and David Hume, Robertson was highly influ-

---

1 Irvine 576-77.

2 Womack 99.

3 Although Williams later translated many works from the French, she draws her quotations of Raynal from Justamond's English translation.

ential in the late eighteenth century, and his *History of America* was considered the standard work on the subject. His philosophical history expanded the traditional narrative form to a larger project, like that of Raynal and Humboldt, aimed at a study of culture, science, and the arts, to illuminate the progress of human history.

Robertson's character-driven history is told primarily from the "civilized" perspective of the Spanish conquistadors, but his take on the Spanish is far from flattering. For example, Robertson describes Francisco Pizarro as a gentleman's bastard son, a hog farmer turned soldier, and an adventurer. For Robertson, Pizarro is both an able commander and a guileful illiterate, selfishly seeking independent fortune and power.[1]

While Williams's chronology follows that of Robertson, she omits an important fact, one clearly elaborated upon by both Robertson and Raynal. When Pizarro arrived in Peru, the noble and harmonious Incas were actually in a state of civil war. The twelfth Inca monarch had divided his kingdom between his eldest son, the pure-blood Inca Huascar, and his mixed-blood son, Atahuallpa.[2] Atahuallpa captured his eldest brother and began a campaign to exterminate the royal bloodline and cement his position as ruler. Williams collapses Inca rulers into the single, idealized figure of Ataliba, defending a united Peru against Spanish barbarism.

Williams also drew from a third major source, but this one more fictionalized—Jean François Marmontel's *Les Incas, ou la destruction de l'empire du Pérou*. Originally published in 1777, Marmontel's immensely popular book was translated into English the same year it appeared in France and was read throughout Europe. This historical novel drew upon both history and philosophy. Marmontel himself struggled to categorize it:

> There is too much truth in it for a mere Romance, at the same time there is too much fiction to admit of its being stiled a History.... It is therefore not so properly a mere fable, as a kind of narrative, of which the ground-work is all along historical, interspersed only with a few such fictions as are not inconsistent with those parts of it that are true.[3]

---

1 Robertson *History*, 148-49.
2 In Robertson, "Atalipa" is spelled "Atahualpa" and in Raynal, "Atabalipa."
3 Marmontel I: xxxi.

As much as it is a melodramatic tragedy, *Les Incas* is an abolitionist work and an indictment of Catholic fanaticism, which Marmontel termed "the cause of all these horrors at which nature stands aghast."[1] Like Raynal and Robertson, Marmontel embodies zealous religious intolerance in the character of the priest, Valverde. He also idealizes the Peruvian Indians and their society, arguing that his "business was to represent doves on one side, and vultures on the other."[2]

From *Les Incas*, Williams took the spelling of "Ataliba" and may have borrowed the characters of Cora, Zorai, and Aciloe, although her plot bears little resemblance to Marmontel's.[3] Like Marmontel, she places the historical figure Las Casas in Peru, a country he never actually visited. Williams's Peruvians, like Marmontel's, speak in an elevated, quasi-Biblical language, while the Spaniards do not. Just as Williams equates liberty and true religion with nature, Marmontel's Las Casas argues that "charity, equality, the natural and sacred right of liberty, all subsist: and throughout the whole surface of the globe, Faith, harmonizing with Nature, offers to a Christian eye nothing but friends and brethren."[4] Finally, Marmontel, unlike Raynal and Robertson, prominently features female characters, and these characters often share the same strength of will, passion, nobility, and even arms, as the men.

Williams did not slavishly draw from these sources. She departs from all three in the initial meeting of Pizarro and Ataliba, an event that is reported nearly identically in Raynal, Robertson, and Marmontel, where it serves as the climax of *Les Incas*. Ataliba, reluctant to take arms against superior forces that are predicted to bring about the fall of the Inca empire, approaches the meeting willing to listen to Pizarro.[5] Valverde,

---

1 Ibid I: xxi.

2 Ibid I: xxxiii. Marmontel claims that he is not "partial" to the Indians, acknowledging them to be "in general weak in mind as well as body," though that weakness comes as a result of the vicissitudes of the climate of the New World (I: xxxii).

3 Williams likely borrowed the name "Zilia" from Françoise de Graffigny's wildly popular *Lettres d'une Péruvienne* (1747), a text that also parallels *Peru* and "Peruvian Tales" in its philosophical exploration of the concept of the "noble savage," bold interrogation of its contemporary society's treatment of women, stark indictment of imperialism, and complex depictions of Christianity and conversion.

4 Marmontel I: 115.

5 In Marmontel, he is even convinced by the noble Pizarro to convert to Christianity (II: 231-37).

however, launches into a didactic harangue of Christian dogmatic law, demanding that Ataliba submit to the Spanish emperor, because Peru had been given to Spain under the authority of the Pope. Ataliba asks by what authority Valverde makes his demand.[1] Valverde hands him a Bible or breviary, which Ataliba holds to his ear, declares to be silent, and, depending upon the source, either throws or drops to the ground. Such perceived sacrilege brings Valverde to shout for vengeance, and Spanish troops, eager for Inca gold, slaughter Ataliba's court and soldiers.[2] In Williams's *Peru*, however, Pizarro's words "charm with eloquence the simple heart" of Ataliba. The Peruvian monarch, "thrill'd with awe" when handed the Bible, trembles so much that he drops it (II: 1-24). Pizarro's army attacks en masse at seeing the Bible drop.[3] In Williams's account, the villainous Valverde is not present at this event and only enters the poem later, in Canto III.

As her treatment of this key event suggests, Williams builds her epic from elements of all three of these major influences, but *Peru* is its own work, blending philosophies, events, and characters into a richly metaphorical poem. From Raynal, she takes landscape description and natural history, as well as a prelapsarian, Edenic setting. From Robertson's "philosophical" history, she draws an historical chronology, novelistic characters, and a passion-driven, blood-soaked plot of greed, revenge, barbarity, and betrayal. From Marmontel she draws romance, passion, characters, and a message of religious tolerance. Yet, in the end, Williams's *Peru* stands on its own as an eloquent and original voice in the late-eighteenth-century conversation about liberty, revolution, and competing civilizations.

Revisions

When *Peru* was first published in 1784, its language was boldly revolutionary. In 1786, Williams refined the language of the poem, tightening tropes, while maintaining and often emphasizing the passion and themes of the original work. An example of Williams's refinement of language between these two editions can be found at the end of Canto I, which concludes with the Genius

---

1 In Raynal and Marmontel, Ataliba retorts that the Pope must be "a very extraordinary man" (Raynal) or "an egregious fool" (Marmontel) to give away what does not belong to him.
2 Raynal II: 477-78; Robertson II: 174-76; Marmontel II: 237-39.
3 In an historical footnote, Williams quotes Robertson, who attributes the attack order to Pizarro.

of Peru witnessing the arrival of the Spanish and foreseeing the tragic events to come. Williams skillfully combined two lines from her 1784 text—"Each gentle Virtue fled the tainted Shore" and "Each sweet Affection, and each moral Grace"—to create one line in 1786: "Each sweet affection fled the tainted shore" (181). She then shifted the excised notion of "Virtue" to the final line of Canto I: "And virtue wander'd, to return no more." This powerful and direct declaration replaced the less memorable line: "While heaps of treasur'd Ore entomb Delight." Such a revision strengthened the finality of the events that took place in Peru, suggesting that the deeds of the Spanish, as well as other European imperialists, will lead to the loss of virtue on European shores—a loss that cannot be rectified. Similar refinements of language appear in each of the six cantos, making Williams's revolutionary message, as well as the overall aesthetic impact of the poem, more powerful.

Between the two editions, Williams also re-enforced the trope of rape. Peru becomes a metaphorical human body, her land forcefully taken and defiled. Williams intensified this trope in Canto II: "unsheath'd Sabres flash a gleamy ray" became the more suggestive and unambiguous "naked sabres flash their streaming ray" (28).

Similarly, Williams strengthened the parent/child trope used throughout the poem. For example, in Canto IV, she altered "the glowing Orb that gives the day" to "his parent orb, that gives the day" (43). The substitution of "parent" for "glowing" makes more explicit her allusion to the Inca myth of *Inti*, the sun God or "parent orb," linked both to gold and to the birth of the Inca leader.

Williams's revisions between 1784 and 1786 mark an overall tightening of language and tropes without the loss of revolutionary fervor and emotional appeal; those made between 1786 and 1823, however, profoundly modify the poem, which became significantly shorter as Williams shifted genre from epic to tale. In 1823, Williams explained that *Peru* as a title "although vague, seemed to promise far more than it performed. I have now adopted what appears to me a more appropriate denomination, that of *Peruvian Tales in Verse*" (x). The increasing popularity of tales in the early nineteenth century may have offered Williams a financial motive. "Tales" was published as part of a volume entitled *Poems on Various Subjects. With Introductory Remarks on the Present State of Science and Literature in France*. Each canto became an individual tale, titled with the name of its female heroine: "Alzira," (Tales I and II); "Zilia" (Tale III); "Cora" (Tales IV and VI); and "Aciloe" (Tale V).

Also in 1823, Williams removed the important final section of Canto V, described in the "Argument" as "A reflection on the influence of Poetry over the human mind." Curiously, in the "Introduction" to *Poems on Various Subjects* (1823), Williams states that it is her "particular purpose at present to plead the cause of the Poets" (xvi), yet she removed a substantial portion of the poem that was originally intended to do just that:

> [Poetry] Can bid the stormy passions backward roll,
> And o'er their low-hung tempests lift the soul;
> With magic touch paint nature's various scene
> Wild on the mountain, in the vale serene:
> Can tinge the breathing rose with brighter bloom,
> Or hang the sombrous rock in deeper gloom;
> Explore the gem, whose pure, reflected ray
> Throws o'er the central cave a paler day;
> Or soaring view the comet's fiery frame
> Rush o'er the sky, and fold the sphere in flame;
> While the charm'd spirit, as her accents move,
> Is wrapt in wonder, or dissolv'd in love. (327-38)

Perhaps it was an oversight that she did not also delete the description of this key section from the "Argument." Williams's excision of these poetic lines illustrates the shift in her view of the role of poetry within the increasingly conservative and violent political sphere. "Peruvian Tales" also shows a remarkable decrease in the political fervor that had imbued *Peru* with such passion, reflecting Williams's tempered vision after having witnessed the complexities of revolution.

Significantly, Williams also altered an important note in Canto VI, which refers to the Andean Rebellion. In the 1784, 1786, and 1791 texts, she writes, "An Indian descended from the Incas, has lately obtained several victories over the Spaniards, the gold mines have been for some time shut up; and there is much reason to hope, that these injured nations may recover the liberty of which they have been so cruelly deprived." But in 1823, the note reads:

> A descendant of the Incas has there reared the feathered
> standard, and obtained some victories over the Spaniards;
> the gold-mines were shut up, and the sound of independence
> was heard; but independence and hope soon vanished, and it

was reserved for the Bolivars of other days to avenge the wrongs of the Peruvians. It was reserved also for Spain to make at present a noble atonement for the past! She has raised an expiatory altar to Liberty over the dungeons of the Inquisition:—may it never be thrown down! May the Old and New World form henceforth an Holy Alliance! And if liberty be menaced in either, may there always be found a Washington in the New World, and a La Fayette in the Old![1]

By 1823, Williams's footnote reflected her having witnessed Peru's slow march to independence, secured by outside forces. The note moved from celebrating Túpac Amaru II, an indigenous revolutionary, to directly referencing Bolivar, an outsider who brought freedom to a reluctant population. After changing the original verbs to past tense to reflect the failure of the indigenous uprising, Williams added "independence and hope soon vanished." The passive construction "it was reserved for the Bolivars of other days to avenge the wrongs of the Peruvians" contrasts with the active presence of 1786's "injured nations" as the avengers of their own wrongs.

In 1823, Williams also decreased her use of natural imagery, which had been abundant in the earlier editions. Jessica Damián believes that Williams did not want to be complicit in the exploitation of South America by making her natural descriptions appealing.[2] Alexander von Humboldt, whose work Williams translated, penned idyllic descriptions of the landscape, which increased the numbers of Europeans drawn to the wealth and beauty of the continent. In her opening description of Peru in Canto I, Williams combined the following three lines from 1786, "The citron, and the glowing orange spring, / And on the gale a thousand odours fling; / The guava, and the soft ananas bloom" (I: 11-13), to create a single line in 1823: "The Orange, and the rich Ananas bloom" (I: 9). She also changed the following lines from 1786:

There, lost Peruvia, rose thy cultur'd scene,
The wave an emblem of thy joy serene:
There nature ever in luxuriant showers
Pours from her treasures, the perennial flowers; (I: 3-6)

---

1 *Poems on Various Subjects* 82.
2 Damián 25.

to become in 1823: "There, lost Peruvia! bloom'd thy cultur'd bowers, / Thy vallies fragrant with perennial flowers" (I: 3-4). Notably, she removed the word "treasures" from these lines, delaying the introduction of the theme of treasure, both natural and monetary. As Damián points out, by 1823, Williams had witnessed the exploitation of Peru's gold and silver by the capitalist vanguard.

Moreover, in 1823, Williams eliminated much of the language of sensibility and included less natural imagery and fewer descriptions of Peru's "body." She also cut descriptions of the simplicity, innocence, and responsiveness of the Peruvian people. For example, in Canto I, she deleted lines 47-54, which contain the phrases "Mild visitant" and "responsive heart." From Canto IV she cut lines such as, "Oh think not, when in thee alone I live, / This breast can bear the pain thy dangers give" (85-86); "Yet her soul spoke expressive in her eye; / Her lord beholds her grief, with tender pain" (94-95); and "A num'rous host along the plain appear, / And hail their monarch with a gen'rous tear" (99-100). Williams's removal of these lines describing the empathy between two lovers, as well as the empathy between a monarch and his troops, shows a shift that may have been motivated by the same forces as the poem's genre shift—to help sales of the poem in a culture that was increasingly critical of sensibility.

Peru's Early Post-Colonial Critique

Nature functions not simply as a setting but as a central character in *Peru*; it is both protector and refuge. The imagery and controlling metaphors, from birds and flowers to water and storms, are emblems of nature, appropriate for a poem written from the point of view of those living in Edenic harmony with the natural world.[1] In Williams's poetic formulation, wilderness offers freedom, and the "fair clime" of the plains offers safety. Her abolitionist work, *A Poem on the Bill Lately Passed for Regulating the Slave Trade*, similarly connects freedom and nature, urging England to spread its anti-slavery resolution throughout the world: "Teach them to make all nature free" (361). In *Peru,* that freedom is threatened by the conquest of Spaniards, who rape the land and destroy the innocence of the pastoral Peruvians. Nature

---

1 Williams terms this climate "the torrid zone." See her "Sonnet to the Torrid Zone" in *Paul and Virginia* (113).

intercedes for the Peruvians and responds to their opposition to Spanish conquest.

The relationship between the Peruvians and their environment suggests the natural virtue of the people, implicitly undermining the justification for imperialism and colonization. This justification rests on the notion that native peoples are savage and immoral, in need of saving, both spiritually and culturally, and that Christians are responsible for saving the Godless people encountered in foreign lands. Williams counters this notion in *Peru* by establishing the Incas as a moral people who seek their own God in nature, while the Spanish are savages whose behavior epitomizes evil. Williams interrogates various aspects of European society by positing them against the Inca equivalent, thus undermining, in a multidimensional way, the notion of European superiority to native cultures and, through metaphor, advancing her anti-colonial, anti-imperial, and abolitionist ideals.

Still, Williams complicates this dichotomy. In Canto III, for example, she introduces a Spanish priest, Las Casas, who is moral and kind. She also creates moments in the poem in which the Spanish are responsive to heartfelt pleas and recognize the chaos caused by their own behavior. Williams's argument about the moral and cultural superiority of the Inca people is also complicated by the conversion of an unnamed Peruvian priest, and the necessity of an intermediary for the liberation of Peru.

While *Peru* offers a direct critique of colonialism and imperialism, it also speaks to the egalitarian issues of the French Revolution. Williams presents the brutality of the European colonist, while also offering what Meyda Yeğenoğlu describes as a "cultural representation of the West to *itself* by way of a detour through the other."[1] The brutal colonization of Peru and the oppression of the Inca serve as a metaphor for the oppression of the working classes. Williams points out problems, not only in the morality of the colonial venture, but with Eurocentric notions of gender, education, and wealth, as well—systems based in hierarchical structures that benefit the privileged and oppress the poor and marginalized.

Canto I opens with a description of the lush, Edenic landscape of Peru and introduces the character Ataliba, based on the historical figure Atahuallpa. According to historians, Atahuallpa and his brother Huascar fought for the throne after the death from smallpox of their father, Sapa Inca Huayna Cápac. Their battle

---

1 Yeğenoğlu 1.

for royal succession in 1525 led to a brutal civil war in which thousands were killed.[1] While both Robertson and Raynal, the major historical sources that Williams consulted, discuss this civil war, Williams ignores it in her account. *Peru* opens, not on a country that has been war torn, but on an innocent and peaceful scene:

> Where the pacific deep in silence laves
> The western shore, with slow and languid waves,
> There, lost Peruvia, rose thy cultur'd scene,
> The wave an emblem of thy joy serene:
> There nature ever in luxuriant showers
> Pours from her treasures, the perennial flowers;
> In its dark foliage plum'd the tow'ring pine
> Ascends the mountain, at her call divine; (I: 1-8)

The poet's ambiguous use of "lost" in "lost Peruvia," indicates a civilization that is unknown to the world. "Lost" also alludes to Milton's *Paradise Lost*, foreshadowing the damage to Peru's culture and landscape at the hands of the Spanish. Williams personifies Peru in these first lines as possessing "joy serene" and as a "cultur'd scene" before European influence. Moreover, as the main character in this first canto, Peru, itself, is wise and possesses a "responsive heart" (I: 52).

The spirit of this personified land and the sea mirror one another; the land is responsive—to the rain offered by the sky as well as to the divine call of the mountain. This mountain voice comes down from "on high"—the perspective of the divine call of God. Psalm 68 says of God "Thou hast ascended on high" (16). The pine "Ascends the mountain," suggesting upward movement to higher realms.

These lines introduce the first of many Christian allusions in the poem that blend with non-Christian ideas of inner virtue and enlightenment. Williams sometimes uses traditional Christian religious language but puts these terms in the context of a nature-based, pantheistic spirituality. Christian virtues play out in the poem by a people "lost" to European influences. Within this scenario, Williams interrogates the notion that the natives are "savages" in need of being saved. Instead, she portrays the Inca as a people who are not only called by the divine spirit, but who answer that call and "ascend."

---

1 Hemming 350.

The culture of Peru is filled with the "treasures" of nature, including "luxuriant showers" and "perennial flowers." Its wealth is not of the Eurocentric, material kind but natural and "perennial," that is to say, enduring. This landscape, a metaphor for Peru's native people, is "unsullied, and sublime" (I: 42).

Over the course of the poem, the hummingbird comes to suggest the Inca. Williams introduces the bird as "plaintive" and reflective of the sun: "His wings their colours to the sun unfold, / The vivid scarlet, and the blazing gold" (I: 31-32). The Inca believed Atahuallpa and his ancestors to be descendants of the sun, and gold, both literally and metaphorically, linked the sun on earth and the Inca leaders.[1] The golden hummingbird, here, suggests natural, cultural, and social wealth. According to Williams, the hummingbird takes "fond delight" in the "social nest" which "Parental care has rear'd, and love has blest" (I: 35-36), and, in her telling, the male bird, rather than the female, proudly feeds the young:

The drops that on the blossom's light leaf hung,
He bears exulting to his tender young;
The grateful joy his happy accents prove,
Is nature, smiling on her works of love. (I: 37-40)

Williams reverses traditional European gender roles in assigning men to the nurturing domestic sphere, which affords them a satisfaction and joy unrelated to acts of control and oppression. The character of Ataliba, a "Descendant of a scepter'd, sacred race" (I: 57), also challenges Eurocentric ideas about male roles. His power does not come through force or economic manipulation but through his mild nature, which "the willing heart obey'd" (I: 56). Williams imagines a social revolution, with leadership emerging from a gentle and family-centered nobility—the "blazing gold" of the hummingbird, rather than metal mined from the earth.

In contrast, Williams describes the "sullen pomp" of the Spanish breaking the "artless bosom's holy ties" (I: 73-74); she juxtaposes this violence to domestic affection against the colorful magnificence of the hummingbird (Inca), whose natural world is full of the treasures of reciprocal love and connectivity. While the Spanish justify their conquest as an effort to bring Christianity and holiness to the "savage" natives, Williams demonstrates that their presence is, in fact, avaricious and unholy. The purity of

---

1 MacQuarrie 100.

Alzira, Ataliba's bride, is, likewise, not dependent upon European notions of spirituality. Alzira's "meek" devotion rises on "wings of purity" (I: 125), suggesting not only Christian ideals—an angelic quality—but purity connected to the natural world—a bird-like quality.

Williams also inverts Christian symbolism in her contrast of the Peruvian leader to Pizarro, the stern Spanish leader, with his "Charms to betray, in Candour's open smile" (II: 4). Ataliba, naïve about the evil he is to encounter, with "native grace" meets Pizarro and his men dressed "In all the savage pomp of armour" (II: 11, 13). Pizarro deceives the Inca with language, charming "with eloquence the simple heart" (II: 16).[1] Alzira's grandfather, a pacifist, dies in the first battle of the poem, ending his "consecrated" life with a prayer (II: 36). The Spanish, who claim to hold "religion's light," murder the old Inca holy man (II: 21). The Spaniards are "human vultures," who attack the "dove-like prey" (II: 70), ironically connecting the Peruvian priest with Christian notions of the Holy Spirit. Unlike the Spanish, the Inca are unconcerned with any treasure other than one another.

In another religious juxtaposition, Williams contrasts two priests: the fanatic Spaniard Valverde and the gentle Spaniard Las Casas. Alice Knight describes the historical figure, Las Casas, as a man who was "not bent on fame and glory, not possessed of that greed for gold that led to so much ruthless cruelty toward the natives of the New World,—a man consumed with one burning desire: to spend himself in the service of others, to protect and save the weak and helpless."[2] Unlike Valverde, Las Casas offers an example of European Christianity capable of empathy, which is, therefore, pure and virtuous. These characters suggest that for Williams, the problem was not Christianity itself, but loss of compassion and disconnection from the natural world.

Indeed, Williams recounts Valverde's brutal capture of a Peruvian priest, and Williams sees "pure religion" defiled by the Spaniard's religious fanaticism:

Fanatic fury rears her sullen shrine,
Where vultures prey, where venom'd adders twine;

---

1   Williams revises history here; the Inca, of course, would not have been able to understand the Spanish language at this early point in their interactions with the conquistadors.

2   Knight 7.

Her savage arm with purple torrents stains ...
And pure religion's sacred voice profane; (III: 15-17,
   24)

The Peruvian priest's "meek spirit humbly sought its God" (III: 34), but Valverde tortures him in an attempt to convert him. The Peruvian remains faithful, even in the face of death, to the "Power" he serves, while Valverde betrays the very qualities that the Bible extols. The priest, like many of the despondent Peruvians in the poem, sees death as a release.[1] Other Peruvian characters in the poem seek death as a way to be reunited with loved ones killed by the Spaniards. Death is more than simply an end to mortal suffering but is a reunion with the earth. This doorway to the afterlife gives meaning to the world and provides eternal existence for the soul. Williams's characters seek not only death but burial in the earth—an act so essential that in Canto VI, the Inca even bury Almagro out of pity, offering the conqueror of nature a return to the earth that he sought to exploit (181-88). Earlier in the same canto, the poet appeals to nature as her muse, invoking sympathy for Cápac, who mourns his beloved Cora:

Oh nature! sure thy sympathetic ties
Shall o'er the ruins of the grave arise;
Undying spring from the relentless tomb,
And shed, in scenes of love, a lasting bloom. (145-48)

This Peruvian burial offers a reunion not with the immortality of the Christian afterlife but with the eternally renewing and inspiring natural world.

Unlike Valverde, the Spanish priest, Las Casas values the Peruvians' naturalistic spirituality. When Las Casas encounters the Peruvian priest, he recognizes his counterpart's purity and connection to the natural world, the "kindred skies" (III: 96). The empathetic Las Casas seems to understand the interconnectedness of life-giving nature. He does not offer a traditional communion, but rather asks the Peruvian priest to receive his tears. While the poem likens Las Casas' tears to the blood of Christ,

---

1   In Canto V, Aciloe "seeks repose in death" (84) and in Canto III, Zilia
    seeks consolation there: "'Weep not for me,' she cried, 'For Zilia's breast /
    Soon in the shelt'ring earth shall find its rest'" (157-58). Similarly, in
    Canto VI, as the Peruvians search the Cuzco battlefield for dead loved
    ones in "mute despair," the mourners "only crave / The deep repose
    which wraps the shelt'ring grave" (35-42).

"poured for the many," this "sacred flood" is drunk by the earth as the good Spanish priest prays to God to forgive the cruelty of Valverde and his "murd'rous band" (III: 106). He saves the old priest from Valverde but is unable to prevent his death. In the final canto of the poem, the Spaniards, Almagro and Pizarro, kill one another out of greed and revenge. They ultimately not only destroy the Inca but themselves as well.

Peru opens and closes with references to shorelines and comes full circle in several ways. The shore at the start is that of Peru, while the final line of the poem refers to the shores of other lands around the world, underlining Peru's role as metaphor. The full circle, or revolution, of the poem suggests that, while it is too late to save the Inca, the events of Peru might bring "triumphs" to other shores.

When Williams described Peru, she clearly had in mind a place closer to home—France, the contemporary political stage for revolution. The poem's praise for the inherent virtue of the Incas also speaks to the marginalized in France and on many "unnumber'd shores" (VI: 356), including that of Britain. While her idealized treatment of the Peruvians contains moments of contradiction, Williams offers their example as a powerful critique of oppression, in the Americas, in Europe, and elsewhere around the globe.

Our hope for this new edition of *Peru* is not only to allow a modern audience to read Williams's remarkable poetic work, but to re-establish Williams's reputation as one of the key figures in the history of the epic. On one of the largest and most ambitious of literary stages, Williams brings to life individual human beings caught in the web of political forces far beyond their control. She is unflinching in depicting psychic injury, not only within the individual but within an entire culture. Moreover, the issues her work addresses so powerfully and movingly are far from having been resolved, even in our own time. We would all do well to consider Williams's commentary on the relationships she explores: between the colonizer and the colonized; between capitalism and greed; and between destruction and the possibility for renewal.

Helen Maria Williams: A Brief Chronology[1]

1761 Helen Maria Williams is born on 17 June in London. Her mother, Helen (née Hay), is a Scotswoman, and her father, Charles Williams, is a Welsh army officer. She has an older sister, Cecilia, and a half-sister, Persis, from her father's first marriage.

1762 Charles Williams dies in December. Some time after her father's death, Williams's family moves to Berwick-upon-Tweed, where she absorbs the culture of the Anglo-Scottish border and receives what she later terms a "confined education."

1781 In the summer, the family moves to Southampton Row in Bloomsbury, London; their Presbyterian minister, Dr. Andrew Kippis, becomes Williams's mentor and introduces her to the city's artistic and intellectual elite.

1782 *Edwin and Eltruda. A Legendary Tale*, Williams's first book of poetry, is published by Thomas Cadell in London with the help of Kippis. She signs it "By a Young Lady." Later, she describes this work about the War of the Roses as "composed to amuse some solitary hours, and without any view to publication." Williams begins composing *Peru*.

1783 *An Ode on the Peace*, celebrating the conclusion of the American Revolution, is published by Cadell and signed "By the Author of *Edwin and Eltruda*."

1784 *Peru, a Poem. In Six Cantos*, bearing Williams's name on the title page, is published by Cadell. Williams meets Samuel Johnson.

1786 *Poems*, including *Peru* in revised form, is published in two volumes by Cadell with a list of more than 1500 subscribers.

1787 William Wordsworth publishes his first poem, "Sonnet, on Seeing Miss Helen Maria Williams Weep at a Tale of Distress" under the pseudonym "Axiologus" in the March issue of *The European Magazine*. Williams's salon

---

1 We are indebted to Deborah Kennedy's important biography, *Helen Maria Williams and the Age of Revolution* for much of the information used in this chronology.

becomes known for hosting some of the most important figures of the period.

1788   *A Poem on the Bill Lately Passed for Regulating the Slave Trade* is published by Cadell.

1790   *Julia, a Novel; Interspersed with Some Poetical Pieces* is published in the spring by Cadell in two volumes and includes "The Bastille, A Vision." Williams visits Paris from July to September. *Letters Written in France, in the Summer of 1790, to a Friend in England; containing Various Anecdotes relative to the French Revolution; and Memoirs of Monsieur and Madame du F,*[1] the first of her eyewitness volumes, is published by Cadell.

1791   *Poems*, second edition, is published by Cadell and includes a reprinting of *Peru*. In August, Williams travels to France. *A Farewell, for Two Years, to England. A Poem*, is published by Cadell.

1792   In June, Williams returns to England. *Letters from France* (first series) volume two is published; this volume and subsequent *Letters* are published by G.G. and J. Robinson, London. In August, Williams leaves England for Paris, never to return. As in London, her salon in Paris becomes an important meeting place for writers, intellectuals, and politicians.

1793   *Letters from France*, volumes 3 and 4, are published anonymously in the summer.
         Williams is rumored to be involved romantically with the radical political reformer, John Hurford Stone, who had subscribed to her *Poems* (1786). In the midst of the Terror, she, along with her mother and sisters, is imprisoned in Paris for a harrowing six weeks (October to November). Many close to her, including Madame Roland, are guillotined.

1794   Williams's sister, Cecilia, marries Marie-Martin-Athanase Coquerel in March. Stone and his wife divorce; he, Williams, and other members of her household spend June to December in Switzerland. Williams composes "Hymn Written among the Alps."

---

1   We refer to later volumes by the title by which they became known—*Letters from France*.

1795   Williams's translation of Bernardin de Saint-Pierre's novel, *Paul et Virginie*, with eight of her own sonnets, appears in Paris and is brought out by Vernor and Hood in London under the title *Paul and Virginia*. Williams invests heavily in Stone's press. *Letters from France* (second series), volumes one to three, are published.

1796   *Letters from France* (second series), volume four is published. An anthology, *Poems, Moral, Elegant and Pathetic*, includes a selection of Williams's poetry.

1798   *A Tour in Switzerland: or, A View of the Present State of the Governments and Manners of Those Cantons, with Comparative Sketches of the Present State of Paris* (2 volumes) is published by G.G. and J. Robinson, London. Williams's sister, Cecilia, dies in September; Williams adopts her two young nephews, Athanase and Charles.

1801   *Sketches of the State of Manners and Opinions in the French Republic, towards the Close of the Eighteenth Century. In a Series of Letters* is published by G.G. and J. Robinson, London. "Ode to Peace" is published in November.

1803   Williams publishes *The Political and Confidential Correspondences of Lewis the Sixteenth* (3 volumes).

1812   Williams's mother dies in April. John Hurford Stone goes bankrupt from the overwhelming cost of publishing the 31-volume *Voyage de Humboldt et de Bonpland*.

1814   Williams translates from the French and publishes in London (with Longman, Hurst, Rees, Orme & Brown; John Murray; Henry Colburn) Alexander von Humboldt's *Researches Concerning the Institutions and Monuments of the Ancient Inhabitants of America, with Descriptions and Views of Some of the Most Striking Scenes in the Cordilleras*, one of the earliest archaeological works on the Aztec and Inca civilizations. She also begins translating the monumental *Personal Narrative of Travels to the Equinoctial Regions of the New Continent, during the years 1799-1804* by Humboldt and Bonpland, in 7 volumes (1814-27).

1815   *A Narrative of the Events Which Have Taken Place in France, From the Landing of Napoleon Bonaparte on the First of March, 1815, Till the Restoration of Louis XVIII* is published by John Murray, London.

1816   *On the Late Persecution of the Protestants in the South of France* is published by Underwood.

1817 Williams becomes a French citizen. Her translation of *The Leper of the City of Aoste* by Xavier de Maistre is published in London by George Cowie. In September, John Hurford Stone becomes seriously ill.

1818 Stone dies on 22 May and is buried in Père Lachaise Cemetery, Paris.

1819 *Letters on the Events Which Have Passed in France since the Restoration in 1815* is published by Baldwin, Cradock and Joy, London. *The Charter, Lines Addressed by Helena Maria Williams to her Nephew, Athanase C.L. Coquerel, on his Wedding Day* is published in Paris.

1820 Dorothy and William Wordsworth meet Williams in Paris.

1823 *Poems on Various Subjects. With Introductory Remarks on the Present State of Science and Literature in France,* which includes a substantially altered version of *Peru,* entitled "Peruvian Tales," is published by G. and W.B. Whittaker, London. Williams moves to Amsterdam to live with Athanase Coquerel and his family. Her half-sister, Persis, dies there on 23 December.

1827 Williams's memoir is translated from English into French by Charles Coquerel and published as *Souvenirs de la Révolution Française.* By May, Williams has returned to Paris, where she dies on 15 December, aged 66; she is buried next to her mother and John Hurford Stone in Père Lachaise Cemetery.

A Note on the Texts of Peru and "Peruvian Tales"

Our preferred copy text of *Peru* was published in the two-volume *Poems* (London: Thomas Cadell, 1786, II: 45-178). We have chosen this text over the first edition of 1784 and the later edition of 1791 for several reasons. When Williams revised *Peru* for its 1786 reprinting in *Poems*, she polished the poem considerably. As a result, the language and word choice are more precise, the meter is improved, and the poem is thematically tighter. This fine tuning resulted in a more emotionally powerful poem than its earlier incarnation. In addition, Williams published it at the height of her London celebrity in a collection of her work which was read and discussed by a wider audience than the 1784 text. It was not only instrumental in shaping her reputation as an advocate for revolution but was also at the forefront of Romanticism. The text of 1791 differs from that of 1786 only in accidentals. We include the dedicatory poem, "To Mrs. Montagu," which appeared in 1784 but was only printed in some copies of *Poems* (1786).

In 1823, toward the end of her life, Williams revised *Peru* from an epic poem in six cantos into a series of six "Peruvian Tales." In doing so, she deleted hundreds of lines, many of them dealing with poetry, revolution, mining, religion, and sensibility. Nature is almost completely written out of the poem as well, and, at this more conservative historical moment, much of the revolutionary energy and fervor of the poem is lost. Even so, the shift in genre, along with its heightened feminism, makes "Peruvian Tales" of interest to modern readers; we reprint it here in full. Williams published "Peruvian Tales" in her collection *Poems on Various Subjects. With Introductory Remarks on the Present State of Science and Literature in France* (London: G. and W.B. Whittaker, 1823: 19-83), which we use as our copy text.

For the most part, Williams's original spelling, punctuation and capitalization have been retained. However, the proper names which were italicized have been set as roman, and words written in all caps have been printed with only the initial letter capitalized. We have preserved the original spelling in the texts even when it is inconsistent. Markers for Williams's own footnotes, such as daggers, crosses, asterisks, and so forth, have been removed from the body of the texts, although her notes themselves have been preserved. Moreover, the long "s" and running open quotation marks at the beginning of each line of poetry within a speech have been modernized, and close quotes have been supplied where a modern reader would expect to find them at the end of a speech. Obvious printer's errors have been corrected silently and periods after headings have been removed.

Textual matters of particular significance are discussed in the notes. Accidental variants are not reported. Helen Maria Williams's name has been abbreviated in the notes as HMW. With regard to texts in the appendices, the table of contents gives the original date of publication, while the appendices themselves give the date and bibliographic information for the copy text used here.

Drawn by Maria Cosway.   Engraved by Isaac Taylor Jun

Frontispiece to *Poems* (1786). Copper plate engraving of a drawing
by Maria Cosway. Published in London, 25 April 1786. Private
collection.

P O E M S,

BY

HELEN MARIA WILLIAMS.

IN TWO VOLUMES.

VOL. I.

LONDON:

Printed by A. RIVINGTON and J. MARSHALL,

FOR THOMAS CADELL IN THE STRAND.

M DCC LXXXVI.

Title page to *Poems* (1786), which contained Williams's revised text of *Peru*. Private collection.

PERU

A Poem, in Six Cantos

To Mrs. Montagu[1]

While, bending at thy honour'd shrine, the Muse
  Pours, Montagu, to thee her votive strain,
Thy heart will not her simple notes refuse,
  Or chill her timid soul with cold disdain.

O might a transient spark of genius fire   5
  The fond effusions of her fearful youth;
Then should thy virtues live upon her lyre,
  And give to harmony the charm of truth.

Vain wish! they ask not the imperfect lay,
  The weak applause her trembling accents breathe;   10
With whose pure radiance glory blends her ray,
  Whom fame has circled with her fairest wreathe.

Thou, who while seen with graceful step to tread
  Grandeur's enchanted round, can'st meekly pause
To rend the veil obscurity had spread   15
  Where his lone sigh deserted Genius draws;

To lead his drooping spirit to thy fane,[2]
  Where attic[3] joy the social circle warms;

---

1 Elizabeth Montagu (1718-1800) cofounded the Blue Stocking Society
in the early 1750s with Elizabeth Vesey. Among other pursuits, the Blue
Stockings sought to increase women's social standing through educa-
tion. Montagu hosted parties at her house on Hill Street, which were
attended by many of London's intellectual and literary elite, including
Samuel Johnson, Sir Joshua Reynolds, Frances Burney, Anna Letitia
Barbauld, and in 1782, HMW. By January 1783, William Hayley records
that HMW planned to dedicate *Peru* to Montagu, whom HMW had
already praised in *An Ode on the Peace* (1783) l. 252 (see Appendix A1).
Montagu read *Peru* in manuscript (Kennedy 27). By the time she enter-
tained HMW, Montagu's mansion had long been the premier salon in
London, a status which HMW's own salon would achieve years later in
Paris.

2 Temple.

3 Marked by simple and refined elegance; pure, classical (*OED*).

Where science loves to pour her hallow'd strain,
  Where wit, and wisdom, blend their sep'rate charms.   20

And sure to cherish intellectual powers,
  To bid the vig'rous tides of genius roll,
Unfold, in fair expansion, fancy's flowers,
  And wake the latent energies of soul;

Far other homage claims than flatt'ry brings   25
  The little triumphs of the proud to grace:
For deeds like these a purer incense springs,
  Warm from the swelling heart its source we trace!

Yet not to foster the rich gifts of mind
  Alone can all thy lib'ral cares employ;   30
Not to the few those gifts adorn, confin'd,
  They spread an ampler sphere of genuine joy.

While pleasure's lucid star illumes thy bower,
  Thy pity views the distant storm that bends
Where want unshelter'd wastes the ling'ring hour;—   35
  And meets the blessing that to heav'n ascends!

For this, while fame thro' each successive age
  On her exulting lip thy name shall breathe;
While woman, pointing to thy finish'd page,
  Claims from imperious man the critic wreathe;   40 ·

Truth on her spotless record shall enroll
  Each moral beauty to her spirit dear;
Paint in bright characters each grace of soul—
  While admiration pours a gen'rous tear.

Helen Maria Williams
London, April the 24th, 1784

Advertisement

That no readers of the following work may entertain expectations respecting it which it would ill satisfy, it is necessary to acquaint them, that the author has not had the presumption even to attempt a full, historical narration of the fall of the Peruvian empire. To describe that important event with accuracy, and to display with clearness and force the various causes which combined to produce it, would require all the energy of genius, and the most glowing colours of imagination. Conscious of her utter inability to execute such a design, she has only aimed at a simple detail of some few incidents that make a part of that romantic story; where the unparalleled sufferings of an innocent and amiable people, form the most affecting subjects of true pathos, while their climate, totally unlike our own, furnishes new and ample materials for poetic description.

PERU
Canto the First

The Argument

General description of the country of Peru, and of its animal, and vegetable productions—the virtues of the people—character of Ataliba, *their Monarch—his love for* Alzira—*their nuptials celebrated—character of* Zorai, *her father—descent of the genius of Peru—prediction of the fate of that empire.*

Canto the First

Where the pacific deep in silence laves
The western shore, with slow and languid waves,
There, lost Peruvia,[1] rose thy cultur'd scene,[2]
The wave an emblem of thy joy serene:
There nature ever in luxuriant showers   5
Pours from her treasures, the perennial flowers;
In its dark foliage plum'd, the tow'ring pine
Ascends the mountain, at her call divine;
The palm's wide leaf its brighter verdure spreads,
And the proud cedars bow their lofty heads;   10
The citron, and the glowing orange spring,
And on the gale a thousand odours fling;
The guava, and the soft ananas[3] bloom,
The balsam[4] ever drops a rich perfume:
The bark, reviving shrub! Oh not in vain   15
Thy rosy blossoms tinge[5] Peruvia's plain;
Ye fost'ring gales, around those blossoms blow,
Ye balmy dew-drops, o'er the tendrils flow.

---

1 The first of many echoes of *Paradise Lost.*
2 HMW depicts Peru as both a natural paradise and a civilized society. Similarly, Edmund and William Burke write in *An Account of the European Settlements in America* that other than Mexico, Peru is the only country in the Americas that ought to be called a "civilized kingdom" (1: 129).
3 Pineapple (*Ananassa sativa*).
4 Like the famous Balm of Gilead, the balsam of Peru is an aromatic, soothing, medicinal vegetable (*OED*).
5 A foreshadowing of the blood that later covers Peru's ground.

Lo, as the health-diffusing plant aspires,
Disease, and pain, and hov'ring death retires;   20
Affection sees new lustre light the eye,
And feels her vanish'd joys again are nigh.
The Pacos,[1] and Vicunnas[2] sport around,
And the meek Lamas,[3] burden'd, press the ground.
Amid the vocal groves, the feather'd throng   25
Pour to the list'ning breeze their native song;
The mocking-bird her varying note essays,
The vain[4] macaw his glitt'ring plume displays.
While spring's warm ray the mild suffusion sheds,
The plaintive humming-bird his pinion[5] spreads;   30
His wings their colours to the sun unfold,
The vivid scarlet, and the blazing gold;
He sees the flower which morning tears bedew,
Sinks on its breast, and drinks th' ambrosial dew:
Then seeks with fond delight the social nest   35
Parental care has rear'd, and love has blest:
The drops that on the blossom's light leaf hung,
He bears exulting to his tender young;
The grateful joy his happy accents prove,
Is nature, smiling on her works of love.   40

        Nor less, Peruvia, for thy favour'd clime
The virtues rose, unsullied, and sublime:
There melting charity, with ardor warm,
Spread her wide mantle o'er th' unshelter'd form;
Cheer'd with the festal song, her lib'ral toils,   45
While in the lap of age[6] she pour'd the spoils.
Simplicity in every vale was found,
The meek nymph smil'd, with reeds, and rushes crown'd;

---

1   The pacos is a domestic animal of Peru. Its wool resembles the colour
    of dried roses [HMW's note].
2   The vicunnas are a species of wild pacos [HMW's note].
3   The lamas are employed as mules, in carrying burdens [HMW's note].
4   The subject of vanity is important in *Peru*, as it is in much of HMW's
    poetry, and she sometimes puns on "vain" and "vein." For more on
    veins and mining, see Jessica Damián's "Helen Maria Williams's Per-
    sonal Narrative of Travels from *Peru* (1784) to *Peruvian Tales* (1823)."
5   A bird's wing (*OED*).
6   The people cheerfully assisted in reaping those fields, whose produce
    was given to old persons, past their labor [HMW's note].

And innocence in light, transparent vest,
Mild visitant! the gentle region blest: 50
As from her lip enchanting accents part,
They thrill with pleasure the responsive heart;[1]
And o'er the ever-blooming vales around,
Soft echoes waft each undulating sound.

    This happy region Ataliba[2] sway'd,   55
Whose mild behest the willing heart obey'd;
Descendant of a scepter'd, sacred race,
Whose origin from glowing suns they trace;
And as o'er nature's form, the solar light[3]
Diffuses beauty, and inspires delight;   60
So, o'er Peruvia flow'd the lib'ral ray
Of mercy, lovelier than the smile of day!
In Ataliba's pure and gen'rous heart
The virtues bloom'd without the aid of art.
His gentle spirit, love's soft power possest,   65
And stamp'd Alzira's image on his breast;
Alzira, form'd each tenderness to prove,
That sooths in friendship, and that charms in love.

---

1   HMW adapts one of the familiar tropes of Sensibility, the sympathetic
    heart, to introduce Peru as the central character in her epic.

2   The thirteenth and last king of the Peruvian Empire. Atahuallpa (1502-
    33), also "Atahualpa," "Atabalipa," and "Atalipa," was King Huayna
    Cápac's younger son. Upon his father's death in 1527, he ruled the
    northern region of the kingdom, while the legitimate heir, Huáscar,
    ruled in the south, which included the capital city of Cuzco. This
    arrangement led to a civil war, still raging when Pizarro landed
    (Hemming 29). HMW would have read about Atahuallpa in Abbé
    Raynal's *Histoire philosophique et politique* and William Robertson's *The
    History of America*, in which he is depicted as cruel and opportunistic. In
    Jean-François Marmontel's *Les Incas*, another important source for
    HMW, Atahuallpa is a hero. HMW ignores Robertson's, Raynal's, and
    Marmontel's record of the conflict between the half-brothers. See
    Appendix B, pp. 188-212, for extracts from these works.

3   Sun worship is central to Inca religion. The character of Ataliba, a ruler
    who is a descendant of the sun, invites comparison with the French Sun
    King, Louis XIV. HMW gathered information on sun worship from
    several sources, including Robertson, Raynal, Marmontel, and Françoise
    de Graffigny's "Historical Introduction" to the 1752 edition of her novel
    Lettres d'une Péruvienne.

But, ah! in vain the drooping muse would paint
(Her accents languid, and her colours faint,)   70
How dear the joys love's early wishes sought,
How mild his spirit, and how pure his thought,
Ere wealth in sullen pomp was seen to rise,
And break the artless bosom's holy ties;
Blast with his touch affection's op'ning flower,   75
And chill the hand that rear'd her blissful bower.
Fortune, light nymph! still bless the sordid heart,
Still to thy venal slave thy gifts impart;
Bright in his view may all thy meteors shine,
And lost Peruvia open every mine;   80
For him the robe of eastern pomp display,
The gems that ripen in the torrid ray;
Collected may their guilty lustre stream
Full on the eye that courts the partial beam:
But Love, oh Love! should haply this late hour,   85
One softer mind avow thy genuine power;
Breathe at thy altar nature's simple strain,
And strew the heart's pure incense on thy fane;
Give to that bosom scorning fortune's toys,
Thy sweet enchantments, and thy virtuous joys;   90
Bid pleasure bloom thro' many a circling year,
Which love shall wing, and constancy endear;
Far from this happy clime avert the woes,
The heart from alienated fondness knows;
And from that agony the spirit save,   95
When unrelenting yawns the op'ning grave;
When death dissolves the ties for ever dear;
When frantic passion pours her parting tear;
With all the cherish'd pains affection feels,
Hangs on the quiv'ring lip, that silence seals;   100
Views fondness struggling in the closing eye,
And marks it mingling in the falt'ring sigh;
As the lov'd form, while folded to her breast,
On earth's cold bosom seeks more lasting rest!
Leave her fond soul in hopeless griefs to mourn, 105
Clasp the pale corse,[1] and bathe th' unconscious urn;—
Mild, to the wounds that pierce her bleeding heart,
Nature's expiring pang, and death's keen dart.

---

1 Corpse.

Pure was the lustre of the orient[1] ray,
That joyful wak'd Alzira's nuptial day: 110
Her auburn hair, spread loosely to the wind,
The virgin train, with rosy chaplets[2] bind;
The scented flowers that form her bridal wreathe,
A deeper hue, a richer fragrance breathe.
The gentle tribe now sought the hallow'd fane,   115
Where warbling vestals pour'd the choral strain:
There aged Zorai, his Alzira prest
With love parental, to his anxious breast:
Priest of the sun, within the sacred shrine
His fervent spirit breath'd the strain divine;   120
With glowing hand, the guiltless off'ring spread,[3]
With pious zeal the pure libation shed;
Nor vain the incense of erroneous praise
When meek devotion's soul the tribute pays;
On wings of purity behold it rise,   125
While bending mercy wafts it to the skies!

    Peruvia! oh delightful land, in vain
The virtues flourish'd on thy beauteous plain;
In vain sweet pleasure there was seen to move,
And wore the smile of peace, the bloom of love;   130
For soon shall burst the unrelenting storm,
Rend her soft robe, and crush her tender form:
Peruvia! soon the fatal hour shall rise,
The hour despair shall waste in tears and sighs;
Fame shall record the horrors of thy fate,   135
And distant ages weep for ills so great.

    Now o'er the deep chill night her mantle flung,
Dim on the wave the moon's faint crescent hung;

---

1 The Far East. In HMW's time, most of the gold and silver mined in
   Peru paid for goods from China. See David Shield's *Oracles of Empire:
   Poetry, Politics, and Commerce in British America, 1690-1750*.
2 Ornamental head wreaths often made of flowers, leaves, gold, and pre-
   cious stones (*OED*).
3 HMW implies that Peruvian worship involves no animal or human sac-
   rifice. She is influenced by Raynal and Marmontel, who argue that
   Peruvians were more advanced for having ended that violent practice.

Peruvia's Genius[1] sought the liquid plain,
Sooth'd by the languid murmurs of the main; 140
When sudden clamour the illusion broke,
Wild on the surface of the deep it spoke;
A rising breeze expands her flowing veil,
Aghast with fear, she spy'd a flying sail—
The lofty mast impends, the banner waves, 145
The ruffled surge th' incumbent vessel laves;
With eager eye she views her destin'd foe
Lead to her peaceful shores th' advent'rous prow;
Trembling she knelt, with wild disorder'd air,
And pour'd with frantic energy her pray'r— 150
"Oh, ye avenging spirits of the deep!
Mount the blue lightning's wing, o'er ocean sweep;
Loud from your central caves the shell resound,
That summons death to your abyss profound;
Call the pale spectre from his dark abode, 155
To print the billow, swell the black'ning flood,
Rush o'er the waves, the rough'ning deep deform,
Howl in the blast, and animate the storm—
Relentless powers! for not one quiv'ring breeze
Has ruffled yet the surface of the seas— 160
Swift from your rocky steeps, ye condors[2] stray,
Wave your black plumes, and cleave th' aërial way;
Proud in terrific force, your wings expand,
Press the firm earth, and darken all the strand;
Bid the stern foe retire with wild affright, 165
And shun the region veil'd in partial night.
Vain hope, devoted land! I read thy doom,
My sad prophetic soul can pierce the gloom;
I see, I see my lov'd, my favour'd clime,
Consum'd, and fading in its early prime. 170

---

1 Genius loci, or "genius of the place," a "presiding deity or spirit." In the
 late eighteenth century, "genius" sometimes referred to an "attendant
 spirit allotted to every person at his birth," while it also described the
 general character, or spirit, of a nation or age. Genius was beginning to
 be used in its more modern sense to mean "native intellectual power of
 an exalted type" (*OED*).
2 The condor is an inhabitant of the Andes. Its wings, when expanded, are
 said to be eighteen feet wide [HMW's note]. HMW makes a subtle polit-
 ical point with her sound play between "condor" and "conquistador."

But not in vain the beauteous realm shall bleed,
Too late shall Europe's race deplore the deed.
Region abhorr'd! be gold the tempting bane,
The curse that desolates thy hostile plain;
May pleasure tinge with venom'd drops the bowl,   175
And luxury unnerve the sick'ning soul."—
Ah, not in vain she pour'd th' impassion'd tear!
Ah, not in vain she call'd the powers to hear!
When borne from lost Peruvia's bleeding land,[1]
The guilty treasures beam'd on Europe's strand;   180
Each sweet affection fled the tainted shore,
And virtue wander'd, to return no more.

---

1 Alzira's wedding celebration ends not with the consummation of love
   but with the rape of the virgin landscape.

PERU
Canto the Second

The Argument
Pizarro, *a Spanish Captain, lands with his forces*—*his meeting with*
Ataliba—*its unhappy consequences*—Zorai *dies*—Ataliba *impris-*
oned, and strangled—Alzira's *despair, and madness.*

Canto the Second

Flush'd with impatient hope, the martial band
By stern Pizarro[1] led, approach the land:
No terrors arm the hostile brow, for guile
Charms to betray, in Candour's open smile.
Too artless[2] for distrust, the monarch springs   5
To meet his latent foe on friendship's wings:
On as he moves, with glitt'ring splendours crown'd,
His feather'd chiefs the golden throne surround;
The waving canopy its plume displays,

---

1 Francisco Pizarro (c. 1475-1541), an illiterate soldier who rose to power
  and riches by leading the Spanish conquest of Peru. Pizarro first sailed
  to the Americas in 1502, and in 1513 he crossed the Isthmus of Panama
  with Vasco Núñez de Balboa. Pizarro was named mayor of Panama City
  in 1519, and in 1524 formed an alliance with Diego de Almagro, a
  soldier, and Hernando de Luque, a priest. Their goal was to explore and
  conquer the lands to the south and divide the riches. Two failed expedi-
  tions followed (1524 and 1526). The *Capitulación de Toledo*, signed in
  July 1529, gave Pizarro license for a third attempt. He left Panama in
  December 1530 and in July 1532, established the first Spanish settle-
  ment in Peru—San Miguel de Piura. In November of that year, Pizarro's
  forces captured the Inca leader Atahuallpa at the Battle of Cajamarca,
  setting in motion the Spanish conquest of Peru. After the conquest,
  Pizarro and Almagro fell out over the division of the country's riches
  and lands. That schism led to Almagro's defeat and execution. However,
  Almagro's son (also called Diego de Almagro) led a rebel group that
  stormed Pizarro's palace in Lima and assassinated the conquistador.
  HMW's depiction of Pizarro—and by extension, the Spanish as a
  whole—foregrounds a lust for riches as motivation for the conquest. Her
  analysis departs from her sources; Robertson, for instance, offers greed
  as a possible subtext rather than an explicit driving force. Interestingly,
  many modern-day readings of Pizarro's motives align more with HMW's
  depiction than with the views of the historians, whom she read.
2 Ataliba's artless innocence contrasts with Pizarro's "guile." See I: 64.

Whose varied hues reflect the morning rays;   10
With native grace he hails the warrior train,
Who stood majestic on Peruvia's plain,
In all the savage pomp of armour drest,
The radiant helmet, and the nodding crest.
Yet themes of joy Pizarro's lips impart,   15
And charm with eloquence the simple heart;
Unfolding to the monarch's wond'ring thought,
All that inventive arts the rude have taught:
And now he bids the purer spirit rise
Above the circle of surrounding skies;   20
Presents the page that shed religion's light
O'er the dark mist of intellectual night;
While thrill'd with awe the monarch trembling stands,
He dropp'd the hallow'd volume from his hands.

Sudden, while frantic zeal[1] each breast inspires,   25
And shudd'ring demons fan the impious fires,

---

1 "Sudden, while frantic zeal, &c." Pizarro, who during a long conference,
had with difficulty restrained his soldiers, eager to seize the rich spoils of
which they had now so near a view, immediately gave the signal of
assault. At once the martial music struck up, the cannon and muskets
began to fire, the horse sallied out fiercely to the charge, the infantry
rushed on sword in hand. The Peruvians, astonished at the suddenness
of an attack which they did not expect, and dismayed with the destruc-
tive effects of the fire-arms, fled with universal consternation on every
side. Pizarro, at the head of his chosen band, advanced directly towards
the Inca; and though his Nobles crowded around him with officious
zeal, and fell in numbers at his feet, while they vied one with another in
sacrificing their own lives, that they might cover the sacred person of
their Sovereign, the Spaniards soon penetrated to the royal seat; and
Pizarro seizing the Inca by the arm, dragged him to the ground, and
carried him a prisoner to his quarters.—Robertson's *History of America*
[HMW's note]. See II: 175-76. The battle described here is the Battle of
Cajamarca, 16 November 1532. While HMW quotes directly from
William Robertson's description of the battle, she drastically changes the
moment that triggers it. Whereas HMW portrays Ataliba as a latent
Christian, whose very reverence makes him lose his grip on the Bible,
Robertson has the Peruvian emperor aggressively desecrate the book:
"The Inca opened it eagerly, and turning over the leaves, lifted it to his
ear: 'This,' says he, 'is silent; it tells me nothing'; and threw it with
disdain to the ground" (II: 175). HMW evidences a strategic and selec-
tive use of historical texts in her poetic adaptation.

The bloody signal waves, the banners play,
The naked sabres flash their streaming ray;
The martial trumpet's animating sound,
And thund'ring cannon, rend the vault around;   30
While fierce in sanguine[1] rage the sons of Spain
Rush on Peru's unarm'd, devoted train;
The fiends of slaughter urg'd their dire career,
And virtue's guardian spirits dropp'd a tear.—
Mild Zorai fell, deploring human strife,   35
And clos'd with prayer his consecrated life.
In vain Peruvia's chiefs undaunted stood,
Shield their lov'd prince, and bathe his robes in blood;
Touch'd with heroic ardor, rush around,
And high of soul, receive each fatal wound: 40
Dragg'd from his throne, and hurry'd o'er the plain,
The wretched monarch swells the captive train;
With iron grasp, the frantic prince they bear,
And bless the omen of his wild despair.

     Deep in the gloomy dungeon's lone domain,   45
Lost Ataliba wore the galling chain;
The earth's cold bed refus'd oblivious rest,
While throbb'd the pains of thousands at his breast;
Alzira's desolating moan he hears,
And with the monarch's, blends the lover's tears—   50
Soon had Alzira[2] felt affliction's dart
Pierce her soft soul, and rend her bleeding heart;
Its quick pulsations paus'd, and, chill'd with dread,
A livid hue her fading cheek o'erspread;
No tear she gave to love, she breath'd no sigh,   55
Her lips were mute, and clos'd her languid eye;
Fainter, and slower heav'd her shiv'ring breast,
And her calm'd passions seem'd in death to rest!—
At length reviv'd, mid rising heaps of slain
She prest with trembling step, the crimson plain;   60
The dungeon's gloomy depth she fearless sought,
For love, with scorn of danger arm'd her thought:
The cell that holds her captive lord she gains,

---

1 As used here, "delighting in bloodshed" (*OED*).

2 Robertson makes little mention of women. Williams may have taken the
    name "Alzira" from Voltaire's tragedy *Alzire, ou les Américains* (1736).
    Alzira is also the name of a town in Valencia, in eastern Spain.

Her tears fall quiv'ring on a lover's chains!
Too tender spirit, check the filial tear,   65
A sympathy more soft, a tie more dear
Shall claim the drops that frantic passion sheds,
When the rude storm its darkest pinion spreads.
Lo! bursting the deep cell where mis'ry lay,
The human vultures seize the dove-like prey!   70
In vain her treasur'd wealth Peruvia gave,
This dearer treasure from their grasp to save:
Alzira! lo, the ruthless murd'rers come,
This moment seals thy Ataliba's doom.
Ah, what avails the shriek that anguish pours!   75
The look, that mercy's lenient aid implores!
Torn from thy clinging arms, thy throbbing breast,
The fatal cord his agony supprest:[1]
In vain the livid corse she fondly clasps,
And pours her sorrows o'er the form she grasps—   80
The murd'rers now their struggling victim tear
From the lost object of her keen despair:
The swelling pang unable to sustain,
Distraction throbb'd in every beating vein:
Its sudden tumults seize her yielding soul,   85
And in her eye distemper'd glances roll—
"They come!" (the mourner cried, with panting breath,)
"To give the lost Alzira rest in death!
One moment more, ye bloody forms, bestow,
One moment more for ever cures my woe—   90
Lo where the purple evening sheds her light
On blest remains! oh hide them, pitying night!
Slow in the breeze I see the verdure wave
That shrouds with tufted grass, my lover's grave:
There, on its wand'ring wing in mildness blows   95
The mournful gale, nor wakes his deep repose—
And see, yon hoary form still lingers there!
Dishevell'd by rude winds his silver hair;
O'er his chill'd bosom falls the winter's rain,
I feel the big drops on my wither'd brain: 100
Not for himself that tear his bosom steeps,

---

1   HMW once again departs from Robertson, who records that Atahuallpa
    did not die at the initial siege but rather was held for ransom and exe-
    cuted later (II: 183-85). Historians now list 26 July 1533 as the date of
    Atahuallpa's death (Hemming 557).

For his lost child it flows, for me he weeps!
No more the dagger's point shall pierce thy breast,
For calm and lovely is thy silent rest;
Yet still in dust these eyes shall see thee roll,   105
Still the sad thought shall waste Alzira's soul—
What bleeding phantom moves along the storm?
It is—it is my lover's well-known form!
Tho' the dim moon is veil'd, his robes of light
Tinge the dark clouds, and gild the mist of night: 110
Approach! Alzira's breast no terrors move,
Her fears are all for ever lost in love!
Safe on the hanging cliff I now can rest,
And press its pointed pillow to my breast—
He weeps! in heav'n he weeps! I feel his tear—   115
It chills my trembling heart, yet still 'tis dear—
To him all joyless are the realms above,
That pale look speaks of pity, and of love!
My love ascends! he soars in azure light;
Stay tender spirit—cruel! stay thy flight—   120
Again descend in yonder rolling cloud,
And veil Alzira in thy misty shroud—
He comes! my love has plac'd the dagger near,
And on its hallow'd point has dropp'd a tear"—
As roll'd her wand'ring glances wide around   125
She snatch'd a reeking sabre from the ground;
Firmly her lifted hand the weapon press'd,
And deep she plung'd it in her panting breast:
"'Tis but a few short moments that divide
Alzira from her love!"—she said—and died.   130

PERU
Canto the Third

The Argument

Pizarro *takes possession of Cuzco—the fanaticism of* Valverde, *a Spanish priest—its dreadful effects—A Peruvian priest put to the torture—his daughter's distress—he is rescued by* Las Casas, *an amiable Spanish ecclesiastic, and led to a place of safety, where he dies—his daughter's narration of her sufferings—her death.*

Canto the Third

Now stern Pizarro seeks the distant plains,
Where beauteous Cuzco[1] lifts her golden fanes:[2]
The meek Peruvians gaz'd in pale dismay,
Nor barr'd the dark oppressor's sanguine way:
And soon on Cuzco, where the dawning light   5
Of glory shone, foretelling day more bright,
Where the young arts had shed unfolding flowers,
A scene of spreading desolation lowers;
While buried deep in everlasting shade,
Those lustres sicken, and those blossoms fade.   10
And yet, devoted land, not gold alone,
Or wild ambition wak'd thy parting groan;
For, lo! a fiercer fiend, with joy elate,
Feasts on thy suff'rings, and impels thy fate.
Fanatic fury rears her sullen shrine,   15
Where vultures prey, where venom'd adders twine;
Her savage arm with purple torrents stains
Thy rocking temples, and thy falling fanes;
Her blazing torches flash the mounting fire,
She grasps the sabre, and she lights the pyre;   20
Her voice is thunder, rending the still air,
Her glance the livid light'ning's fatal glare;
Her lips unhallow'd breathe their impious strain,
And pure religion's sacred voice profane;

---

1 Capital of the Inca Empire, founded around 1200. It was mainly a center for ceremonial and political activities rather than a residential area (*Concise Oxford Dictionary of Archaeology* 120). Francisco Pizarro invaded Cuzco 15 November 1533 (Lockhart *Spanish Peru*, 4).

2 Flags, banners, pendants (*OED*).

Whose precepts, pity's mildest deeds approve,   25
Whose law is mercy, and whose soul is love.
Fanatic fury wakes the rising storm—
She wears the stern Valverda's[1] hideous form;
His bosom never felt another's woes,
No shriek of anguish breaks its dark repose.   30
The temple nods—an aged form appears—
He beats his breast—he rends his silver hairs—
Valverda drags him from the blest abode
Where his meek spirit humbly sought its God:
See, to his aid his child, soft Zilia,[2] springs,   35
And steeps in tears the robe to which she clings,
Till bursting from Peruvia's frighted throng,
Two warlike youths impetuous rush'd along;
One, grasp'd his twanging bow with furious air,
While in his troubled eye sat fierce despair.   40
But all in vain his erring weapon flies,
Pierc'd by a thousand wounds, on earth he lies.
His drooping head the heart-struck Zilia rais'd,
And on the youth in speechless anguish gaz'd;
While he, who fondly shar'd his danger, flew,   45
And from his breast a reeking sabre drew.
"Deep in my faithful bosom let me hide

---

1   Vicente de Valverde (1501?-41) was one of only six Dominican friars
    accompanying Pizarro who survived the journey to central Peru. Because
    he did not receive spoils from Atahuallpa's capture, Valverde's presence at
    the Battle of Cajamarca is not recorded on a list of participants in the
    battle, which James Lockhart calls "the roll of Cajamarca." The absence of
    Valverde's name from this list may explain HMW's omission of Valverde
    from her depiction of the battle in Canto II. Valverde was also present at
    the execution of Atahuallpa, where he succeeded in baptizing the last Inca
    ruler. This conversion meant that Atahuallpa would be garroted (executed
    by strangulation) rather than being burnt alive. Valverde was appointed
    Bishop of Cuzco in January 1537. After Pizarro's assassination (26 June
    1541) during the Spanish Civil War, Valverde fled Peru to escape the
    Almagrists. He was executed by natives of the Island of Puná sometime
    after 11 November 1541 (Lockhart *Men*, 90-102, 202, 204-06; Stirling
    56). Marmontel portrayed Valverde as the central villain in *Les Incas*.
2   Zilia is the name of a character in Françoise de Graffigny's epistolary
    novel *Lettres d'une Péruvienne* (1747; see Appendix B5). Although she
    differs from HMW's character, there are clear thematic parallels
    between the two works, including meditations on friendship, suicide,
    and conversion.

The fatal steel, that would our souls divide,"
He quick exclaims—the dying warrior cries,
"Ah, yet forbear!—by all the sacred ties,   50
That bind our hearts, forbear"—In vain he spoke,
Friendship with frantic zeal impels the stroke:
"Thyself for ever lost, thou hop'st in vain,"
The youth replied, "my spirit to detain;
From thee, my soul, in childhood's earliest year,   55
Caught the light pleasure, and the starting tear;
Thy friendship then my young affections blest,
The first pure passion of my infant breast;
That passion, which o'er life delight has shed,
By reason cherish'd, and by virtue fed: 60
And still in death I feel its strong controul;
Its sacred impulse wings my fleeting soul,
That only lingers here till thou depart,
Whose image lives upon my fainting heart."—
In vain the gen'rous youth, with panting breath,   65
Pour'd these lost murmurs in the ear of death;
He reads the fatal truth in Zilia's eye,
And gives to friendship his expiring sigh.—
But now with rage Valverda's glances roll,
And mark the vengeance rankling in his soul: 70
He bends his wrinkled brow—his lips impart
The brooding purpose of his venom'd heart;
He bids the hoary priest in mutter'd strains,
Abjure his faith, forsake his falling fanes,
While yet the ling'ring pangs of torture wait,   75
While yet Valverda's power suspends his fate.
"Vain man," the victim cried, "to hoary years
Know death is mild, and virtue feels no fears:
Cruel of spirit, come! let tortures prove
The Power I serv'd in life, in death I love."—   80
He ceas'd——with rugged cords his limbs they bound,
And drag the aged suff'rer on the ground;
They grasp his feeble form, his tresses tear,
His robe they rend, his shrivell'd bosom bare.
Ah, see his uncomplaining soul sustain   85
The sting of insult, and the dart of pain;
His stedfast spirit feels one pang alone;
A child's despair awakes one suff'ring groan—
The mourner kneels to catch his parting breath,
To sooth the agony of ling'ring death;   90

No moan she breath'd, no tear had power to flow,
Still on her lip expir'd th' unutter'd woe:
Yet ah, her livid cheek, her stedfast look,
The desolated soul's deep anguish spoke—
Mild victim! close not yet thy languid eyes;   95
Pure spirit! claim not yet thy kindred skies;
A pitying angel comes to stay thy flight,
Las Casas[1] bids thee view returning light:
Ah, let that sacred drop to virtue dear,
Efface thy wrongs—receive his precious tear;   100
See his flush'd cheek with indignation glow,
While from his lips the tones of pity flow.
"Oh suff'ring Lord!" he cried, "whose streaming blood
Was pour'd for man—Earth drank the sacred flood—
Whose mercy in the mortal pang forgave   105
The murd'rous band, thy love alone could save;
Forgive—thy goodness bursts each narrow bound,
Which feeble thought, and human hope surround;
Forgive the guilty wretch, whose impious hand
From thy pure altar flings the flaming brand,[2]   110
In human blood that hallow'd altar steeps,
Libation dire! while groaning nature weeps—
The limits of thy mercy dares to scan,
The object of thy love, his victim,—Man;
While yet I linger, lo, the suff'rer dies—   115

---

1 "Las Casas, &c." that amiable Ecclesiastic, who obtained by his human-
   ity the title of Protector of the Indies [HMW's note]. Bartolomé de las
   Casas (1484-1566), Dominican priest, Spanish missionary, and writer,
   whose works, including *Brevísima relación de la destrucción de las Indias*
   (commonly translated into English as *The Tears of the Indians*), argued
   for the humane treatment of the indigenous populations of the New
   World. Placing Las Casas in Peru is HMW's invention. Las Casas, the
   bishop of Chiapas in Mexico, never journeyed to Peru; neither Robert-
   son nor Raynal place him there. But he was widely read in colonial
   Peru (Starn et al. 107). Although HMW gives the title of "Protector" to
   Las Casas, *The Catholic Encyclopedia* (15: 265) reports that Charles V
   gave Valverde the official title "Protector of the Natives." HMW's depic-
   tion of Las Casas is entirely positive, but modern historians see Las
   Casas as a more controversial figure. See Daniel Castro's *Another Face of
   Empire*.
2 Burning piece of wood.

I see his frame convuls'd—I hear his sighs—
Whoe'er controuls the purpose of my heart
First in this breast shall plunge his guilty dart:"
With anxious step he flew, with eager hands
He broke the fetters, burst the cruel bands.   120
As the fall'n angel heard with awful fear
The cherub's grave rebuke, in grace severe,
And fled, while horror plum'd his impious crest,[1]
The form of virtue, as she stood confest;
So fierce Valverda sullen mov'd along,   125
Abash'd, and follow'd by the guilty throng.
At length the hoary victim, freed from chains,
Las Casas gently leads to safer plains;
Soft Zilia's yielding soul the joy opprest,
She bath'd with floods of tears her father's breast.   130
Las Casas now explores a secret cave
Whose shaggy sides the languid billows lave;
"There rest secure," he cried, "the Christian God
Will hover near, will guard the lone abode."
Oft to the gloomy cell his steps repair,   135
While night's chill breezes wave his silver'd hair;
Oft in the tones of love, the words of peace,
He bids the bitter tears of anguish cease;
Bids drooping hope uplift her languid eyes,
And points a dearer bliss beyond the skies.   140
Yet ah, in vain his pious cares would save
The hoary suff'rer from the op'ning grave;
For deep the pangs of torture pierc'd his frame,
And sunk his wasted life's expiring flame;
To his cold lip Las Casas' hand he prest,   145
He faintly clasp'd his Zilia to his breast;
Then cried, "the God, whom now my vows adore,

---

1 ———————————————On his crest
   Sat horror plum'd.   *Par. Lost*, iv. 988 [HMW's note].

In her only direct allusion in *Peru* to any literary text, HMW reempha-
sizes the connections to Milton's *Paradise Lost* begun in Canto I. This
quotation comes at the end of Book IV, after Satan has visited the
Garden of Eden for the first time. Satan hesitates in tempting Eve, and
Gabriel confronts him, expelling Satan from the Garden. Unlike
Valverda in HMW's *Peru*, Satan in *Paradise Lost* stands defiant with his
crest, poised to fight Gabriel. Milton's Satan does not flee until Gabriel
shows him the astronomical sign that he is destined to lose this fight.

My heart thro' life obey'd, unknowing more;
His mild forgiveness then my soul shall prove,
His mercy share—Las Casas' God, is Love!"   150
He spoke no more—his Zilia's frantic moan
Was heard responsive to his dying groan.
"Victim of impious zeal," Las Casas cries,
"Accept departed shade, a Christian's sighs;
And thou, soft mourner, tender, drooping form,   155
What power shall guard thee from the fearful storm?"
"Weep not for me," she cried, "for Zilia's breast
Soon in the shelt'ring earth shall find its rest.
Hope not the victim of despair to save,
I ask but death—I only seek a grave—   160
Witness thou mangled form that earth retains,
Witness a murder'd lover's cold remains.
I liv'd my father's pangs to sooth, to share;
I bore to live, tho' life was all despair—
In vain my lover, urg'd by fond desire   165
To shield from torture, and from death my sire,
Flew to the fane where stern Valverda rag'd,
And fearless, with unequal force engag'd;
I saw him bleeding, dying press the ground,
I drew the poison from each fatal wound;   170
I bath'd those wounds with tears—he pour'd a sigh—
A drop hung trembling in his closing eye—
Ah, still his mournful sigh I shiv'ring hear,
In every pulse I feel his parting tear—
I faint—an icy coldness chills each vein,   175
No more these feeble limbs their load sustain:
Spirit of pity! catch my fleeting breath,
A moment stay—and close my eyes in death—
Las Casas, thee, thy God in mercy gave
To sooth my pangs—to find the wretch a grave."—   180
She ceas'd—her spirit fled to purer spheres—
Las Casas bathes the pallid corse with tears—
Fly, minister of good! nor ling'ring shed
Those fruitless sorrows o'er the unconscious dead;
Ah fly—'tis innocence, 'tis virtue bleeds,   185
And heav'n will listen, when an angel pleads;
I view the sanguine flood, the wasting flame,
I hear a suff'ring world Las Casas claim![1]

---

1 This line may be read "I hear Las Casas claim a suff'ring world."

PERU
Canto the Fourth

The Argument

Almagro*'s expedition to Chili—his troops suffer great hardships from cold, in crossing the Andes—they reach Chili—the Chilese make a brave resistance—the revolt of the Peruvians in Cuzco—they are led on by* Manco-Capac, *the successor of* Ataliba—*his parting with* Cora, *his wife—the Peruvians regain half their city—Almagro leaves Chili—to avoid the Andes, he crosses a vast desert—his troops can find no water—the rest divide in two bands—*Alphonso *leads the second band, which soon reaches a fertile valley—the Spaniards observe the natives are employed in searching the streams for gold— they resolve to attack them.*

Canto the Fourth

Now the stern partner of Pizarro's[1] toils,
Almagro,[2] lur'd by hope of golden spoils,
To distant Chili's[3] ever-verdant meads,
Thro' paths untrod, a band of warriors leads;
O'er the high Andes' frozen steeps they go,   5

---

1   See note to Canto II. 2.

2   The Spaniard Diego de Almagro (1475-1538) settled in Panama before being chosen by Pizarro as part of a company that would explore and later conquer Peru. The men were given joint authority over the army and conquered land, but bitter disagreements developed between them over the division of conquest spoils, leading to the Battle of Salinas referenced in Canto VI and Almagro's execution. HMW's characterization draws from Raynal: "Pizarro was to command the troops, Almagro conduct the succors, and Luques prepare the means. This plan of ambition, avarice, and ferociousness was completed by fanaticism.... all three swearing, by the blood of their God, that, to enrich themselves, they would not spare the blood of man" (Raynal II: 472).

3   On 3 July 1535, Almagro marched from Cuzco to Chile with nearly 600 soldiers and 12,000 natives provided by one of Huayna Cápac's surviving sons, Paullu. After twenty months, Almagro and his "men of Chile," as they were later called, returned to Peru deeply disillusioned. They suffered privation and defeat by the natives and had not discovered the treasure, which they had so eagerly sought. When Almagro heard of Manco Cápac's rebellion in Cuzco, he saw it as his chance to unseat Pizarro (Klarén 40).

And wander mid' eternal hills of snow:
In vain the vivifying orb of day
Darts on th' impervious ice his fervent ray;
Cold, keen as chains the oceans of the Pole,
Numbs the shrunk frame, and chills the vig'rous soul—   10
At length they reach luxuriant Chili's plain,
Where ends the dreary bound of winter's reign;
Where spring sheds odours thro' th' unvaried year,
And bathes the flower of summer, with her tear.

    When first the brave Chilese,[1] with eager glance,   15
Behold the hostile sons of Spain advance;
Heard the loud thunder of the cannon[2] crash,
And view'd the light'ning of the instant flash,
The threat'ning sabre red with purple streams,
The lance that quiver'd in the solar beams;   20
With pale surprise they saw the low'ring storm,
Where hung dark danger, in an unknown form:
But soon their spirits, stung with gen'rous shame,
Renounce each terror, and for vengeance flame;
Pant high with sacred freedom's ardent glow,   25
And met intrepid, the superiour foe.
Long unsubdu'd by stern Almagro's train,
Their valiant tribes unequal fight maintain;

---

1 According to Robertson: "the survivors [of Almagro's band], when they
descended into the fertile plains of Chili, had new difficulties to
encounter. They found there a race of men very different from the
people of Peru, intrepid, hardy, independent, and in their bodily consti-
tution, as well as vigour of spirit, nearly resembling the warlike tribes in
North America. Though filled with wonder at the first appearance of the
Spaniards, and still more astonished at the operations of their cavalry
and the effects of their firearms, the Chilese soon recovered so far from
their surprise, as not only to defend themselves with obstinacy, but to
attack their new enemies with more determined fierceness than any
American nation had hitherto discovered" (Robertson *History*, II: 195).

2 In her "Historical Introduction" to the 1752 edition of *Lettres d'une
Péruvienne*, which HMW read, de Graffigny writes: "Thunder, which
they called Yalpor, and lightning passed among them for ministers of the
Sun's justice, and this notion contributed more than a little to the
sacred respect inspired in them by the first Spaniards, whose firearms
they took for instruments of thunder." Translation by David Kornacker,
Letters from a Peruvian Woman 11.

Long victory hover'd doubtful o'er the field,
And oft she forc'd Iberia's band to yield;   30
Oft tore from Spain's proud head her laurel bough,
And bade it blossom on Peruvia's brow;
When sudden tidings reach'd Almagro's ear
That shook the warrior's soul with doubt and fear.

Of murder'd Ataliba's[1] royal race   35
There yet remain'd a youth of blooming grace,
Who pin'd, the captive of relentless Spain,
And long in Cuzco[2] dragg'd her galling chain;
Capac[3] his name, whose soul indignant bears
The rankling fetters, and revenge prepares.   40
But since his daring spirit must forego
The hope to rush upon the tyrant foe,
Led by his parent orb,[4] that gives the day,
And fierce as darts the keen, meridian ray,
He vows to bend unseen his hostile course,   45
Then on the victors rise with latent force,
As sudden from its cloud the brooding storm,
Bursts in the thunder's voice, the lightning's form—
For this, from stern Pizarro he obtains
The boon, enlarg'd, to seek the neighb'ring plains,   50
For one bless'd day, and with his friends unite
To crown with solemn pomp an antient rite;
Share the dear pleasures of the social hour,
And mid' their fetters twine one festal flower.
So spoke the Prince[5]—far other thoughts possest,   55
Far other purpose animates his breast:
For now Peruvia's nobles he commands
To lead, with silent step, her martial bands

---

1   See note to Canto I. 55.
2   See note to Canto III. 2.
3   Title given to the first ruler of the Incas and several subsequent rulers,
    meaning "King" or "Prince." Considered the son of the sun god Inti,
    the *sapa*, or "supreme Inca," was both "man and god" and his subjects
    were the "children of God" (Klarén 19).
4   The sun god, or Inti. Atahuallpa and his ancestors were believed to be
    descended from Inti. Gold was linked to both the sun and the Inca
    leader (MacQuarrie 100). The Incas invoked the power of Inti as a
    symbol of authority over conquered ethnic groups (Klarén 24).
5   Manco Cápac. See notes to Canto IV. 3 and IV. 39 above.

Forth to the destin'd spot, prepar'd to dare
The fiercest shock of dire, unequal war;   60
While every tender, human interest pleads,
And urges the firm soul to lofty deeds.
Now Capac hail'd th' eventful morning's light,
Rose with its dawn, and panted for the fight;
But first with fondness to his heart he prest   65
The tender Cora,[1] partner of his breast;
Who with her lord, had sought the dungeon's gloom,
And wasted there in grief, her early bloom.
"No more," he cried, "no more my love shall feel
The mingled agonies I fly to heal;   .   70
I go, but soon exulting shall return,
And bid my faithful Cora cease to mourn:
For oh, amid' each pang my bosom knows,
What wastes, what wounds it most, are Cora's woes.
Sweet was the love that crown'd our happier hours,   75
And shed new fragrance o'er a path of flowers;
But sure divided sorrow more endears
The tie, that passion seals with mutual tears"—
He paus'd—fast-flowing drops bedew'd her eyes,
While thus in mournful accents she replies: 80
"Still let me feel the pressure of thy chain,
Still share the fetters which my love detain;
Those piercing irons to my soul are dear,
Nor will their sharpness wound while thou art near.
Oh think not, when in thee alone I live,   85
This breast can bear the pain thy dangers give,
Look on our helpless babe in mis'ry nurst—
My child—my child, thy mother's heart will burst!
Methinks I see the raging battle rise,
And hear this harmless suff'rer's feeble cries;   90
I view the blades that pour a sanguine flood,
And plunge their cruel edge in infant blood."—
She could no more; her falt'ring accents die,
Yet her soul spoke expressive in her eye;

---

1 In Marmontel's *Les Incas*, a woman named Cora is one of the three
   virgins of the sun. Another possible origin for this name is the Inca word
   "coya," meaning queen. The coya's husband was believed to be the son
   of Inti, and she was believed to be the daughter of the moon, represent-
   ing womankind. There is evidence that the coya may have had influence
   in the politics of the empire, mainly over the women (Klarén 20).

Her lord beholds her grief, with tender pain,   95
And leads her breathless, to a shelt'ring fane.
Now high in air his feather'd standard waves,
And soon from shrouding woods, and hollow caves,
A num'rous host along the plain appear,
And hail their monarch with a gen'rous tear: 100
To Cuzco's gate now rush th' increasing throngs,
And such their ardor, rouz'd by sense of wrongs,
That vainly would Pizarro's vet'ran force
Arrest the torrent in its raging course;
In vain his murd'ring bands terrific stood,   105
And plung'd their sabres in a sea of blood:
Danger and death Peruvia's sons disdain,
And half their captive city soon regain.
With such pure joy the natives view their lord
To the warm wishes of their souls restor'd   110
As feels the tender child whom force had torn
From his lov'd home, and bruis'd the flower of morn,
When his fond searching eye again beholds
His mother's form, when in her arms she folds
The long lost child, who bathes with tears her face,   115
And finds his safety in her dear embrace.—

　　Soon as Almagro heard applauding fame
The triumphs of Peruvia, loud proclaim,
Unconquer'd Chili's vale he swift forsakes,
And his bold course to distant Cuzco takes;   120
Shuns Andes' icy shower, its chilling snows,
The arrowy gale that on its summit blows;
A burning desart undismay'd he past,
And meets the ardours of the fiery blast.
Now as along the sultry waste they move,   125
The keenest pang of raging thirst they prove:
No cooling fruit its grateful juice distils,
Nor flows one balmy drop from crystal rills;
For nature sickens in th' oppressive beam,
That shrinks the vernal bud, and dries the stream;   130
While horror, as his giant stature grows,
O'er the drear void his spreading shadow throws.

　　Almagro's band now pale, and fainting stray,
While death oft barr'd the sinking warrior's way:
At length the chief divides his martial force,   135

And bids Alphonso,[1] by a sep'rate course,
Lead o'er the hideous desart half his train—
"And search," he cried, "this drear, uncultur'd plain:
Perchance some fruitage withering in the breeze,
The pains of lessen'd numbers may appease;   140
Or Heav'n in pity, from some genial shower,
On the parch'd lip one precious drop may pour."

    Not far the troops of young Alphonso went,
When sudden, from a rising hill's ascent,
They view a valley, fed by fertile springs,   145
Which Andes from his lofty summit flings;
Where summer's flowers their mingled odours shed,
And wildly bloom, a waste by beauty spread—
To the charm'd warrior's eye, the vernal scene
That 'mid the howling desart, smil'd serene,   150
Appear'd like nature rising from the breast
Of chaos,[2] in her infant graces drest:
When warbling angels hail'd the lovely birth,
And stoop'd from heav'n to bless the new-born earth.

    And now Alphonso, and his martial band,   155
On the rich border of the valley stand;
They quaff the limpid stream with eager haste,
And the pure juice that swells the fruitage taste;
Then give to balmy rest the night's still hours,
Fann'd by the sighing gale that shuts the flowers.   160
Soon as the purple beam of morning glows,
Refresh'd from all their toils, the warriors rose;
And saw the gentle natives of the mead
Search the clear currents for the golden seed;
Which from the mountain's height with headlong sweep   165
The torrents bear, in many a shining heap—
Iberia's sons beheld with anxious brow
The tempting lure, then breathe th' unpitying vow
O'er those fair lawns to pour a sanguine flood,

---

1 According to Robertson, Francisco Pizarro sent Alonso de Alvarado to
   oppose Almagro's army. During the battle, Alvarado's army was scat-
   tered, and he was captured (Robertson *History*, II: 201-03). This event is
   not treated in Raynal's brief gloss of the Spanish civil wars in Peru.

2 See *Paradise Lost*: "That Shepherd, who first taught the chosen Seed, /
   In the Beginning how the Heav'ns and Earth / out of Chaos" (I: 8-10).

And dye those lucid streams with waves of blood.　　170
Thus, while the humming bird in beauty drest,
Enchanting offspring of the ardent West,[1]
Attunes his soothing song to notes of love,
Mild as the murmurs of the mourning dove;
While his soft plumage glows with brighter hues,　　175
And while with tender bill he sips the dews,
The savage Condor, on terrific wings,
From Andes' frozen steep relentless springs;
And quiv'ring in his fangs, his hapless prey
Drops his gay plume, and sighs his soul away.　　180

1　Reference to Peru's geographical location west of Spain.

PERU
Canto the Fifth

The Argument

Character of Zamor, *a Bard—his passion for* Aciloe, *daughter of the* Cazique *who rules the valley—the Peruvian tribe prepare to defend themselves—a battle—the Peruvians are vanquished—*Aciloe's *father is made a prisoner, and* Zamor *is supposed to have fallen in the engagement—*Alphonso *becomes enamoured of* Aciloe—*offers to marry her; she rejects him—in revenge he puts her father to the torture—she appears to consent, in order to save him—meets* Zamor *in a wood—*Las Casas *joins them—leads the two lovers to* Alphonso, *and obtains their freedom—*Zamor *conducts* Aciloe *and her father to* Chili—*a reflection on the influence of Poetry over the human mind.*

Canto the Fifth

In this sweet scene, to all the virtues kind,
Mild Zamor own'd the richest gifts of mind;
For o'er his tuneful breast the heav'nly muse
Shed from her sacred spring, inspiring dews.
She loves to breathe her hallow'd flame, where art   5
Has never veil'd the soul, or warp'd the heart;
Where fancy glows with all her native fire,
And passion lives on the exulting lyre.
Nature, in terror rob'd, or beauty drest,
Could thrill with dear enchantment Zamor's breast: 10
He lov'd the languid sigh the zephyr pours,
He lov'd the murm'ring rill that fed the flow'rs;
But more the hollow sound the wild winds form,
When black upon the billow hangs the storm;
The torrent rolling from the mountain steep,   15
Its white foam trembling on the darken'd deep—
And oft on Andes' height[1] with eager gaze,
He view'd the sinking sun's reflected rays,
Glow like unnumber'd stars, that seem to rest
Sublime, upon his ice-encircled breast.   20
Oft his wild warblings charm'd the festal hour,

---

1 The Spanish army nearly perishes in the harsh mountains, while Zamor safely admires the Andes and extolls their sublimity.

Rose, in the vale, and languish'd in the bower;
The heart's responsive tones he well could move,
Whose song was nature, and whose theme was love.

Aciloe's beauties his fond eye confest,   25
Yet more Aciloe's virtues warm'd his breast.
Ah stay, ye tender hours of young delight,
Suspend ye moments your impatient flight;
For sure if aught on earth can bliss impart,
Can shed the genuine joy that sooths the heart,   30
'Tis felt, when early passion's pure controul
Unfolds the first affections of the soul;
Bids her soft sympathies the bosom move,
And wakes the mild emotions dear to love.

The gentle tribe Aciloe's sire obey'd   35
Who still in wisdom, and in mercy sway'd.
From him the dear illusions long had fled,
That o'er the morn of life enchantment shed;
Yet virtue's calm reflections cheer'd his breast,
And life was joy serene, and death was rest.   40
Tho' sweet the early spring, her blossoms bright,
When first she swells the heart with pure delight,
Yet not unlovely is the sober ray
That meekly beams o'er autumn's temper'd day;
Dear are her fading beauties to the soul,   45
While scarce perceiv'd the deep'ning shadows roll.

Now the charm'd lovers dress their future years
In forms of joy, then weep delicious tears,
Expressive on the glowing cheek that hung,
And spoke the fine emotions whence they sprung—   50
'Twas truth's warm energy, love's sweet controul,
'Twas all that virtue whispers to the soul.
When lo, Iberia's ruthless sons advance,
Roll the stern eye, and shake the pointed lance:
Oh Nature! the destroying band oppose,   55
Nature, arrest their course—they come thy foes—
Benignant power, where thou with lib'ral care
Hast planted joy, they come to plant despair—
Peruvia's tribe beheld the hostile throng
With desolating fury pour along;   60
With horror their ensanguin'd path they trac'd,

And now to meet the murd'ring band they haste;
The hoary chief to the dire conflict leads
His death devoted train—the battle bleeds.

      Aciloe's searching eye can now no more   65
The form of Zamor, or her sire explore;
She hears the moan of death in every gale,
She sees a purple torrent stain the vale;
While destin'd all the bitterness to prove
Of mourning duty, and of bleeding love,   70
Each name that's dearest wakes her bursting sigh,
Throbs at her soul, and trembles in her eye.
Now, pierc'd by wounds, and breathless from the fight,
Her friend, the valiant Omar, struck her sight:
"Omar" (she cried) "you bleed, unhappy youth,   75
And sure that look unfolds some fatal truth:
Speak, pitying speak, my frantic fears forgive,
Say, does my father, does my Zamor live?"
"All, all is lost," (the dying Omar said)
"And endless griefs are thine, dear wretched maid;   80
I saw thy aged sire a captive bound,
I saw thy Zamor press the crimson ground"—
He could no more, he yields his fleeting breath,
While all in vain she seeks repose in death.
But, oh, how far each other pang above   85
Throbs the wild agony of hopeless love;
That grief, for which in vain shall comfort shed
Her healing balm, or time in pity spread
The veil, that throws a shade o'er other care;
For here, and here alone, profound despair   90
Casts o'er the suff'ring soul a lasting gloom,
And slowly leads her victim to the tomb.

      Now rude tumultuous sounds assail her ear,
And soon Alphonso's victor train[1] appear:
Then, as with ling'ring step he mov'd along,   95
She saw her father mid' the captive throng;
She saw with dire dismay, she wildly flew,
Her snowy arms around his form she threw:
"He bleeds" (she cries) "I hear his moan of pain,
My father will not bear the galling chain;   100

---

1 See note to Canto VI. 1.

"Alphonso and Aciloe." Stipple etching by Francesco Bartolozzi, after Johann Heinrich Ramberg. Published in London by Mary Ryland, 1 May 1788. Private collection.

My tender father will his child forsake,
His mourning child, but soon her heart will break.
Cruel Alphonso, let not helpless age
Feel thy hard yoke, and meet thy barb'rous rage;
Or, oh, if ever mercy mov'd thy soul,   105
If ever thou hast felt her blest controul,
Grant my sad heart's desire, and let me share
The load, that feeble frame but ill can bear."

    While the young victor, as she falt'ring spoke,
With fix'd attention, and with ardent look,   110

Hung on her tender glance, that love inspires,
The rage of conquest yields to milder fires.
Yet, as he gaz'd enraptur'd on her form,
Her virtues awe the heart her beauties warm;
And, while impassion'd tones his love reveal,   115
He asks with holy rites his vows to seal—
"Hop'st thou," she cried, "those sacred ties shall join
This bleeding heart, this trembling hand to thine?
To thine, whose ruthless heart has caus'd my pains,
Whose barb'rous hands the blood of Zamor stains!   120
Can'st thou—the murd'rer of my peace, controul
The grief that swells, the pang that rends my soul?
That pang shall death, shall death alone remove,
And cure the anguish of despairing love."

       In vain th' enamour'd youth essay'd each art   125
To calm her sorrows, and to sooth her heart;
While, in the range of thought, her tender breast
Could find no hope, on which her griefs might rest,
While her soft soul, which Zamor's image fills,
Shrinks from the cruel author of its ills.   130
At length to madness stung by fix'd disdain,
The victor gives to rage the fiery rein;
And bids her sorrows flow from that fond source
Where strong affection feels their keenest force,
Whose breast, when most it suffers, only heeds   135
The sharper pangs by which another bleeds:
For now his cruel mandate doom'd her sire
Stretch'd on the bed of torture, to expire;
Bound on the rack, unmov'd the victim lies,
Stifling in agony weak nature's sighs.   140
But oh, what form of language can impart
The frantic grief that wrung Aciloe's heart,
When to the height of hopeless sorrow wrought,
The fainting spirit feels a pang of thought,
Which never painted in the hues of speech,   145
Lives at the soul, and mocks expression's reach!
At length she trembling cried, "the conflict's o'er,
My heart, my breaking heart can bear no more—
Yet spare his feeble age—my vows receive,
And oh, in mercy, bid my father live!"—   150
"Wilt then be mine?" the enamour'd chief replies,
"Yes, cruel! see, he dies, my father dies—

Save, save, my father"—"Dear, angelic maid,"
The charm'd Alphonso cried, "be swift obey'd:
Unbind his chains—Ah, calm each anxious pain,   155
Aciloe's voice no more shall plead in vain;
Plac'd near his child, thy aged sire shall share
Our joys still cherish'd by thy tender care"—
"No more" (she cried) "will fate that bliss allow,
Before my lips shall breathe the nuptial vow,   160
Some faithful guide shall lead his aged feet,
To distant scenes that yield a safe retreat;[1]
Where some soft heart, some gentle hand, will shed
The drops of comfort on his hoary head:—
My Zamor, if thy spirit trembles near,   165
Forgive!"—she ceas'd, and pour'd her hopeless tear.

    Now night descends, and steeps each weary breast,
Save sad Aciloe's, in the balm of rest.
Her aged father's beauteous dwelling stood
Near the cool shelter of a waving wood: 170
But now the gales that bend its foliage die,
Soft on the silver turf[2] its shadows lie;
While, slowly wand'ring o'er the scene below,
The gazing moon look'd pale as silent woe.
The sacred shade, amid whose fragrant bowers   175
Zamor oft sooth'd with song the evening hours,
Pour'd to the lunar orb, his magic lay,
More mild, more pensive than her musing ray,
That shade with trembling step, the mourner sought,
And thus she breath'd her tender, plaintive thought.   180
"Ah where, dear object of these piercing pains,
Where rests thy murder'd form, thy lov'd remains?
On what sad spot, my Zamor, flow'd the wound
That purpled with thy streaming blood the ground?
Oh had Aciloe in that hour been nigh,   185
Had'st thou but fix'd on me thy closing eye;
Told with faint voice, 'twas death's worst pang to part,
And dropp'd thy last, cold tear upon my heart!

---

1 HMW implies that Aciloe's impending coerced "nuptial" to Alphonso, a
    man she sees as "ruthless," "barb'rous," a "murd'rer," and "cruel,"
    would be rape, a notion reinforced by line 282.
2 Apart from gold, silver was the most desired commodity from Peruvian
    mines.

A pang less bitter then would waste this breast,
That in the grave alone shall seek its rest.   190
Soon as some friendly hand, in mercy leads
My aged father, safe to Chili's meads;
Death shall for ever, seal the nuptial tie,
The heart belov'd by thee is fix'd to die."
She ceas'd, when dimly thro' a flood of tears   195
She sees her Zamor's form, his voice she hears.—
"'Tis he," she cried, "he moves upon the gale,
My Zamor's sigh is deep—his look is pale—
I faint"—his arms receive her sinking frame,
He calls his love by every tender name,   200
He stays her fleeting spirit—life anew
Warms her cold cheek—his tears her cheek bedew—
"Thy Zamor lives," he cried: "as on the ground
I senseless lay, some child of pity bound
My bleeding wounds, and bore me from the plain—   205
But thou art lost, and I have liv'd in vain."
"Forgive," she cried, in accents of despair,
"Zamor forgive thy wrongs, and oh forbear
The mild reproach that fills thy mournful eye,
The tear that wets thy cheek—I mean to die!   210
Could I behold my aged sire endure
The pains his wretched child had power to cure?
Still, still my father, stretch'd in death, I see,
His grey locks trembling, as he gaz'd on me:
My Zamor, soft—breathe not so loud a sigh—   215
Some list'ning foe may pityless deny
This parting hour—hark, sure some step I hear,
Zamor again is lost—for now 'tis near"—
She paus'd, when sudden from the shelt'ring wood
A venerable form before them stood: 220
"Fear not, soft maid," he cry'd, "nor think I come
To seal with deeper miseries thy doom;
To bruise the breaking heart that sorrow rends,
Ah not for this Las Casas hither bends—
He comes to bid those rising sorrows cease,   225
To pour upon thy wounds the balm of peace.
I rov'd with dire Almagro's ruthless train
Thro' scenes of death, to Chili's verdant plain;
Their wish, to bathe that verdant plain in gore,
Then from its bosom drag the golden ore;   230
But mine, to check the stream of human blood,

Or mingle drops of anguish with the flood.
When from those fair unconquer'd vales they fled,
This frame was stretch'd upon the languid bed
Of pale disease:[1] when helpless, and alone,   235
The Chilese spy'd their friend, the murd'rers gone,
With eager fondness round my couch they drew,
And my cold hand with gushing tears bedew;
By day, they sooth my pains with sweet delight,
And give to watchings the chill hours of night;   240
For me their tender spirits joy to prove
The cares of pity, and the toils of love.
Soon as I heard, that o'er this gentle scene,
Where peace and virtue mingled smile serene,
The foe, like clouds that fold the tempest, hung,   245
I hither flew, my breast with anguish wrung.
A Chilese band the pathless desert trac'd,
And softly bore me o'er its dreary waste;
Then parting, at my feet they bend, and clasp
These aged knees—my soul yet feels their grasp.   250
Now o'er the vale with painful step I stray'd,
And reach'd the shelt'ring grove: there, hapless maid,
My list'ning ear has caught thy piercing wail,
My heart has trembled to thy moving tale."—[2]
"And art thou he!" the mournful pair exclaim,   255
"How dear to mis'ry's soul, Las Casas' name!
Spirit benign, who every grief can share,
Whose pity stoops to make the wretch its care;
Weep not for us—in vain thy tear shall flow
For hopeless anguish, and distracting woe"—   260
They ceas'd; in accents mild, the saint returns,
"Yet let me sooth the pains my bosom mourns:
Come, gentle suff'rers, follow to yon fane,

---

1 Between 1524 and 1527, smallpox killed 200,000 Incas out of an esti-
   mated population of six million. Pizarro's success was greatly aided by
   the death from smallpox of the emperor, Huayna Cápac, and his heir.
   The disease remained rampant and deadly in England, as well as
   Europe, during HMW's time; for example, Mary Shelley contracted
   smallpox in Paris in 1828.
2 Aciloe's "moving tale" not only inspires Alphonso to free Zamor, but
   also anticipates HMW's title change in 1823 from *Peru* to "Peruvian
   Tales."

Where rests Alphonso, with his victor train;
My voice shall urge his soul to gen'rous deeds, 265
And bid him hear, when truth, and nature pleads."
While in soft tones, Las Casas thus exprest
His pious purpose, o'er Aciloe's breast
A dawning ray of cheering comfort streams,
But faint the hope that on her spirit beams; 270
Faint, as when ebbing life must soon depart,
The pulse that trembles, while it warms the heart.

Before Alphonso now the lovers stand;
The aged suff'rer join'd the mournful band;
While with the look that guardian seraphs wear, 275
When sent to calm the throbs of mortal care,
The story of their woes Las Casas told,
Then cry'd, "the wretched Zamor here behold—
Hop'st thou, fond man, a passion to controul
Fix'd in the breast, and woven in the soul? 280
But know, mistaken youth, thy power in vain
Would bind thy victim in the nuptial chain:
That faithful heart will rend the galling tie,
That heart will break, that tender form will die—
Then by each sacred name to nature dear, 285
By her strong shriek, her agonizing tear;
By every horror bleeding passion knows,
By the wild glance that speaks her frantic woes;
By all the wasting pangs that rend her breast,
By the deep groan that gives her spirit rest! 290
Let mercy's pleading voice thy bosom move,
And fear to burst the bonds of plighted love"—
He paus'd—now Zamor's moan Alphonso hears,
Now sees the cheek of age bedew'd with tears:
Palid, and motionless, Aciloe stands, 295
Fix'd was her mournful eye, and clasp'd her hands;
Her heart was chill'd—her trembling heart, for there
Hope slowly sinks in cold, and dark despair.
Alphonso's soul was mov'd—"No more," he cried,
"My hapless flame shall hearts like yours divide. 300
Live, tender spirit, soft Aciloe, live,
And all the wrongs of mad'ning rage forgive.
Go from this desolated region far,
These plains, where av'rice spreads the waste of war;

Go, where pure pleasures gild the peaceful scene,　　　　305
. Go where mild virtue sheds her ray serene."

　　　In vain th' enraptur'd maid would now impart,
The rising joy that swells, that pains her heart;
Las Casas' feet in floods of tears she steeps,
Looks on her sire and smiles, then turns, and weeps;　　310
Then smiles again, while her flush'd cheek reveals
The mingled tumult of delight she feels.
So fall the crystal showers of fragrant spring,
And o'er the pure, clear sky, soft shadows fling;
Then paint the drooping clouds from which they flow　　315
With the warm colours of the lucid bow.
Now, o'er the barren desert, Zamor leads
Aciloe, and her sire, to Chili's meads:
There, many a wand'ring wretch, condemn'd to roam
By hard oppression, found a shelt'ring home:　　　　320
Zamor to pity, tun'd the vocal shell,
. Bright'ning the tear of anguish, as it fell.
Did e'er the human bosom throb with pain
The heav'nly muse has sought to sooth in vain?
She, who can still with harmony its sighs,　　　　325
And wake the sound, at which affliction dies;
Can bid the stormy passions backward roll,
And o'er their low-hung tempests lift the soul;
With magic touch paint nature's various scene
Wild on the mountain, in the vale serene:　　　　330
Can tinge the breathing rose with brighter bloom,
Or hang the sombrous rock in deeper gloom;
Explore the gem, whose pure, reflected ray
Throws o'er the central cave a paler day;
Or soaring view the comet's fiery frame　　　　335
Rush o'er the sky, and fold the sphere in flame;
While the charm'd spirit, as her accents move,
Is wrapt in wonder, or dissolv'd in love.

PERU
Canto the Sixth

The Argument

The troops of Almagro *and* Alphonso *meet on the plains of*
*Cuzco—*Manco-Capac *attacks them by night—his army is defeated,*
*and he is forced to fly with its scattered remains—*Cora *goes in*
search of him—her infant in her arms—overcome with fatigue, she
rests at the foot of a mountain—an earthquake—a band of Indians
*fly to the mountains for shelter—*Cora *discovers her husband—their*
*interview—her death—he escapes with his infant—*Almagro *claims*
a share of the spoils of Cuzco—*his contention with* Pizarro—*the*
Spaniards *destroy each other—*Almagro *is taken prisoner, and put to*
death—his soldiers, in revenge, assassinate Pizarro *in his palace—*
Las Casas *dies—*Gasca, *a* Spanish *ecclesiastic, arrives in* Peru—
invested with great power—his virtuous conduct—the annual festival
of the Peruvians—their late victories over the Spaniards in Chili—a
wish for the restoration of their liberty—the Poem concludes.

Canto the Sixth

At length Almagro, and Alphonso's train,[1]
Each peril past, unite on Cuzco's plain:
Capac, who now beheld with anxious woe,
Th' increasing numbers of the powerful foe,
Resolves to pierce beneath the shroud of night   5
The hostile camp, and brave the vent'rous fight;
Tho' weak the wrong'd Peruvians arrowy showers,
To the dire weapons stern Iberia pours.
Fierce was th' unequal contest, for the soul
When rais'd by some high passion's strong controul,   10
New strings the nerves, and o'er the glowing frame
Breathes the warm spirit of heroic flame.

---

1 Francisco Pizarro sent for Alonso de Alvarado to reinforce his army at
   Cuzco, then under control of Manco Cápac. Almagro returned from his
   disastrous expedition in Chili, taking Cuzco in an attempt to usurp
   power from Pizarro. Almagro routed Alvarado's army before he reached
   the city. Alvarado and his men joined Pizarro's army to retake Cuzco
   from Almagro (Stirling 100-11). See note to Canto IV: 136.

But from the scene where raging slaughter burns,
The timid muse with pallid horror turns:
The sounds of frantic woe she panting hears,   15
Where anguish dims a mother's eye with tears;
Or where the maid, who gave to love's soft power
Her faithful spirit, weeps the parting hour:
And ah, till death shall ease the tender woe,
That soul must languish, and those tears must flow;   20
For never with the thrill that rapture proves
Shall bless'd affection hail the form she loves;
Her eager glance no more that form shall view,
Her quiv'ring lip has breath'd the last adieu!
Now night, that pour'd upon her hollow gale   25
The moan of death, withdrew her mournful veil;
The sun rose lovely from the sleeping flood,
And morning glitter'd o'er the field of blood;
Where bath'd in gore, Peruvia's vanquish'd train
Lay cold and senseless on the sanguine plain.   30
Capac, their gen'rous chief, whose ardent soul
Had sought the rage of battle to controul,
Beheld with keen despair his warriors yield,
And fled indignant from the conquer'd field.
From Cuzco now a wretched throng repair,   35
Who tread mid' slaughter'd heaps in mute despair,
O'er some lov'd corse the shroud of earth to spread,
And drop the sacred tear that sooths the dead.
No shriek was heard, for agony supprest
The fond complaints which ease the swelling breast: 40
Each hope for ever lost, they only crave
The deep repose which wraps the shelt'ring grave.
So the meek Lama, lur'd by some decoy
Of man, from all his unembitter'd joy;
Ere while, as free as roves the wand'ring breeze,   45
Meets the hard burden on his bending knees;[1]

---

1   The Lamas bend their knees and stoop their body in such a manner as
    not to discompose their burden. They move with a slow but firm pace,
    in countries that are impracticable to other animals. They are neither
    dispirited by fasting nor drudgery, while they have any strength remain-
    ing; but, when they are totally exhausted, or fall under their burden, it is
    to no purpose to harrass and beat them: they will continue striking their
    heads on the ground, first on one side, then on the other, till they kill
    themselves.—*Abbé* Raynal's *History of the European Settlements* [HMW's
    note]. Raynal II: 529.

O'er rocks, and mountains, dark, and waste he goes,
Nor shuns the path where no soft herbage grows;
Till worn with toil, on earth he prostrate lies,
Heeds not the barb'rous lash, but patient dies.   50
Swift o'er the field of death sad Cora flew,
Her infant to his mother's bosom grew;
She seeks her wretched lord, who fled the plain
With the last remnant of his vanquish'd train:
Thro' the lone vale, or forest's sombrous shade   55
A dreary solitude, the mourner stray'd;
Her timid heart can now each danger dare,
Her drooping soul is arm'd by deep despair—
Long, long she wander'd, till oppress'd with toil,
Her trembling footsteps track with blood the soil;   60
In vain with moans her distant lord she calls,
In vain the bitter tear of anguish falls;
Her moan expires along the desert wood,
Her tear is mingled with the crimson flood.

      Where o'er an ample vale a mountain rose,   65
Low at its base her fainting form she throws;
"And here, my child," (she cried, with panting breath)
"Here let us wait the hour of ling'ring death:
This famish'd bosom can no more supply
The streams that nourish life, my babe must die!   70
In vain I strive to cherish for thy sake
My failing strength; but when my heart-strings break,
When my chill'd bosom can no longer warm,
My stiff'ning arms no more enfold thy form,
Soft on this bed of leaves my child shall sleep,   75
Close to his mother's corse he will not weep:
Oh weep not then, my tender babe, tho' near,
I shall not hear thy moan, nor see thy tear;
Hope not to move me by thy piercing cry,
Nor seek with searching look my answering eye."   80
As thus the dying Cora's plaints arose,
O'er the fair valley sudden darkness throws
A hideous horror; thro' the wounded air
Howl'd the shrill voice of nature in despair;
The birds dart screaming thro' the fluid sky,   85
And, dash'd upon the cliff's hard surface die;
High o'er their rocky bounds the billows swell,
Then to their deep abyss affrighted fell;

"The Death of Cora." Stipple etching by Francesco Bartolozzi, after Johann Heinrich Ramberg. Published in London by Mary Ryland, 1 May 1788. Private collection.

Earth groaning heaves with dire convulsive throws,
While yawning gulphs her central caves disclose:[1]   90
Now rush'd a frighted throng with trembling pace
Along the vale, and sought the mountain's base;

---

1 The earthquake description in lines 82-90 draws heavily on Raynal's *History*:

The birds are then observed to dart in their flight. Neither their tails nor their wings serve them any longer as oars and helm *(continued)*

Purpos'd its perilous ascent to gain,
And shun the ruin low'ring o'er the plain.
They reach'd the spot where Cora clasp'd her child,   95
And gaz'd on present death with aspect mild;
They pitying paus'd—she lifts her mournful eye,
And views her lord!—he hears his Cora's sigh—
He meets her look—their melting souls unite,
O'erwhelm'd, and agoniz'd with wild delight—   100
At length she faintly cried, "we yet must part!
Short are these rising joys—I feel my heart,
My suff'ring heart is cold, and mists arise
That shroud thy image from my closing eyes:
Oh save my child!—our tender infant save,   105
And shed a tear upon thy Cora's grave"—
The flutt'ring pulse of life now ceas'd to play,
And in his arms a pallid corse she lay:
O'er her dear form he hung in speechless pain,
And still on Cora call'd, but call'd in vain;   110
Scarce could his soul in one short moment bear
The wild extreme of transport, and despair.

    Now o'er the west[1] in melting softness streams
A lustre, milder than the morning beams;
A purer dawn dispell'd the fearful night,   115
And nature glow'd in all the blooms of light;
The birds awake the note that hails the day,
And spread their pinions in the purple ray;
A zone of gold the wave's still bosom bound,
And beauty shed a placid smile around.   120
Then, first awaking from his mournful trance,

---

to swim in the fluid of the skies. They dash themselves in pieces
against the walls, the trees, and the rocks.... To this tumult in the air is
added the rumbling of the earth, whose cavities and deep recesses re-
echo each other's noises.... Upon these indications, the inhabitants
instantly run out of their houses, with terror impressed on their coun-
tenances, and fly to search in the enclosures of public places, or in the
fields, an asylum from the fall of their roofs. (II: 513)

1 Cuzco is located in a mountain valley, so the morning light must first
clear the mountain to the east, shining on the western mountains before
it lights the valley.

The wretched Capac cast an eager glance
On his lov'd babe; th' unconscious infant smil'd,
And showers of softer sorrow bath'd his child.
The hollow voice now sounds in fancy's ear,   125
She sees the dying look, the parting tear,
That sought with anxious tenderness to save
That dear memorial from the closing grave:
He clasps the object of his love's last care,
And vows for him the load of life to bear;   130
To rear the blossom of a faded flower,
And bid remembrance sooth each ling'ring hour.
He journey'd o'er a dreary length of way,
To plains where freedom shed her hallow'd ray;
O'er many a pathless wood, and mountain hoar,   135
To that fair clime her lifeless form he bore.
Ye who ne'er suffer'd passion's hopeless pain,
Deem not the toil that sooths its anguish vain;
Its fondness to the mould'ring corse extends,
Its faithful tear with the cold ashes blends.   140
Perchance, the conscious spirit of the dead
Numbers the drops affection loves to shed;
Perchance a sigh of holy pity gives
To the sad bosom, where its image lives.
Oh nature! sure thy sympathetic ties   145
Shall o'er the ruins of the grave arise;
Undying spring from the relentless tomb,
And shed, in scenes of love, a lasting bloom.

    Not long Iberia's sullied trophies wave,
Her guilty warriors press th' untimely grave;   150
For av'rice, rising from the caves of earth,
Wakes all her savage spirit into birth;
Bids proud Almagro feel her baleful flame,
And Cuzco's treasures from Pizarro claim:
Pizarro holds the rich alluring prize,   155
With firmer grasp, the fires of discord rise.
Now fierce in hostile rage, each warlike train
Purple with issuing gore Peruvia's plain;
There, breathing hate, and vengeful death they stood,
And bath'd their impious hands in kindred blood;   160
While pensive on each hill, whose lofty brow
O'erhung with sable woods the vale below;

Peruvia's hapless tribes[1] in scatter'd throngs,
Beheld the fiends of strife avenge their wrongs.
Now conquest, bending on her crimson wings,   165
Her sanguine laurel to Pizarro brings;
While bound, and trembling in her iron chain,
Almagro swells the victor's captive train.
In vain his pleading voice, his suppliant eye,
Conjure his conqu'ror, by the holy tie   170
That seal'd their mutual league with sacred force,
When first to climes unknown they bent their course;
When danger's rising horrors lowr'd afar,
The storms of ocean, and the toils of war,
The sad remains of wasted life to spare,   175
The shrivell'd bosom, and the silver'd hair:—
But vainly from his lips these accents part,
Nor move Pizarro's cold, relentless heart,
That never trembled to the suff'rer's sigh,
Or view'd the suff'rer's tear with melting eye.   180
Almagro dies[2]—the victor's savage pride
To his pale corse funereal rites denied.
Chill'd by the heavy dews of night it lay,
And wither'd in the sultry beam of day,
Till Indian bosoms, touch'd with gen'rous woe,   185
In the pale form forgot the tyrant foe;
The last sad duties to his ashes paid,
And sooth'd with pity's tear the hov'ring shade.
With unrelenting hate the conqu'ror views
Almagro's band, and vengeance still pursues;   190
Condemns the victims of his power to stray
In drooping poverty's chill, thorny way;
To pine with famine's agony severe,

---

1 According to Robertson, Peruvian warriors crowd the mountain slopes,
   observing the battle of Cuzco, but fail to attack the weakened Spanish
   armies as planned. Robertson explains this outcome as lack of courage
   on the part of the Indians (Robertson *History*, II: 207). HMW omits
   these details.
2 Almagro was 73 at the time of his execution. He was garroted (stran-
   gled) on 8 July 1538, and his body was brought out in front of a crowd
   of Peruvians and Spaniards for beheading. His severed head was
   paraded through Cuzco and his headless corpse was taken by his
   African slave for burial in La Merced (Stirling 110-12). HMW has the
   Peruvians bury Almagro's body.

And all the ling'ring forms of death to fear;
Till by despair impell'd, the rival train[1]   195
Rush to the haughty victor's glitt'ring fane;
Swift on their foe with rage impetuous dart,
And plunge their daggers in his guilty heart.
How unavailing now the treasur'd ore
That made Peruvia's rifled bosom poor?   200
He falls—no mourner near to breathe a sigh,
Catch the last breath, and close the languid eye;
Deserted, and refus'd the holy tear
That warm affection sheds o'er virtue's bier;
Denied those drops that stay the parting breath,   205
That sooth the spirit on the verge of death;
Tho' now the pale expiring form would buy
With Andes' glitt'ring mines, one faithful sigh!

Now faint with virtue's toil, Las Casas' soul
Sought with exulting hope, her heav'nly goal: 210
A bending angel consecrates his tears,
And leads his kindred mind to purer spheres.
But, ah! whence pours that stream of lambent light,
That soft-descending on the raptur'd sight,
Gilds the dark horrors of the raging storm—   215
It lights on earth—mild vision! gentle form—
'Tis Sensibility! she stands confest,
With trembling step she moves, and panting breast;
Wav'd by the gentle breath of passing sighs
Loose in the air her robe expanded flies;   220
Wet with the dew of tears her soft veil streams,
And in her eye the ray of pity beams;
No vivid roses her mild cheek illume,
Sorrow's wan touch has chas'd the purple bloom:
Yet ling'ring there in tender, pensive grace,   225
The softer lily fills the vacant place;
And ever as her precious tears bedew
Its modest flowers, they shed a paler hue.

---

1 Almagro's son by a Peruvian woman, Diego, plotted to assassinate Fran-
  cisco Pizarro in June of 1541 (Klarén 40-41). In Robertson's account,
  Almagro's followers, many of whom are destitute, sought revenge after
  Pizarro divided the Peruvian provinces among Spanish leaders, giving
  nothing to them (Robertson *History*, II: 211-12).

To yon deserted grave, lo swift she flies
Where her lov'd victim, mild Las Casas lies: 230
Light on the hallow'd turf I see her stand,
And slowly wave in air her snowy wand;
I see her deck the solitary haunt,
With chaplets twin'd from every weeping plant.
Its odours mild the simple vi'let shed,   235
The shrinking lily hung its drooping head;
A moaning zephyr sigh'd within the bower,
And bent the yielding stem of every flower:
"Hither" (she cried, her melting tone I hear
It vibrates full on fancy's raptur'd ear)   240
"Ye gentle spirits whom my soul refines,
Where all its animating lustre shines;
Ye who can exquisitely feel the glow
Whose soft suffusion gilds the cloud of woe;
Warm as the colours varying Iris pours   245
That tinge with streaming rays the chilling showers;
Ye to whose yielding hearts my power endears
The transport blended with delicious tears,
The bliss that swells to agony the breast,
The sympathy that robs the soul of rest;   250
Hither with fond devotion pensive come,
Kiss the pale shrine, and murmur o'er the tomb;
Bend on the hallow'd turf the tear-full eye
And breathe the precious incense of a sigh.
Las Casas' tear has moisten'd mis'ry's grave,   255
His sigh has moan'd the wretch it fail'd to save!
He, while conflicting pangs his bosom tear
Has sought the lonely cavern of despair;
Where desolate she fled, and pour'd her thought,
To the dread verge of wild distraction wrought.   260
While drops of mercy bath'd his hoary cheek,
He pour'd by heav'n inspir'd its accents meek;
In truth's clear mirror bade the mourner's view
Pierce the deep veil which darkling error drew;
And vanquish'd empire with a smile resign,   265
While brighter worlds in fair perspective shine."—
She paus'd—yet still the sweet enthusiast bends
O'er the cold turf, and still her tear descends;
The ever-falling tears her beauties shroud,
Till slow she vanish'd in a fleecy cloud.   270

Mild Gasca[1] now, the messenger of peace,
Suspends the storm, and bids the tumult cease.
Pure spirit! in Religion's garb he came,
And all his bosom felt her holy flame;
'Twas then her vot'ries[2] glory, and their care   275
To bid oppression's harpy talons spare;
To bend the crimson banner he unfurl'd,
And shelter from his grasp a suff'ring world:
Gasca, the guardian minister of woe,
Bids o'er her wounds the balms of comfort flow   280
While rich Potosi rolls the copious tide
Of wealth, unbounded as the wish of pride;
His pure, unsullied soul with high disdain
For virtue spurns the fascinating bane;
Her seraph form can still his breast allure   285
Tho' drest in weeds, she triumph'd to be poor—
Hopeless ambition's murders to restrain,
And virtue's wrongs, he sought Iberia's plain,
Without one mean reserve he nobly brings
A massive treasure, yet unknown to kings: 290
No purple pomp around his dome was spread
No gilded roofs hung glitt'ring o'er his head;
Yet peace with milder radiance deck'd his bower,
And crown'd with dearer joy life's evening hour;
While virtue whisper'd to his conscious heart   295
The sweet reflexion of its high desert.

Ah, meek Peruvia, still thy murmur'd sighs
Thy stifled groans in fancy's ear arise;
Sadd'ning she views thy desolated soul,
As slow the circling years of bondage roll,   300
Redeem from tyranny's oppressive power
With fond affection's force, one sacred hour,

---

1 See a delightful representation of the incorruptible integrity of this
Spaniard in Robertson's History of America [HMW's note, not present
in 1784]. Pedro de las Gasca, a Spanish royal official, arrived in Peru in
1547 to resolve the civil war between Spanish conquistadors (Klarén
42). An aged priest, he settled the conflict without committing troops to
battle and granted clemency to all but Francisco Pizarro's brother,
Gonzalo, and a small number of officers. Gasca maintained the peace by
partitioning Peru (Robertson *History*, II: 247-51).

2 A devout worshipper (*OED*).

And consecrate its fleeting, precious space,
The dear remembrance of the past to trace.
Call from her bed of dust joy's buried shade;   305
She smiles in mem'ry's lucid robes array'd,
O'er thy creative scene[1] majestic moves,
And wakes each mild delight thy fancy loves.
But soon the image of thy wrongs in clouds
The fair and transient ray of pleasure shrouds;   310
Far other visions melt thy mournful eye,
And wake the gushing tear, th' indignant sigh;
There Ataliba's sacred, murder'd form,
Sinks in the billow of oppression's storm;
Wild o'er the scene of death thy glances roll,   315
And pangs tumultuous swell thy troubled soul;
Thy bosom burns, distraction spreads her flames,
And from the tyrant foe her victim claims.

But, lo! where bursting desolation's night,
A sudden ray of glory cheers my sight;   320
From my fond eye the tear of rapture flows,
My heart with pure delight exulting glows:
A blooming chief of India's royal race,
Whose soaring soul, its high descent can trace,
The flag of freedom rears on Chili's plain,[2]   325
And leads to glorious strife his gen'rous train:
And see Iberia bleeds! while vict'ry twines
Her fairest blossoms round Peruvia's shrines;
The gaping wounds of earth disclose no more
The lucid silver, and the glowing ore;   330

---

1   "O'er thy creative scene." The Peruvians have solemn days on which
    they assume their antient dress. Some among them represent a tragedy,
    the subject of which is the death of Atabalipa. The audience, who begin
    with shedding tears, are afterwards transported into a kind of madness.
    It seldom happens in these festivals, but that some Spaniard is slain.—
    Abbé Raynal's *History* [HMW's note]. See Raynal II: 519.
2   "On Chili's plain."—An Indian descended from the Incas, has lately
    obtained several victories over the Spaniards, the gold mines have been
    for some time shut up; and there is much reason to hope, that these
    injured nations may recover the liberty of which they have been so
    cruelly deprived [HMW's note]. While Raynal briefly treats a 1742
    insurrection (II: 507), Williams is most likely recalling the more recent
    1781 Cuzco rebellion of Túpac Amaru II.

A brighter glory gilds the passing hour,
While freedom breaks the rod of lawless power:
Lo on the Andes' icy steep she glows,
And prints with rapid step th' eternal snows;
Or moves majestic o'er the desart plain,   335
And eloquently pours her potent strain.
Still may that strain the patriot's soul inspire,
And still this injur'd race her spirit fire.
O Freedom, may thy genius still ascend,
Beneath thy crest may proud Iberia bend;   340
While roll'd in dust thy graceful feet beneath,
Fades the dark laurel of her sanguine wreath;
Bend her red trophies, tear her victor plume,
And close insatiate slaughter's yawning tomb.
Again on soft Peruvia's fragrant breast   345
May beauty blossom, and may pleasure rest.
Peru, the muse that vainly mourn'd thy woes,
Whom pity robb'd so long of dear repose;
The muse, whose pensive soul with anguish wrung
Her early lyre for thee has trembling strung;   350
Shed the weak tear, and breath'd the powerless sigh,
Which soon in cold oblivion's shade must die;
Pants with the wish thy deeds may rise to fame,
Bright on some living harp's immortal frame!
While on the string of extasy, it pours   355
Thy future triumphs o'er unnumber'd shores.

POEMS

ON

VARIOUS SUBJECTS.

WITH

INTRODUCTORY REMARKS

ON

THE PRESENT STATE

OF

SCIENCE AND LITERATURE

IN

FRANCE.

By HELEN MARIA WILLIAMS.

LONDON:

G. AND W. B. WHITTAKER, AVE-MARIA LANE.

1823.

Title page to *Poems on Various Subjects* (1823), the volume in which "Peruvian Tales" first appeared. Private collection.

PERUVIAN TALES

ALZIRA
Tale I[1]

*Description of Peru, and of its Productions—Virtues of the People;
and of their Monarch,* Ataliba—*His love for* Alzira—*Their Nuptials
celebrated—Character of* Zorai, *her Father—Descent of the Genius of
Peru—Prediction of the Fall of that Empire.*

Where the Pacific deep in silence laves
The western shore, with slow, and languid waves,
There, lost Peruvia! bloom'd thy cultur'd bowers,
Thy vallies fragrant with perennial flowers;
There, far above, the Pine unbending rose,   5
Along the pathway of thy mountain snows;
The Palms fling high in air their feather'd heads,
While each broad leaf an ample shadow spreads;
The Orange, and the rich Ananas bloom,
And humid Balsams ever shed perfume;   10
The Bark, reviving shrub! Ah, not in vain
Thy rosy blossoms tinge Peruvia's plain;
Ye fost'ring gales around those blossoms blow,
Ye balmy dew-drops o'er the tendrils flow!
Lo, as the health-diffusing plant aspires,   15
Disease relents, and hov'ring death retires;
Affection sees new lustre light the eye,
And feels her vanish'd peace again is nigh.
The Pacas,[2] and Vicunnas[3] sport around,
And the meek Lamas,[4] burden'd, press the ground.   20
The Mocking-bird his varying note essays,
And charms the grove with imitative lays;

---

1 This first tale is fifty-two lines shorter than Canto I of *Peru* (1786),
upon which it is based. Most of the cuts appear in the tale's first half.
For instance, in the poem's opening lines, HMW deletes some grand
descriptions of nature. Also absent are images of nature pouring treas-
ures and mines opening before Ataliba.
2 The Paca is a domestic animal of Peru [HMW's note].
3 The Vicunna is a species of wild goat [HMW's note].
4 The Lamas are employed as mules in carrying burdens [HMW's note].

The plaintive Humming-bird unfolds his wing
Of vivid plumage to the ray of spring;
Then sinks, soft burthen, on the humid flower,   25
His food, the dewdrops of the morning hour.[1]

　Nor less, Peruvia, for thy favour'd clime,
The Virtues rose unsullied and sublime;
There melting Charity, with ardour warm,
Spreads her wide mantle o'er the shiv'ring form;   30
Cheer'd with the festal song her rural toils,[2]
While in the lap of age she pour'd the spoils;[3]
There the mild Inca, Ataliba sway'd,
His high behest the willing heart obey'd;
Descendant of a scepter'd, sacred race,   35
Whose origin from glowing suns they trace.
Love's soft emotions now his soul possest,
And fix'd Alzira's image in his breast.
In that blest clime affection never knew
A selfish purpose, or a thought untrue;   40
Not as on Europe's shore, where wealth and pride,
From mourning love the venal breast divide;
Yet Love, if there from sordid shackles free,
One faithful bosom yet belongs to thee;[4]
On that fond heart the purest bliss bestow,   45
Or give, for thou canst give, a charm to woe;
Ah, never may that heart in vain deplore
The pang that tortures when belov'd no more.
And from that agony the spirit save,
When unrelenting yawns th' untimely grave;   50

1　In lines 23-26, HMW truncates *Peru*'s treatment of birds for "Peruvian
　Tales." She removes the macaw; the hummingbird remains but is no
　longer described as a loving father. The language of golden brightness
　("glitt'ring" and "blazing") that describes the macaw's and humming-
　bird's feathers in *Peru* is absent, which delays introducing the subject of
　natural treasure.
2　*Peru*'s "liberal toils" become "rural toils" in "Peruvian Tales." "Liberal"
　is also cut from HMW's description of Ataliba's reign. These changes
　suggest that the poet had become less willing to use language associated
　with revolution.
3　The people cheerfully assisted in reaping those fields of which the
　produce was given to old persons past their labour [HMW's note].
4　After introducing Alzira, HMW added four new lines (41-44) to critique
　European society.

When death dissolves the ties for ever dear,
When frantic passion pours her parting tear;
With all the wasting pains she only feels,
Hangs on the quiv'ring lip that silence seals;
Views fondness struggling in the closing eye,   55
And marks it mingling in the falt'ring sigh;
As the lov'd form, while folded to her breast,
Breathes the last moan that gives its struggles rest;
Leaves her to pine in grief that none can share,
And find the world a desert to despair.   60

   Bright was the lustre of the orient ray
That joyful wak'd Alzira's nuptial day;
Her auburn hair spread loosely on the wind,
The virgin train with rosy chaplets bind;
While the fresh flowers that form her bridal wreathe   65
Seem deeper hues and richer scents to breathe.
The gentle tribe now sought the hallow'd fane,
Where warbling vestals pour'd the choral strain;
There aged Zorai his Alzira prest,
With love parental, to his anxious breast;   70
Priest of the Sun! within the sacred shrine
His fervent spirit breath'd the strain divine;
With careful hand the guiltless off'ring spread,
With pious zeal the clear libation shed.
Nor vain the incense of erroneous praise   75
When meek devotion's soul the tribute pays;
On wings of purity behold it rise,
While bending mercy wafts it to the skies!
Peruvia! O delightful land, in vain
The virtues flourish'd on thy beauteous plain;   80
For soon shall burst the unrelenting storm
O'er thy mild head, and crush thy prostrate form!
Recording Fame shall mark thy desp'rate fate,
And distant ages weep for ills so great!
Now o'er the deep dull Night her mantle flung,   85
Dim on the wave the moon's faint crescent hung;
Peruvia's Genius sought the liquid plain,
Sooth'd by the languid murmurs of the main;
When sudden clamour the illusion broke,
Wild on the surface of the deep it spoke;   90
A rising breeze expands her flowing veil,
Aghast with fear, she spies a flying sail—

The lofty mast impends, the banner waves,
The ruffled surge th' incumbent vessel laves;
With eager eye she views her destin'd foe   95
Lead to her peaceful shores th' advent'rous prow;
Trembling she knelt, with wild, disorder'd air,
And pour'd with frantic energy her prayer:
"O, ye avenging spirits of the deep!
Mount the blue lightning's wing, o'er ocean sweep;   100
Loud from your central caves the shell resound,
That summons death to your abyss profound;
Call the pale spectre from his dark abode,
To print the billow, swell the black'ning flood,
Rush o'er the waves, the rough'ning deep deform,   105
Howl in the blast, and animate the storm—
Relentless powers! for not one quiv'ring breeze
Has ruffled yet the surface of the seas—
Swift from your rocky steeps ye Condors[1] stray,
Wave your black plumes, and cleave th' aerial way;   110
Proud in terrific force your wings expand,
Press the firm earth, and darken all the strand;
Bid the stern foe retire with wild affright,
And shun the region veil'd in partial night.
Vain hope, devoted land! I read thy doom,   115
My sad prophetic soul can pierce the gloom;
I see, I see my lov'd, my favour'd clime
Consum'd, and wasted in its early prime.
But not in vain this beauteous land shall bleed,
Too late shall Europe's race deplore the deed.   120
Region abhorr'd! be gold the tempting bane,
The curse that desolates thy hostile plain;
May pleasure tinge with venom'd drops the bowl,
And luxury unnerve the sick'ning soul."

  Ah, not in vain she pour'd th' impassion'd tear;   125
Ah, not in vain she call'd the powers to hear!
When borne from lost Peruvia's bleeding land,
The guilty treasures beam'd on Europe's strand;
Each sweet affection fled the tainted shore,
And virtue wander'd, to return no more.   130

---

1   The Condor is an inhabitant of the Andes. Its wings, when expanded,
    are said to be eighteen feet wide [HMW's note].

ALZIRA
Tale II

Pizarro lands with the Forces—*His* meeting with Ataliba—*Its*
unhappy consequences—*Zorai dies*—Ataliba *imprisoned, and*
strangled—Despair of Alzira.

Flush'd with impatient hope, the martial band,
By stern Pizarro led, approach the land;
No terrors arm his hostile brow, for guile
Seeks to betray with candour's open smile.
Too artless for distrust, the Monarch springs   5
To meet his latent foe on friendship's wings.
On as he moves, with dazzling splendour crown'd,
His feather'd chiefs the golden throne surround;
The waving canopy its plume displays,
Whose waving hues reflect the morning rays;   10
With native grace he hails the warrior train,
Who stood majestic on Peruvia's plain,
In all the savage pomp of armour drest,
The frowning helmet, and the nodding crest.
Yet themes of joy Pizarro's lips impart,   15
And charm with eloquence the simple heart;
Unfolding to the monarch's wond'ring thought
All that inventive arts the rude have taught.
And now he bids the musing spirit rise
Above the circle of surrounding skies;   20
Presents the page that sheds Religion's light
O'er the dark mist of intellectual night:
While, thrill'd with awe, the monarch trembling stands,
He dropp'd the hallow'd volume from his hands.
Sudden,[1] while frantic zeal each breast inspires,   25

---

1 Pizarro, who during a long conference had with difficulty restrained his
soldiers, eager to seize the rich spoils of which they had now so near a
view, immediately gave the signal of assault. At once the martial music
struck up, the cannon and muskets began to fire, the horse sallied out
fiercely to the charge, the infantry rushed on sword in hand. The Peru-
vians, astonished at the suddenness of an attack which they did not
expect, and dismayed with the destructive effects of the fire-arms, fled
with universal consternation on every side. Pizarro, at the head of his
chosen band, advanced directly towards the Inca; and though his nobles
crowded around him with officious zeal, and fell in numbers (*continued*)

And shudd'ring demons fan the rising fires,
The bloody signal waves, the banners play,
The naked sabres flash their streaming ray;
The trumpet rolls its animating sound,
And the loud cannon rend the vault around;   30
While fierce in sanguine rage, the sons of Spain
Rush on Peru's unarm'd, defenceless train!
The fiends of slaughter urg'd their dire career,
And virtue's guardian spirits dropped a tear!
Mild Zorai fell, deploring human strife,   35
And clos'd with prayer his consecrated life!—
In vain Peruvia's chiefs undaunted stood,
Shield their lov'd Prince, and bathe his robes in blood;—
Touch'd with heroic ardour, cling around,
And high of soul, receive each fatal wound;   40
Dragg'd from his throne, and hurried o'er the plain,
The wretched Monarch swells the captive train;
With iron grasp the frantic Prince they bear,
And feel their triumph in his wild despair.—
Deep in the gloomy dungeon's lone domain,   45
Lost Ataliba wore the galling chain;
The earth's cold bed refus'd oblivious rest,
While throbb'd the woes of thousands at his breast;
Alzira's desolating moan he hears,
And with the monarch's blends the lover's tears.   50
Soon had Alzira felt affliction's dart
Pierce her soft soul, and rend her bleeding heart;
Its quick pulsations paus'd, and chill'd with dread,
A livid hue her fading cheek o'erspread;
No tear the mourner shed, she breath'd no sigh,   55
Her lips were mute, and clos'd her languid eye;
Fainter, and slower heav'd her shiv'ring breast,
And her calm'd passions seem'd in death to rest.—
At length reviv'd, 'mid rising heaps of slain,
She prest with hurried step the crimson plain;   60

---

at his feet, while they vied one with another in sacrificing their own lives
that they might cover the sacred person of their sovereign, the Spaniards
soon penetrated to the royal seat; and Pizarro, seizing the Inca by the
arm, dragged him to the ground and carried him a prisoner to his quar-
ters. *Robertson's History of America* [HMW's note]. Drawn from Robert-
son *History*, II: 175-76.

The dungeon's gloomy depth she fearless sought,
For love with scorn of danger arm'd her thought:
She reach'd the cell where Ataliba lay,
Where human vultures haste to seize their prey.—
In vain her treasur'd wealth Peruvia gave,   65
This dearer treasure from their grasp to save;
Alzira! lo, the ruthless murd'rers come,
This moment seals thy Ataliba's doom.
Ah, what avails the shriek that anguish pours?
The look that mercy's lenient aid implores?   70
Torn from thy clinging arms, thy throbbing breast,
The fatal cord his agony supprest!—
In vain the livid corpse she firmly clasps,
And pours her sorrows o'er the form she grasps,
The murd'rers soon their struggling victim tear   75
From the lost object of her soul's despair!
The swelling pang unable to sustain,
Distraction throbb'd in every beating vein;
Its sudden tumults seize her yielding soul,
And in her eye distemper'd glances roll—   80
"They come!" the mourner cried with panting breath,
"To give the lost Alzira rest in death!
One moment more, ye bloody forms, bestow,
One moment more for ever cures my woe—
Lo! where the purple evening sheds her light   85
On blest remains! O! hide them, pitying night!
Slow in the breeze I see the verdure wave,
That shrouds with tufted grass my lover's grave;
Hark! on its wand'ring wing in mildness blows
The murm'ring gale, nor wakes his deep repose—   90
And see, yon hoary form still lingers there!
Dishevell'd by rude winds his silver hair;
O'er his chill'd bosom falls the winter rain,
I feel the big drops on my wither'd brain.
Not for himself that tear his bosom steeps,   95
For his lost child it flows—for me he weeps!
No more the dagger's point shall pierce thy breast,
For calm and lovely is thy silent rest;
Yet still in dust these eyes shall see thee roll,
Still the sad thought shall waste Alzira's soul—   100
What bleeding phantom moves along the storm?
It is my Ataliba's well-known form!
Approach! Alzira's breast no terrors move,

Her fears are all for ever lost in love.
Safe on the hanging cliff I now can rest, 105
And press its pointed pillow to my breast—
He weeps! in heaven he weeps!—I feel his tear—
It chills my trembling heart, yet still 'tis dear.
To him all joyless are the realms above,
That pale look speaks of pity and of love! 110
Ah come, descend in yonder bending cloud,
And wrap Alzira in thy misty shroud!"
As roll'd her wand'ring glances wild around,
She snatch'd a reeking sabre from the ground;
Firmly her lifted hand the weapon prest, 115
And deep she plung'd it in her panting breast!
"'Tis but a few short moments that divide"—
She falt'ring said—then sunk on earth and died!

ZILIA
Tale III[1]

Pizarro *takes possession of Cuzco—The fanaticism of* Valverda, *a
Spanish priest—Its dreadful effects—A Peruvian priest put to the
torture—His Daughter's distress—He is rescued by* Las Casas, *a
Spanish ecclesiastic—And led to a place of safety, where he dies—His
daughter's narration of her sufferings—Her death.*

Now stern Pizarro seeks the distant plains,
Where beauteous Cuzco lifts her golden fanes.
The meek Peruvians gaz'd in wild dismay,
Nor barr'd the dark Oppressor's sanguine way;
And soon on Cuzco, where the dawning light   5
Of glory shone, foretelling day more bright,
Where the young arts had shed unfolding flowers,
A scene of spreading desolation lowers!
While buried deep in everlasting shade,
That lustre sickens, and those blossoms fade.   10
And yet, devoted land, not gold alone,
Or dire ambition wak'd thy rising groan;
For lo! a fiercer fiend, with joy elate,
Feasts on thy suff'rings, and impels thy fate:
Fanatic Fury rears her sullen shrine,   15
Where vultures prey, where venom'd adders twine;
Her savage arm with purple torrents stains
Thy rocking temples, and thy falling fanes;
Her blazing torches flash the mounting fire,
She grasps the sabre, and she lights the pyre;   20
Her voice is thunder rending the still air,
Her glance the baleful lightning's lurid glare;
Her lips unhallow'd breathe their impious strain,
And pure Religion's sacred voice profane;
Whose precepts pity's mildest deeds approve,   25
Whose law is mercy, and whose soul is love.
And see, fanatic Fury wakes the storm—

---

1 Of the six tales, this one has the fewest substantive textual changes from
Peru (1786), with alterations in only 38 of the 188 lines; most of those
revisions are to words or short phrases. HMW did remove four passages
from Canto III of *Peru* (lines 59-60, 129-30, 165-72, 185-86), reflecting
her wish to distance her writing from the cult of Sensibility to which she
belonged nearly four decades earlier.

She wears the stern Valverda's hideous form;
His bosom never felt another's woes,
No shriek of anguish breaks its dark repose.   30
The temple nods—an aged form appears—
He beats his breast, he rends his silver hairs—
Valverda drags him from the blest abode,
Where his meek spirit humbly sought its God;
See, to his aid his child, soft Zilia, springs,   35
And steeps in tears the robe to which she clings!
Now bursting from Peruvia's frighted throng,
Two warlike youths impetuous rush'd along;
One grasp'd his twanging bow with furious air,
While in his troubled eye sat fierce despair;   40
But all in vain his erring weapon flies,
Pierc'd by a thousand wounds, on earth he lies.
His drooping head the trembling Zilia rais'd,
And on the youth in speechless anguish gaz'd;
While he who fondly shared his danger flew,   45
And from his bleeding breast a poignard drew.
"Deep in my faithful bosom let me hide
The fatal steel that would our souls divide,"—
He quick exclaims—the dying warrior cries
"Ah yet forbear!—by all the sacred ties   50
That bind our hearts, forbear!"—in vain he spoke,
Friendship with frantic zeal impels the stroke!
"Thyself for ever lost, thou hop'st in vain,"
The youth replied, "my spirit to detain;
From thee my soul, in childhood's earliest year,   55
Caught the light pleasure and the passing tear;
Thy friendship then my young affections blest
The first pure passion of my infant breast;
And still in death I feel its strong controul,
Its sacred impulse wings my fleeting soul,   60
That only lingers here till thou depart,
Whose image lives upon my fainting heart!"—
In vain the gen'rous youth, with panting breath,
Pour'd these last murmurs in the ear of death;
He reads the fatal truth in Zilia's eye,   65
And gives to friendship his expiring sigh.—
But now with rage Valverda's glances roll,
And mark the vengeance rankling in his soul;
He bends his gloomy brow—his lips impart
The brooding purpose of his venom'd heart;   70

He bids the hoary priest in mutter'd strains
Abjure his faith, forsake his native fanes,
While yet the ling'ring pangs of torture wait,
While yet Valverda's power suspends his fate.
"Vain man," the victim cried, "to hoary years   75
Know death is mild, and virtue feels no fears;
Cruel of spirit, come! let tortures prove
The power I serv'd in life in death I love."
He ceas'd—with rugged cords his limbs they bound,
And drag the aged suff'rer on the ground;   80
They grasp his feeble frame, his tresses tear;
His robe they rend, his shrivell'd bosom bare.
Ah, see his uncomplaining soul sustain
The sting of insult and the dart of pain!
His stedfast spirit feels one pang alone,   85
A child's despair awakes one bitter groan—
The mourner kneels to catch his parting breath,
To soothe the agony of ling'ring death:
No moan she breath'd, no tear had power to flow,
Still on her lip expir'd th' unutter'd woe;   90
Yet ah, her livid cheek, her stedfast look,
The desolated soul's deep anguish spoke—
Mild victim! close not yet thy languid eyes;
Pure spirit! claim not yet thy kindred skies;
A pitying angel comes to stay thy flight,   95
Las Casas[1] bids thee view returning light;
Ah, let that sacred drop, to virtue dear,
Efface thy wrongs—receive his precious tear;
See his flush'd cheek with indignation glow,
While from his lips the tones of pity flow.—   100
"Oh, suff'ring Lord!" he cried, "whose streaming blood,
Was pour'd for man—earth drank the sacred flood,
Whose mercy in the mortal pang forgave
The murd'rous band, Thy love alone could save;
Forgive—thy goodness bursts each narrow bound   105
Which feeble thought, and human hope surround;
Forgive the guilty wretch, whose impious hand
From thy pure altar flings the flaming brand;
In human blood that hallow'd altar steeps,
Libation dire! while groaning nature weeps;   110

---

1 Las Casas, that admirable ecclesiastic, who obtained by his humanity
   the title of Protector of the Indies [HMW's note].

The limits of thy mercy dares to scan,
The object of thy love, his victim,—man.
While yet I linger, lo, the suff'rer dies,
I see his frame convuls'd,—I hear his sighs!
Whoe'er controuls the purpose of my heart,   115
First in this breast shall plunge his guilty dart."
With hurried step he flew, with eager hands
He broke the fetters, burst the cruel bands.
As the fall'n angel heard with awful fear,
The cherub's grave rebuke, in grace severe,   120
And fled, while horror plum'd his impious crest,[1]
The form of virtue as she stood confest;
So fierce Valverda sullen mov'd along,
Abash'd, and follow'd by the hostile throng.
At length the hoary victim, freed from chains,   125
Las Casas gently leads to safer plains;
His searching eye explores a secret cave,
Whose shaggy sides the languid billows lave;
"There rest secure," he cried, "the Christian's God
Will hover near, will guard the lone abode."   130
Oft to the gloomy cell his steps repair,
While night's chill breezes wave his silver'd hair;
Oft in the tones of love, the words of peace,
He bids the bitter tears of anguish cease;
Bids drooping hope uplift her languid eyes,   135
And points to bliss that dwells beyond the skies.
Yet ah! in vain his pious cares would save
The aged suff'rer from the op'ning grave;
For deep the pangs of torture pierc'd his frame,
And sunk his wasted life's expiring flame;   140
To his cold lip Las Casas' hand he prest,
He faintly clasp'd his Zilia to his breast;
Then cried, "the God, whom now my vows adore,
My heart through life obey'd, unknowing more;
His mild forgiveness then my soul shall prove,   145
His mercy share, Las Casas' God is love."
He spoke no more, his Zilia's hopeless moan
Was heard responsive to his dying groan.
"Victim of impious zeal," Las Casas cries,
"Accept, departed shade, a Christian's sighs;   150

---

1 "————on his crest
  Sat horror plum'd." *Par. Lost*, xiv. 988 [HMW's note].

And thou, soft mourner, tender, drooping form,
What power shall guard thee from the fearful storm?"
"Weep not for me," she cried, "for Zilia's breast
Soon in the shelt'ring earth shall find its rest;
Seek not the victim of despair to save,   155
I ask but death—I only wish a grave.
Witness, thou mangled form, that earth retains,
Witness a murder'd lover's cold remains;
I liv'd my father's pangs to soothe, to share,
I bore to live, though life was all despair.   160
Ah! still my lover's dying moan I hear,
In every pulse I feel his parting tear—
I faint—an icy coldness chills each vein,
No more these feeble limbs their load sustain;
Spirit of pity! catch my fleeting breath,   165
A moment stay—and close my eyes in death.
Las Casas, thee thy God in mercy gave,
To soothe my pangs, to find the wretch a grave."
She ceas'd, her spirit fled to purer spheres,
Las Casas bathes the pallid corse with tears;   170
Fly, minister of good! nor ling'ring shed
Those fruitless sorrows o'er th' unconscious dead;
I view the sanguine flood, the wasting flame,
I hear a suff'ring world Las Casas claim.

CORA

Tale IV[1]

Almagro's expedition to Chili—His troops suffer great hardships from cold, in crossing the Andes—They reach Chili—The Chilians make a brave resistance—The revolt of the Peruvians in Cuzco—They are led on by Manco Capac, *the successor of* Ataliba—*Parting with* Cora, *his wife—The Peruvians regain half their city—Almagro leaves Chili—To avoid the Andes, he crosses a vast desert—His troops can find no water—They divide into two bands—Alphonso leads the second band, which soon reaches a fertile valley—The Spaniards observe that the natives are employed in searching the streams for gold—They resolve to attack them.*

Now the stern partner of Pizarro's toils,
Almagro, lur'd by hope of golden spoils,
To distant Chili's ever-verdant meads,
Through paths untrod, a band of warriors leads;
O'er the high Andes' frozen steeps they go,   5
And wander 'mid eternal hills of snow:
In vain the vivifying orb of day
Darts on th' impervious ice his fervent ray;
Cold, keen as chains the oceans of the pole,
Numbs the shrunk frame, and chills the vig'rous soul;   10
At length they reach luxuriant Chili's plain,
Where ends the dreary bound of winter's reign.

When first the brave Chilese, with eager glance,
Beheld the hostile sons of Spain advance,
Their threat'ning sabres red with purple streams,   15
Their lances quiv'ring in the solar beams,
With pale surprise they saw th' impending storm,
Where low'ring danger wore an unknown form;
But soon their spirits, stung with gen'rous shame,
Renounce each terror, and for vengeance flame;   20
Pant high with sacred freedom's ardent glow,
And meet intrepid the superior foe.

---

1   The inspiration for the character, Cora, probably came, at least in part, from Marmontel's *The Incas*, in which a woman named Cora is one of the three virgins of the sun. Cora is also a character in Elizabeth Scot's poem "Alonzo and Cora" (1801). The name may have origins in the Inca word *coya*, or "daughter of the sun" (see Robertson *History*, II: 243).

Long unsubdued by stern Almagro's train,
Their valiant tribes unequal fight maintain;
Long vict'ry hover'd doubtful o'er the field,   25
And oft she forc'd Iberia's band to yield;
Oft love from Spain's proud head her laurel bough,
And bade it blossom on Peruvia's brow;
When sudden tidings reach'd Almagro's ear,
That shook the warrior's soul with doubt and fear.   30
Of murder'd Ataliba's royal race
There yet remain'd a youth of blooming grace,
Who pin'd, the captive of relentless Spain,
And long in Cuzco dragg'd her galling chain;
Capac, whose lofty soul indignant bears   35
The rankling fetters, and revenge prepares.
But since his daring spirit must forego
The hope to rush upon the tyrant foe,
Led by his parent orb, that gives the day,
And fierce as darts the keen meridian ray,   40
He vows to bend unseen his hostile course,
Then on the victors rise with latent force,
As sudden from its cloud, the brooding storm,
Bursts in the thunder's voice, the light'ning's form.
For this, from stern Pizarro he obtains   45
The boon, enlarg'd, to seek the neighb'ring plains,
For one bless'd day, and with his friends unite,
To crown with solemn pomp an antient rite;
Share the dear pleasures of the social hour,
And 'mid their fetters twine one festal flower.   50
So spoke the Prince—far other thoughts possest,
Far other purpose animates his breast:
For now Peruvia's Nobles he commands
To lead, with silent step, her martial bands
Forth to the destin'd spot, prepared to dare   55
The fiercest shock of dire, unequal war;
While every sacred human interest pleads,
And urges the firm soul to lofty deeds.
Now Capac hail'd th' eventful morning's light,
Rose with its dawn, and panted for the fight;   60
But first with fondness to his heart he prest
The tender Cora, partner of his breast,
Who with her lord had sought the dungeon's gloom,
And wasted there in grief her early bloom.
"No more," he cried, "no more my love shall feel   65

The mingled agonies I fly to heal;—
I go, but soon exulting shall return,
And bid my faithful Cora cease to mourn;
For O, amid each pang my bosom knows,
What wastes, what wounds it most are Cora's woes!   70
Sweet was the love that crown'd our happier hours,
And shed new fragrance o'er a path of flowers:
But sure divided sorrow more endears
The tie that passion seals with mutual tears!"
He paus'd. Fast-flowing drops bedew'd her eyes,   75
While thus in mournful accents she replies:—
"Still let me feel the pressure of thy chain,
Still share the fetters which my love detain;
The piercing iron to my soul is dear,
Nor will its sharpness wound while thou art near.   80
Look on our helpless babe, in mis'ry nurst—
My child! my child, thy mother's heart will burst!
O, wherefore bid the raging battle rise,
Nor hear this harmless suff'rer's feeble cries?
Look on those blades that pour a crimson flood,   85
And plunge their cruel edge in infant blood!"
She could no more—he sees with tender pain
Her grief, and leads her to a shelt'ring fane.
Now high in air his feather'd standard waves,
And soon from shrouding woods and hollow caves   90
To Cuzco's gate advance increasing throngs,
And, such their ardour, rous'd by sense of wrongs,
That vainly would Pizarro's vet'ran force
Arrest the torrent in its raging course;[1]
Danger and death Peruvia's sons disdain,   95
And half their captive city soon regain.

When stern Almagro heard the voice of fame
The triumphs of Peruvia loud proclaim,
Unconquer'd Chili's vale he swift forsakes,
And his bold course to distant Cuzco takes.   100
But now he shuns the Andes' frozen snows,
The arrowy gale that on their summit blows;

---

1 When she prepared the text of "Peruvian Tales," HMW removed the
    lines which follow in *Peru*: "Yet her soul spoke expressive in her eye; /
    Her lord beholds her grief, with tender pain"—one of many examples of
    Williams revising to downplay sensibility.

A burning desert undismay'd he past,
And meets the ardors of the fiery blast.
As o'er the sultry waste they slowly move,   105
The keenest pang of raging thirst they prove;
No cooling fruit its grateful juice distils,
Nor flows one balmy drop from crystal rills;
For nature sickens in the parching beam
That shrinks the vernal bud and dries the stream;   110
While horror, as his giant stature grows,
O'er the drear void his spreading shadow throws.

Almagro's band now pale and fainting stray,
While death oft barr'd the sinking warrior's way;
At length the chief divides his martial force,   115
And bids Alphonso by a sep'rate course
Lead o'er the hideous desert half his train—
"And search," he cried, "this vast, untrodden plain,
Perchance some fruitage, with'ring in the breeze,
The pains of lessen'd numbers may appease;   120
Or heaven in pity from some genial shower
On the parch'd lip one precious drop may pour."
Not far the troops of young Alphonso went,
When sudden from a rising hill's ascent
They view a valley fed by fertile springs,   125
Which Andes from his snowy summit flings;
Where summer's flowers humected odours shed,
And wildly bloom, a waste by beauty spread.
And now Alphonso and his martial band
On the rich border of the valley stand;   130
They quaff the limpid stream with eager haste,
And the pure juice that swells the fruitage taste;
Then give to balmy rest the night's still hours,
Fann'd by the cooling gale that shuts the flowers.
Soon as the purple beam of morning glows,   135
Refresh'd from all their toils, the warriors rose;
And saw the gentle natives of the mead
Search the clear currents for the golden seed,
Which from the mountain's height with headlong sweep
The torrents bear in many a shining heap;   140
Iberia's sons beheld with anxious brow
The tempting lure, then breathe th' unpitying vow
O'er those fair lawns to pour a sanguine flood,
And dye those lucid streams with guiltless blood.

Thus while the humming-bird, in beauty drest,   145
Enchanting offspring of the ardent west,
Attunes his tender song to notes of love,
Mild as the murmurs of the morning dove,
While his rich plumage glows with brighter hues,[1]
And with soft bill he sips the scented dews,   150
The savage condor on terrific wings,
From Andes' frozen steeps relentless springs;
And, quiv'ring in his fangs, his helpless prey
Drops his weak wing, and sighs his soul away.

---

1 By the time HMW was working on "Peruvian Tales," Alexander von
   Humboldt's writings describing the virginal lands of South America had
   been exploited by the "capitalist vanguard." HMW may well have
   removed the following lines from *Peru* that characterize the region as
   unsullied to avoid encouraging more exploitation: "To the charm'd
   warrior's eye, the vernal scene ... smil'd serene, ... warbling angels ...
   stoop'd from heav'n to bless the new-born earth" (IV: 149-54). See
   Damián 1-27.

ACILOE
Tale V

Character of Zamor, *a bard—His passion for* Aciloe, *daughter of the Cazique who rules the valley—The Peruvian tribe prepare to defend themselves—A battle—The Peruvians are vanquished— Aciloe's father is made a prisoner, and Zamor is supposed to have fallen in the engagement—Alphonso becomes enamoured of Aciloe—Offers to marry her—She rejects him—In revenge he puts her father to the torture—She appears to consent, in order to save him—Meets Zamor in a wood—Las Casas joins them—Leads the two lovers to Alphonso, and obtains their freedom—Zamor conducts Aciloe and her father to Chili—A reflection on the influence of Poetry over the human mind.*

In this sweet scene, to all the virtues kind,
Mild Zamor own'd the richest gifts of mind;
For o'er his tuneful breast the heav'nly muse
Shed from her sacred spring inspiring dews;
She loves to breathe her hallow'd strain where art   5
Has never veil'd the soul, or warp'd the heart;
Where fancy glows with all her native fire,
And passion lives on the exulting lyre.
Nature, in terror rob'd or beauty drest,
Could thrill with dear enchantment Zamor's breast;   10
He lov'd the languid sigh the zephyr pours,
He lov'd the placid rill that feeds the flowers,—
But more the hollow sound the wild winds form,
When black upon the billow hangs the storm;
The torrent rolling from the mountain steep,   15
Its white foam trembling on the darken'd deep—
And oft on Andes' heights with earnest gaze
He view'd the sinking sun's reflected rays
Glow like unnumber'd stars, that seem to rest
Sublime upon his ice-encircled breast.   20
Oft his wild warblings charm'd the festal hour,
Rose in the vale, and languish'd in the bower;
The heart's reponsive tones he well could move,
Whose song was nature, and whose theme was love.

Aciloe's beauties his fond soul confest,   25
Yet more Aciloe's virtues warm'd his breast.
Ah stay, ye tender hours of young delight,

Suspend, ye moments, your impatient flight;
Prolong the charm when passion's pure controul
Unfolds the first affections of the soul!   30
This gentle tribe Aciloe's sire obey'd,
Who still in wisdom and in mercy sway'd.
From him the dear illusions long had fled
That o'er the morn of life enchantment shed;
But virtue's calm remembrance cheer'd his breast,   35
And life was joy serene, and death was rest:
Bright is the blushing Summer's glowing ray,
Yet not unlovely Autumn's temper'd day.

　　Now stern Iberia's ruthless sons advance,
Roll the fierce eye, and shake the pointed lance.   40
Peruvia's tribe behold the hostile throng
With desolating fury pour along;
The hoary chief to the dire conflict leads
His death-devoted train—the battle bleeds.
Aciloe's searching eye can now no more   45
The form of Zamor or her sire explore;
While destin'd all the bitterness to prove
Of anxious duty and of mourning love,
Each name that's dearest wakes her bursting sigh,
Throbs at her soul, and trembles in her eye.   50
Now pierc'd by wounds, and breathless from the fight,
Her friend, the valiant Omar, struck her sight:—
"Omar," she cried, "you bleed, unhappy youth!
And sure that look unfolds some fatal truth;
Speak, pitying speak, my frantic fears forgive,   55
Say, does my father, does my Zamor live?"—
"All, all is lost!" the dying Omar said,
"And endless griefs are thine, dear, wretched maid;
I saw thy aged sire a captive bound,
I saw thy Zamor press the crimson ground!"—   60
He could no more, he yields his fleeting breath,
While all in vain she seeks repose in death.
But O, how far each other pang above
Throbs the wild agony of hopeless love!
That woe, for which in vain would comfort shed   65
Her healing balm, or time in pity spread
The veil that throws a shade o'er other care,
For here, and here alone, profound despair

Casts o'er the suff'ring soul a lasting gloom,
And slowly leads her victim to the tomb.   70

Now rude tumultuous sounds assail her ear,
And soon Alphonso's victor train appear;
Then, as with ling'ring step he mov'd along,
She saw her father 'mid the captive throng;
She saw with dire dismay, she wildly flew,   75
Her snowy arms around his form she threw;—
"He bleeds!" she cries; "I hear his moan of pain!
My father will not bear the galling chain!
Cruel Alphonso, let not helpless age
Feel thy hard yoke, and meet thy barb'rous rage;   80
Or, O, if ever mercy mov'd thy soul,
If ever thou hast felt her blest controul,
Grant my sad heart's desire, and let me share
The fetters which a father ill can bear."
While the young warrior, as she falt'ring spoke,   85
With fix'd attention and with ardent look
Hung on her tender glance, that love inspires,
The rage of conquest yields to milder fires.
Yet as he gaz'd enraptur'd on her form,
Her virtues awe the heart her beauties warm;   90
And while impassion'd tones his love reveal,
He asks with holy rites his vows to seal.
"Hops't thou," she cried, "those sacred ties shall join
This bleeding heart, this trembling hand to thine?
To thine, whose ruthless heart has caus'd my pains,   95
Whose barb'rous hand the blood of Zamor stains!
Canst thou, the murd'rer of my peace, controul
The grief that swells, the pang that rends my soul?—
That pang shall death, shall death alone remove,
And cure the anguish of despairing love."   100

At length, to madness stung by fixed disdain,
Alphonso now to fury gives the rein;
And with relentless mandate dooms her sire,
Stretch'd on the bed of torture to expire;
But O, what form of language can impart   105
The frantic grief that wrung Aciloe's heart!
When to the height of hopeless sorrow wrought,
The fainting spirit feels a pang of thought,
Which, never painted in the hues of speech,

Lives at the soul, and mocks expression's reach!   110
At length she falt'ring cried, "the conflict's o'er,
My heart, my breaking heart can bear no more!
Yet spare his feeble age—my vows receive,
And O, in mercy bid my father live!"
"Wilt thou be mine?" th' enamour'd chief replies—   115
"Yes, cruel!—see, he dies! my father dies!—
Save, save my father!"—"Dear, unhappy maid,"
The charm'd Alphonso cried, "be swift obey'd—
Unbind his chains—Ah, calm each anxious pain,
Aciloe's voice no more shall plead in vain;   120
Plac'd near his child, thy aged sire shall share
Our joys, still cherished by thy tender care."—
"No more," she cried, "will fate that bliss allow;
Before my lips shall breathe the impartial vow,
Some faithful guide shall lead his aged feet   125
To distant scenes that yield a safe retreat;
Where some soft heart, some gentle hand will shed
The drops of comfort on his hoary head.
My Zamor, if thy spirit hovers near,
Forgive!"—she ceas'd, and shed no more a tear.   130

    Now night descends, and steeps each weary breast,
Save sad Aciloe's, in the balm of rest.
Her aged father's beauteous dwelling stood
Near the cool shelter of a waving wood;
But now the gales that bend its foliage die,   135
Soft on the silver turf its shadows lie;
While slowly wand'ring o'er the vale below,
The gazing moon look'd pale as silent woe.
The sacred shade, amid whose fragrant bowers
Zamor oft sooth'd with song the evening hours,   140
Pour'd to the lunar orb his magic lay,
More mild, more pensive than her musing ray,
That shade with trembling step the mourner sought,
And thus she breath'd her tender, plaintive thought:—
"Ah where, dear object of these piercing pains,   145
Where rests thy murder'd form, thy lov'd remains?
On what sad spot, my Zamor, flow'd the wound
That purpled with thy streaming blood the ground?
O, had Aciloe in that hour been nigh,
Hadst thou but fix'd on me thy closing eye,—   150
Told with faint voice, 'twas death's worst pang to part,
And dropp'd thy last cold tear upon my heart!

A pang less bitter then would waste this breast,
That in the grave alone shall seek its rest.
Soon as some friendly hand in mercy leads   155
My aged father safe to Chili's meads,
Death shall for ever seal the nuptial tie,
The heart belov'd by thee is fix'd to die."—
She ceas'd, when dimly thro' her flowing tears
She sees her Zamor's form, his voice she hears.   160
"'Tis he!" she cries, "he moves upon the gale!
My Zamor's sigh is deep—his look is pale—
I faint—" his arms receive her sinking frame,—
He calls his love by every tender name;
He stays her fleeting spirit—life anew   165
Warms her cold cheek—his tears her cheek bedew.
"Thy Zamor lives," he cried: "as on the ground
I senseless lay, some child of pity bound
My bleeding wounds, and bore me from the plain,—
But thou art lost, and I have liv'd in vain!"   170
"Forgive," she cried, in accents of despair,
"Zamor, forgive thy wrongs, and O forbear,
The mild reproach that fills thy mournful eye,
The tear that wets thy cheek—I mean to die.
Could I behold my aged sire endure   175
The pains his wretched child had power to cure?
Still, still my father, stretch'd in death, I see,
His grey locks trembling while he gaz'd on me;
My Zamor, soft, breathe not so loud a sigh,
Some list'ning foe may pityless deny   180
This parting hour—hark, sure some step I hear,
Zamor again is lost—for now 'tis near."—
She paus'd, when sudden from the shelt'ring wood
A venerable form before them stood:
"Fear not, soft maid," he cried, "nor think I come   185
To seal with deeper miseries thy doom;
To bruise the broken heart that sorrow rends,
Ah, not for this Las Casas hither bends—
He comes to bid those rising sorrows cease,
To pour upon thy wounds the balm of peace.   190
I rov'd with dire Almagro's ruthless train,
Through scenes of death, to Chili's verdant plain;
Their wish to bathe that verdant plain in gore,
Then from its bosom drag the golden ore:
But mine to check the stream of human blood,   195

Or mingle drops of pity with the flood;
When from those fair, unconquered vales they fled,
This languid frame was stretch'd upon the bed
Of pale disease; when, helpless and alone,
The Chilese 'spied their friend, the murd'rers gone,   200
With eager fondness round my couch they drew,
And my cold hand with gushing tears bedew;
By day they soothe my pains with sweet delight,
And give to watchings the dull hours of night;
For me their gen'rous bosoms joy to prove   205
The cares of pity, and the toils of love—
At length for me the pathless wild they trac'd,
And softly bore me o'er its dreary waste;
Then parting, at my feet they bend, and clasp
These aged knees—my soul yet feels their grasp!   210
Now o'er the vale with painful step I stray'd,
And reach this shelt'ring grove; here, hapless maid,
My list'ning ear has caught thy piercing wail,
My heart has trembled to thy moving tale."—[1]
"And art thou he?" the mournful pair exclaim,   215
"How dear to mis'ry's soul Las Casas' name!
Spirit benign, who every grief can share,
Whose pity stoops to make the wretch its care,
Weep not for us—in vain thy tears shall flow
For cureless evils, and for hopeless woe!"—   220
"Come," he replied, "mild suff'rers, to the fane
Where rests Alphonso with his martial train;
My voice shall urge his soul to gen'rous deeds,
And bid him hear when truth and nature pleads."
While in meek tones Las Casas thus exprest   225
His pious purpose, o'er Aciloe's breast
A dawning ray of cheering comfort streams,
But faint the hope that on her spirit beams;
Faint as when ebbing life must soon depart,
The pulse that trembles while it warms the heart.   230

---

1   This line remains the same in all editions of *Peru*, and HMW retains it
    in "Peruvian Tales." It marks her only use of the word "tale" in any of
    these works. Although HMW revised Canto V of *Peru* into Aciloe's tale,
    it is still both Aciloe's *and* Zamor's words that Las Casas overhears.
    Notably, it is Las Casas' "voice"—his retelling of the tale—that changes
    Alphonso's mind.

Before Alphonso now the lovers stand,
The aged suff'rer joined the mournful band;
While, with the look that guardian seraphs wear,
When sent to calm the throbs of mortal care,
The story of their woes Las Casas told, 235
Then cried, "the wretched Zamor here behold—
Hop'st thou, fond man, a passion to controul
Fix'd in the breast, and woven in the soul?
Ah, know, mistaken youth, thy power in vain
Would bind thy victim in the nuptial chain; 240
That faithful heart will rend the galling tie,
That heart will break, that tender frame will die!
Then, by each sacred name to nature dear,
By faithful passion's agonizing tear,
By all the wasting pangs that tear her breast, 245
By the deep groan that gives the suff'rer rest,
Let mercy's pleading voice thy bosom move,
And fear to burst the bonds of plighted love!"
He paus'd—now Zamor's moan Alphonso hears;
Now sees the cheek of age bedew'd with tears. 250
Pallid and motionless Aciloe stands,
Fix'd was her lifted eye, and clasp'd her hands;
Her heart was chill'd—her fainting heart—for there
Hope slowly sinks in cold and dark despair.
Alphonso's soul was mov'd—"No more," he cried, 255
"My hapless flame shall hearts like yours divide.
Live, tender spirit, soft Aciloe live,
And all the wrongs of madd'ning rage forgive!
Go from this desolated region far,
These plains, where av'rice spreads the waste of war; 260
Go where pure pleasures gild the peaceful scene,
Go where mild virtue sheds her ray serene!"

In vain th' enraptur'd lovers would impart
The rising joy that swells, that pains the heart;
Las Casas' feet in tears Aciloe steeps, 265
Looks on her sire and smiles, then turns and weeps;
Then smiles again, while her flush'd cheek reveals
The mingled tumult of delight she feels;—
So fall the crystal showers of fragrant Spring,
And o'er the pure, clear sky, soft-shadows fling; 270
Then paint the drooping clouds from which they flow
With the warm colours of the lucid bow.

Now o'er the barren desert Zamor leads
Aciloe and her sire to Chili's meads;
There many a wand'ring wretch, condemn'd to roam   275
By hard oppression, found a shelt'ring home:
Zamor to pity tun'd the vocal shell,
Bright'ning the tear of anguish as it fell.
Did e'er the human bosom throb with pain
The heav'nly muse has sought to soothe in vain?   280
She, who can still with harmony its sighs,
And wake the sound at which affection dies![1]

---

1   Although HMW retained from *Peru* "A reflection on the influence of
    Poetry over the human mind" in the "Argument" to this tale, she
    deleted the concluding sixteen lines (V: 323-38) that originally followed
    this one and that constituted the substance of that argument.

CORA
Tale VI

The troops of Almagro *and* Alphonso *meet on the plain of Cuzco—* Manco-Capac *attacks them by night—His army is defeated, and he is forced to fly with its scattered remains—*Cora *goes in search of him—Her infant in her arms—Overcome with fatigue, she rests at the foot of a mountain—An earthquake—A band of Indians fly to the mountain for shelter—*Cora *discovers her husband—Their interview—Her death—He escapes with his infant—*Almagro *claims a share of the spoils of Cuzco—His contention with* Pizarro*—The Spaniards destroy each other—*Almagro *is taken prisoner, and put to death—His soldiers, in revenge, assassinate* Pizarro *in his palace—* Las Casas *dies—The annual festival of the Peruvians—Their victories over the Spaniards in Chili—A wish for the restoration of their liberty—Conclusion.*

At length Almagro and Alphonso's train,
Each peril past, unite on Cuzco's plain;
Capac resolves beneath the shroud of night
To pierce the hostile camp, and brave the fight;[1]
Though weak the wrong'd Peruvians' arrowy showers   5
To the dire weapons stern Iberia pours,
Fierce was th' unequal contest, for the soul,
When rais'd by some high passion's strong controul,
New strings the nerves, and o'er the glowing frame
Breathes the warm spirit of heroic flame.   10

But from the scene where raging slaughter burns,
The timid muse with silent horror turns;
The blended sounds of grief she panting hears,
Where anguish dims a mother's eye with tears;
Or where the maid, who gave to love's soft power   15
Her faithful spirit, weeps the parting hour;
And O, till death shall ease the tender woe,
That soul must languish, and those tears must flow;
For never with the thrill that rapture proves,
Her voice again shall hail the youth she loves!   20

---

1 "Cora" underwent the most extensive revision of any of the six tales in
   the transition from *Peru* to "Peruvian Tales." For example, in *Peru,*
   HMW included here a description of Cápac's "anxious woe" when he
   beheld "Th' increasing numbers of the powerful foe" (VI: 3-6).

Her earnest eye no more his form shall view,
Her quiv'ring lip has breath'd the last adieu!

Now night, that pour'd upon the hollow gale
The din of battle, dropp'd her mournful veil.
The sun rose lovely from the sleeping flood,   25
And morning glitter'd o'er the field of blood;
Where, bath'd in gore, Peruvia's vanquish'd train
Lay cold and senseless on the sanguine plain.
The gen'rous Capac saw his warriors yield,
And fled indignant from the conquer'd field.[1] 30
A wretched throng from Cuzco now repair,
Who tread 'mid slaughter'd heaps in mute despair;
O'er some lov'd corse the shroud of earth to spread,
And breathe some ritual that may soothe the dead.
No moan was heard, for agony supprest   35
The fond complaints which ease the swelling breast;
Each hope for ever lost, they only crave
The deep repose that wraps the shelt'ring grave:—
So the meek lama, lur'd by some decoy
Of man, from all his unembitter'd joy,   40
Erewhile as free as roves the wand'ring breeze,
Meets the hard burden on his bending knees;[2]
O'er rocks and mountains, dark and waste he goes,
Nor shuns the path where no fresh herbage grows;
Till, worn with toil, on earth he prostrate lies, 45
Heeds not the barb'rous lash, and scornful dies.
Swift o'er the field of death sad Cora flew,
Her infant to his mother's bosom grew;
She seeks her wretched lord, who fled the plain

---

1 HMW revised four lines of *Peru* (VI: 31-34) into two here, cutting a
 description of Cápac's emotional turmoil.
2 The Lamas bend their knees and stoop their body in such a manner as
 not to discompose their burden. They move with a slow but firm pace,
 in countries that are impracticable to other animals. They are neither
 dispirited by fasting or drudgery, while they have any strength remain-
 ing; but when they are totally exhausted, or fall under their burdens, it is
 to no purpose to harass and beat them, they will continue striking their
 heads on the ground till they kill themselves. *Raynal's History of the
 European Settlements* [HMW's note]. This passage is somewhat loosely
 drawn from Raynal (II: 529).

With the last remnant of his vanquish'd train: 50
Thro' the long glen, or forest's gloomy shade,
A dreary solitude, the mourner stray'd;
Her timid heart can now each danger dare,
Her drooping soul is arm'd by deep despair—
Long, long she wander'd, till oppress'd with toil, 55
Her trembling footsteps track with blood the soil.[1]

Where o'er an ample vale a mountain rose,
Low at its base her fainting form she throws:
"And here, my child," she cried, with panting breath,
"Here let us wait the hour of ling'ring death; 60
This famish'd bosom can no more supply
The streams that nourish life—my babe must die!
In vain I strive to cherish, for thy sake,
My failing strength; but when my heart-strings break,
When my cold bosom can no longer warm, 65
My stiff'ning arms no more enfold thy form,
Soft on this bed of leaves my child shall sleep—
Close to his mother's corse, he will not weep!
O! weep not then, my tender babe—tho' near,
I shall not hear thy moan, nor see thy tear; 70
Hope not to move me by thy mournful cry,
Nor seek with earnest look my answering eye."
As thus the dying Cora's plaints arose,
O'er the fair valley sudden darkness throws
A hideous horror; thro' the wounded air 75
Howl'd the shrill voice of nature in despair;
The birds dart screaming thro' the fluid sky,
And, dash'd upon the cliff's hard surface, die;
High o'er their rocky bounds the billows swell,
Then to their deep abyss affrighted fell; 80
Earth groaning heaves with dire convulsive throes,
While yawning gulphs its central caves disclose.
Now rush'd a frighted throng with trembling pace

---

1 This stanza concludes in *Peru* with four powerful lines that HMW
deleted in her revision of the tale:
    In vain with moans her distant lord she calls,
    In vain the bitter tear of anguish falls;
    Her moan expires along the desert wood,
    Her tear is mingled with the crimson flood. (VI: 61-64)

Along the vale, and sought the mountain's base;
Purpos'd its perilous ascent to gain,   85
And shun the ruin low'ring o'er the plain.
They reach'd the spot where Cora clasp'd her child,
And gaz'd on present death with aspect wild:
They pitying pause—she lifts her mournful eye,
And views her lord!—he hears his Cora's sigh—   90
He meets her look—their melting souls unite,
O'erwhelmed, and agoniz'd with wild delight.
At length she faintly cried, "we yet must part!
Short are these rising joys—I feel my heart,
My suff'ring heart is cold, and mists arise,   95
That shroud thy image from my closing eyes!
O, save my child!—our helpless infant save,
And shed a tear upon thy Cora's grave."
The fluttering pulse of life now ceas'd to play,
And in his arms a pallid corse she lay!   100
O'er her dear form he hung in speechless pain,
And still on Cora call'd—but call'd in vain;
Scarce could his soul in one short moment bear
The wild extremes of transport and despair.

Now o'er the west in melting softness streams   105
A lustre, milder than the morning beams;
A purer dawn dispell'd the fearful night,
And nature glow'd in all the blooms of light;[1]
Then first the mourner, waking from his trance,
Cast on his smiling babe an eager glance:[2]   110
Then rose the hollow voice on fancy's ear,
The parting words he hears, or seems to hear!
That sought with anxious tenderness to save
That dear memorial from the closing grave;
He clasps the object of his love's last care,   ·   115
And vows for him the load of life to bear.[3]
He journey'd o'er a dreary length of way,

---

1 This passage was followed in *Peru* by four lines describing birds and
   beauty (VI: 117-20).
2 HMW cut the two lines which follow in *Peru* (VI: 123-24), describing
   an emotional exchange between Cápac and his child.
3 HMW excised the two lines which follow in *Peru*:
      To rear the blossom of a faded flower,
      And bid remembrance sooth each ling'ring hour. (VI: 131-32)

To plains where freedom shed her hallow'd ray;
There, o'er the pathless wood, and mountain hoar,
His faithful band the lifeless Cora bore: 120
Ye who ne'er pin'd in sorrow's hopeless pain,
Deem not the toil that soothes its anguish vain;[1]
Perchance the conscious spirit hovers near,
And love's fond tribute to the dead is dear.
Not long Iberia's sullied trophies wave,   125
Her guilty warriors press th' untimely grave;
For av'rice rising from the caves of earth,
Wakes all her savage spirit into birth:
Bids proud Almagro feel her baleful flame,
And Cuzco's treasures from Pizarro claim.[2]   130
Now fierce in hostile rage each warlike train,
Purple with kindred blood Peruvia's plain;[3]
While pensive on the hills, whose lofty brow
O'erhung with waving woods the vale below,
Peruvia's hapless tribes in scatter'd throngs,   135
Behold the fiends of strife avenge their wrongs:
Till, fetter'd in Pizarro's iron chain,
Almagro swells the victor's captive train.
In vain his pleading voice, his suppliant eye,
Conjure his conqu'ror by the holy tie   140
That seal'd their mutual league with sacred force,
When first to climes unknown they bent their course;
When danger's rising horrors low'r'd afar,
The storms of ocean, and the toils of war,
The sad remains of wasted life to spare,   145
The shrivell'd bosom, and the silver'd hair—[4]
Almagro dies—the victor's barb'rous pride
To his pale corpse funereal rites denied;

---

1 The two following lines in *Peru* are absent here:
      Its fondness to the mould'ring corse extends,
      Its faithful tear with the cold ashes blends. (VI: 139-40)
2 In *Peru*, these lines follow:
      Pizarro holds the rich alluring prize,
      With firmer grasp, the fires of discord rise. (VI: 155-56)
3 Eleven lines in *Peru* have been excised here (VI: 159-69), beginning:
      There, breathing hate, and vengeful death they stood,
      And bath'd their impious hands in kindred blood;
4 Four lines from *Peru* (VI: 177-80), describing Pizarro's coldness and
   lack of sympathy, have been cut following this line.

Chill'd by the heavy dews of night it lay,
And wither'd in the sultry beam of day; 150
Till Indian bosoms, touch'd with gen'rous woe,
Paid the last duties to a prostrate foe.[1]
With unrelenting hate the conqu'ror views
Almagro's band, and vengeance still pursues.
Condemns the victims of his power to stray 155
In drooping poverty's chill, thorny way;
To pine with famine's agony severe,
And all the ling'ring forms of death to fear;
Till, by despair impell'd, the rival train,
Rush to the haughty victor's splendid fane; 160
Swift on their foe with rage impetuous dart,
And plunge their daggers in his guilty heart.
How unavailing now the treasur'd ore
That made Peruvia's rifled bosom poor!
He falls—unpitied, and would vainly buy[2] 165
With Andes' mines, the tribute of a sigh.

    Now faint with virtue's toil, Las Casas' soul
Sought, with exulting hope, her heavenly goal:—[3]
But whence descends, in streams of lambent light,
That lovely vision on the raptur'd sight? 170
'Tis Sensibility! she stands confest:
With trembling step she moves, and panting breast;[4]
To yon deserted grave, lo, swift she flies,
Where her lov'd victim, mild Las Casas lies!
I see her deck the solitary haunt 175
With chaplets twin'd from every weeping plant:
Its odours soft the simple violet shed,
The shrinking lily hung its drooping head;
A moaning zephyr sigh'd within the bower,
And bent the frail stem of the pliant flower: 180
"Hither," she cried, her melting tone I hear,
It vibrates full on fancy's wakeful ear;[5]

---

1 HMW eliminated a couplet in *Peru* (VI: 187-88) mentioning pity's tear.

2 Seven lines in *Peru* (VI: 201-08) are revised into this single line.

3 HMW cut the two following lines from *Peru* (VI: 211-12), concerning an attending angel.

4 HMW cut ten lines from *Peru* following this one, as well as another couplet following line 170 and one more following line 174, all describing Sensibility (VI: 215-16, 219-28, 231-32).

5 HMW deleted six lines in *Peru* (VI: 241-46) from this speech.

"Ye to whose yielding hearts my power endears,
The transport blended with delicious tears,
The bliss that swells to agony the breast,   185
The sympathy that robs the soul of rest;
Hither, with fond devotion, pensive come,
Kiss the pale shrine, and murmur o'er the tomb;
Bend on the hallow'd turf the tearful eye,
And breathe the precious incense of a sigh.   190
Las Casas' tear has moisten'd misery's grave,
His sigh has moan'd the wretch he fail'd to save!
He, while conflicting pangs his bosom tear,
Has sought the lonely cavern of despair,
Where desolate she pin'd, and pour'd her thought   195
To the dread verge of wild distraction wrought.
While drops of mercy bath'd his hoary cheek,
He pour'd, by heav'n inspir'd, its accents meek;
In truth's clear mirror bade the mourner's view
Pierce the deep veil which error darkly drew,   200
And vanquish'd empire with a smile resign,
While brighter worlds in fair perspective shine."
She paus'd—yet still the sweet enthusiast bends
O'er the cold turf, and still her tear descends.[1]

Ah, weak Peruvia! oft thy murmur'd sighs,   205
Thy stifled groans in fancy's ear arise;
She views, as slow the years of bondage roll,
On solemn days[2] when sorrow mocks controul,
Thy captive sons their antique garb assume,
And wake remember'd images of gloom.   210
Lo! Ataliba's murder'd form appears,
The mournful object of eternal tears!
Wild o'er the scene indignant glances dart,

---

1   HMW cut twenty-eight lines which follow in *Peru* celebrating "Mild
    Gasca ... the messenger of peace" (VI: 269-96).
2   The Peruvians have solemn days, on which they assume their ancient
    dress. Some among them represent a tragedy, the subject of which is the
    Death of Ataliba; the audience, who begin with shedding tears, are after-
    wards transported into a kind of madness: it seldom happens in these
    festivals but that some Spaniard is slain. —*Raynal's History* [HMW's
    note]. Drawn from Raynal (II: 519).

And pangs convulsive seize the throbbing heart—
Distraction soon each burning breast inflames,   215
And from the tyrant foe a victim claims![1]

But now, dispersing desolation's night,
A ray benignant cheers my gladden'd sight![2]
A blooming Chieftain of Peruvian race,
Whose soaring soul its high descent can trace,   220
The feather'd standard rears on Chili's[3] plain,
And leads to glorious strife his gen'rous train.
And see, Iberia bleeds! while Vict'ry twines
Her fairest garlands round Peruvia's shrines;
The gaping wounds of earth disclose no more   225
The lucid silver, and the blazing ore;
A brighter radiance gilds the passing hour,
While Freedom breaks the rod of lawless power;
On Andes' icy steep exulting glows,
And prints with rapid step th' eternal snows;[4]   230
While, roll'd in dust her graceful feet beneath,

---

1 The concluding nine lines of this stanza are a major reworking of sixteen
   lines in *Peru* (VI: 301-16).
2 Following this line, HMW deletes a couplet from *Peru*:
       From my fond eye the tear of rapture flows,
       My heart with pure delight exulting glows: (VI: 321-22)
3 A descendant of the Incas had there reared the feathered standard, and
   obtained some victories over the Spaniards; the gold-mines were shut
   up, and the sound of independence was heard; but independence and
   hope soon vanished, and it was reserved for the Bolivars of other days to
   avenge the wrongs of the Peruvians. It was reserved also for Spain to
   make at present a noble atonement for the past! She has raised an expi-
   atory altar to Liberty over the dungeons of the Inquisition:—may it
   never be thrown down! May the Old and New World form henceforth
   an Holy Alliance! And if liberty be menaced in either, may there always
   be found a Washington in the New World, and a La Fayette in the Old!
   [HMW's note].
4 Missing after this line is HMW's stirring suggestion that Peru might yet
   attain freedom:
       Or moves majestic o'er the desert plain,
       And eloquently pours her potent strain.
       Still may that strain the patriot's soul inspire,
       And still this injur'd race her spirit fire.
       O Freedom, may thy genius still ascend,
       Beneath thy crest may proud Iberia bend; (VI: 335-40)

Fades the dark laurel of Iberia's wreath!—[1]
Peru! the timid muse who mourn'd thy woes,
Whom pity robb'd so long of dear repose,
The muse whose pensive soul with anguish wrung,   235
Her early lyre for thee has trembling strung;
Shed the vain tear, and breath'd the powerless sigh,
Which in oblivion with her song must die;
Pants with the wish thy deeds may rise to fame;
Bright on some high-ton'd harp's immortal frame,   240
While on the string of ecstacy it pours
Thy future triumphs o'er unnumber'd shores.

---

1   HMW excises after this line the wish she expresses in *Peru*:
        Bend her red trophies, tear her victor plume,
        And close insatiate slaughter's yawning tomb.
        Again on soft Peruvia's fragrant breast
        May beauty blossom, and may pleasure rest. (VI: 343-46)

Appendix A: Related Poetic Works by Helen Maria Williams

[*An Ode on the Peace*, commemorating the end of the American Revolutionary War, was published pseudonymously in 1783 "by the author of Edwin and Eltruda." In modified Spenserian stanzas, the poem follows personified Peace from America to Britain. Samuel Johnson admired the poem, as did other critics. Williams published *A Poem on the Bill Lately Passed for Regulating the Slave Trade* shortly after the Slave Trade Regulation Act became law in July 1788. Despite Williams's abolitionist efforts and those of many of her contemporaries, the British slave trade, as well as slavery throughout the empire, would not be abolished until 1807 and 1834, respectively.]

1. *An Ode on the Peace* (London: T. Cadell, 1783)

As wand'ring late on Albion's shore
That chains the rude tempestuous deep,
I heard the hollow surges roar
Whose tears her rocky bosom steep;
Loud on the storm's wild pinion flow   5
The sullen sounds of mingled woe,
And softly vibrate on the trembling Lyre,
That wakes to sorrow's moan each sad responsive wire.

From Shores the wide Atlantic laves
The Spirit of the Ocean bears,   10
In moanings o'er his western waves,
Fond Passion's shrieks, and Nature's tears;
Enchanting climes of young delight,
How chang'd since first ye rush'd in sight!
Since first ye rose, in infant glories drest,   15
Fresh from the sparkling wave, and rear'd your ample breast.

His crested Serpents Discord bears
O'er scenes Affection's roses grac'd.
Her flowery Chain he frantic tears,
And scatters o'er the howling waste.   20
His glance her soothing smile deforms,
His voice awakes the mental storms,
His blazing torches spread their sanguine fires,
While Passion's trembling flame in seas of blood expires.

Now burns the savage soul of War,   25
While Terror flashes from his eyes,
Lo! waving o'er his fiery car
Aloft his bloody banner flies.
The battle wakes: with shrilling sound
He thunders o'er the groaning ground,   30
He grasps his reeking blade, while streams of blood
Tinge the impurpled plain, and swell the ample flood.

Hark! softer sounds of sorrow flow:
On drooping wing the murm'ring gales
Now pour the plaints of hopeless woe   35
That rise along the lonely vales:
They waft the tender Orphan's cries,
They tremble to parental sighs,
And drink a tear these mingled griefs above,
The wild impassion'd tear of fond Connubial Love;   40

The Object of her shiv'ring fear
Lies bleeding, panting on the ground,
She frantic pours her gushing tear
That bathes the fatal gaping wound:
The blood-stained hand she trembling grasps,   45
Hangs on the quiv'ring lip, and clasps
The fainting Form that slowly sinks in death,
And meets the parting glance, and sucks the fleeting breath.

Pale as the livid Corse her cheeks,
Her tresses torn, her glances wild,   50
In frantic tones she fault'ring speaks,
She wept—and then in horrors smil'd—
She gazes now with wild affright,
Lo! bleeding Phantoms rush in sight—
Hark! on yon mangled form she faintly calls,   55
Then on the flinty earth the Mourner senseless falls.

And lo! o'er hapless Andre's tomb[1]
Mild victim of his soft despair!
Whose soul in Life's exulting bloom
Deem'd not that Life deserv'd a care,   60
O'er the cold earth his relicks prest

---

1   Major John André (1750-80) was hanged in America for conspiring with
    Benedict Arnold. Anna Seward wrote a long elegy, *Monody on the Death of
    Major André* (1781). She considered him a "Martyr in the Cause of his King
    and Country."

Lo! Britain's drooping Legions rest;
For him the blades they sternly grasp, appear
Dim'd with a rising sigh, and sullied with a tear.

While Seward sweeps her plaintive strings,   65
    While pensive round his sable shrine
    A radiant zone she graceful flings,
    Where full emblaz'd his virtues shine,
    The mournful Loves that tremble nigh
    Shall catch her warm melodious sigh,   70
And drink the precious thrilling drops that flow
From Pity's hov'ring soul, that pants dissolv'd in woe.

And hark! in Albion's flow'ry Vale
    A Parent's moans I shiv'ring hear—
    A Sister calls the western Gale   75
    To drink her soul-expressive tear!
    The throbbing sigh for Asgill[1] flows
    That breathes Affection's mingled woes,
While on the rack of Doubt, and Terror, rest
The dearest fondest ties that tremble at her breast.   80

How oft' in every dawning grace
    That blossom'd in his early hours,
    Her soul some comfort lov'd to trace,
    And deck'd Futurity in flowers!
    But lo! in shudd'ring Fancy's sight   85
    The dear illusions sink in night—
She views the murder'd form—the quiv'ring breath—
The rising Virtues chill'd in the cold shade of death—

Cease, cease, ye throbs of frantic woe!
    He lives parental love to bless,   90
    To wake the pure extatic glow
    The thrill of transport's sweet excess—
    Again his smile shall life endear,
    And Pleasure pour her brightest tear!
The private pang shall Albion trembling share,   95
And breathe with fervid zeal, a warm accepted prayer.

---

1 Sir Charles Asgill (1762-1823), a captain in the British Army, was captured by
   American forces in 1781. In retaliation for the unrelated execution of an
   American soldier, Asgill was sentenced to die. His mother wrote to the King
   and Queen of France, begging that they use their influence to have him
   released. The monarchy's support, together with other factors, resulted in
   Asgill gaining his freedom in December 1782.

And lo! a lucid stream of light
Descends o'er Horror's sable cloud,
While Desolation's gloomy night
Retiring, folds her sullen shroud—   100
It flashes o'er the limpid deep—
It rests on Britain's rocky steep—
'Tis mild benignant Peace, enchanting form!
That gilds the black Abyss, that lulls the raging Storm.

So, thro' the dark and misty Sky,   105
Where clouds and sullen vapours roll'd,
Their curling wreathes dissolving fly
As the faint hues of light unfold:
The Sky with spreading azure streams—
The Sun now darts his orient beams—   110
And now he glows insufferably bright,
And sheds o'er Nature's form the rays of living light.

Mild Peace! from Albion's fairest Bowers,
Soft Spirit! cull with snowy hands,
The buds that drink the morning showers,   115
And bind the Realms in flow'ry bands.
Thy smiles th' infuriate Passions chase,
Thy glance is Pleasure's sportive grace,
Around thy form th' exulting Virtues move,
Thy voice the thrilling strain of mild melodious Love. 120

Bless, all ye Powers! the patriot name
That courts, fair Peace, thy smiling stay;
Ah gild with Glory's light his Fame,
His Life with Pleasure's roseate ray!
While, like th' affrighted Dove, thy form   125
Still shrinks, and fears some latent storm,
His cares shall soothe thy panting soul to rest,
And spread thy flowery couch on Albion's fost'ring breast.

Ah! see tumultuous transports move
The faithful heart, with Passion warm;   130
With frantic joy Connubial Love
Clasps to her soul the well-known form,
That long, in all her throbbing veins,
Wak'd fond Affection's cherish'd pains—
She weeps—the gushing drops her joys endear,   135
'Tis glowing Rapture speaks, expressive in a tear.

Ye who have mourn'd the parting hour
Which Love in darker horrors drew,
When ardent Passion fear'd to pour,
With quiv'ring lip, her last adieu,   140
When the fix'd glance, the bursting sigh,
The soul that trembled in the eye,
Express'd the frantic fears of hopeless Love—
Ah! paint the swelling joys your panting bosoms prove.

Yon hoary form with aspect mild,   145
Deserted kneels, by sorrows prest,
And seeks from heav'n his long-lost child
To smooth the path that leads to rest!—
He comes—to close the sinking eye,
To catch the faint expiring sigh;   150
A moment transport stays the fleeting breath
And sooths the ling'ring soul on the pale verge of death.

The milder Passions dear controul,
The purer Pleasures vivid bloom,
That bathe in bliss th' exulting soul,   155
Soft Peace! are couch'd beneath thy Plume:
It floats in Rapture's glowing ray,
O'er wilder'd Life's low, thorny way,
And wakes the softest balms, the fairest flowers,
That shed their odours mild in sweet Affection's Bowers.   160

Tho' the red Trophies Vict'ry twines[1]
Now drooping fade in Stygian glooms,
Yet hung around thy simple Shrines,
Fair Peace, each milder Glory blooms.
Lo! Commerce rears her languid head   165
Triumphal, Thames! from thy deep bed,
High o'er the subject wave she sails sublime,
To bless with Albion's wealth, each less indulgent Clime.

---

1   The ensanguined spoils of war. HMW conjures a similar image in *Peru*:
    "Bend her red trophies, tear her victor plume,
    And close insatiate slaughter's yawning tomb." (VI: 343-44)

She fearless prints the Polar snows
Where Horror shrouds the struggling day,   170
Along the burning Line she glows,
Nor shrinks beneath the Torrid ray:
She opes the glitt'ring Indian mine
Where the warm beams reflected shine;
Bears the bright Gems to Britain's temp'rate Vale,   175
And breathes Sabean[1] sweets o'er the chill Northern Gale.

While from the far-divided Shore
Where Liberty exulting roves,
Her ardent glance shall oft' explore
The Parent-Isle her spirit loves—   180
Lo! rushing o'er the western main,
She spreads fair Concord's golden chain,
And sternly pours on prostrate Gallia's[2] strand,
From Albion's[3] pendent Cliff, her firm united Band.

Yet hide the Sabre's horrid glare   185
That steeps its edge in streams of blood,
The Lance that quivers high in air,
And falling drinks a purple flood;
For, Britain! fears shall seize thy foes.
While freedom in thy senate glows,   190
While Peace shall scatter o'er thy cultur'd plain
Each Glory, Pleasure, Grace, her fair attendant train.

Enchanting Visions soothe my sight—
The finer Arts in Beauty drest,
Benignant source of pure delight!   195
Reclining on her bosom rest.
While each discordant sound expires,
Strike, Harmony! thy warbling wires,
The fine vibrations of the spirit move,
Wake Extasy's pure thrill, and touch the springs of Love. 200

---

1   The ancient Sabean people of the Arabian Peninsula lived in the warmth of
    what is present day Yemen.
2   France.
3   Britain.

Bright Painting's living forms shall rise,
And still for Ugolino's woe[1]
Shall Reynolds wake unbidden sighs,
And Romney's soothing Pencil flow,
    That Nature's look benign pourtrays,[2]   205
    When, to her infant Shakspeare's gaze,
The smiling form "unveil'd her awful face,"[3]
And bade his "colours clear"[4] each glowing feature trace.

    And Poesy! thy deep-ton'd shell
    The heart shall sooth, the spirit fire,   210
    And all th' according passions swell
    While rapture trembles on thy lyre;
    Awake its sweetly-thrilling sound,
    And call enchanting Visions round,
    Strew the soft path of Peace with Fancy's flowers,   215
And lead the glowing heart to Joy's Elysian bowers.

    While Hayley wakes thy magic strings,
    His shades shall no rude sound prophane,
    But stillness on her tender wings,
    Enamour'd drink the potent strain.   220
    Tho' Genius flash the vivid flame
    Around his Lyre's enchanting frame,
    Where Fancy's warbled tones melodious roll,
More warm his friendship glows, more harmoniz'd his soul!

---

1 "Ugolino's woe"—a celebrated picture by Sir Joshua Reynolds, taken
    from Dante [HMW's note]. Sir Joshua Reynolds (1723-92) was a portrait
    painter, friend of Samuel Johnson, and first president of the Royal Academy.
2 "Nature's look benign pourtrays"—a subject Mr. Romney has taken
    from Gray's Progress of Poesy [HMW's note]. George Romney (1734-1802)
    was the most celebrated portrait painter of his day.
3 From "The First of April: Or, the Triumphs of Folly: a Poem" (1777) by
    William Combe. The full passage reads:
        There the great Bacon, whose sagacious eye
        Pierc'd through the gloom of dark Philosophy,
        And to the World unveil'd her awful face,
        Crouch'd a low, servile Courtier in disgrace. (65-68)
4 See Thomas Gray's lines on Shakespeare in "The Progress of Poesy: A
    Pindaric Ode" (1757):
        "This pencil take ... whose colours clear
        Richly paint the vernal year" (89-90)

While Taste instructs a polish'd age   225
With luxury of mind to trace
The lustre of th' unerring page,
Where Symmetry sheds finish'd grace;
Judgment shall point to Fancy's gaze,
As wild the sportive wand'rer strays,   230
Perfection's fairest form, where mimic Art
With Nature softly blends, and leads the subject heart.

Th' historic Muse illumes the maze[1]
Oblivion veil'd in deep'ning night,
Where empire with meridian blaze   235
Once trod Ambition's lofty height:
Tho' headlong from the dizzy steep
It rolls with wide, and wasteful sweep,
Her tablet still records the deeds of Fame,
And swells the Patriot's soul, and wakes the Hero's flame. 240

While meek Philosophy explores
Creation's vast stupendous round,
With piercing gaze sublime she soars,
And bursts the system's distant bound.
Lo! 'mid the dark deep void of space,   245
A rushing World[2] her glance can trace!
It moves majestic in its ample sphere,
Sheds its refracted light, and rolls its ling'ring year.

Ah! still diffuse thy mental ray,
Fair Science! on my Albion's plain,   250
While oft' thy step delights to stray
Where Montagu has rear'd her Fane;[3]
Where Eloquence shall still entwine
Rich attic flowers around the shrine,
View hallow'd Learning ope his treasured store,   255
And with her signet stamp the mass of classic ore.

---

1 Edward Gibbon (1737-94), English historian, author of *The Decline and Fall of the Roman Empire* (1776-88).

2 Alluding to Mr. Herschel's wonderful discoveries; and particularly to his discovery of a new planet, called the "Georgium Sidus" [HMW's note]. William Herschel (1738-1822), the English astronomer who discovered Uranus in 1781, named it "Georgium Sidus" (George's Star) in honor of his patron, King George III.

3 Elizabeth Montagu, to whom HMW dedicated *Peru* in 1784. See HMW's poem "To Mrs. Montagu" and accompanying note (pp. 47-48).

Auspicious Peace! for thine the hours
Meek Wisdom decks in moral grace,
And thine each tenderness that pours
Enchantment o'er their destin'd space.   260
Benignant form! in silence laid
Beneath the olive's silken shade,
Shed each mild bliss that charms the tuneful mind,
And in the zone of love the hostile spirit bind.

While Albion on her parent deep   265
Shall rest, may glory gild her shore,
And blossom on her rocky steep
Till Time shall wing his course no more;
Till angels wrap the spheres in fire,
Till Earth and yon fair Orbs expire,   270
While Chaos mounting in the rushing flame,
Shall spread his cold deep shade o'er Nature's sinking frame.

2. *A Poem on the Bill Lately Passed for Regulating the Slave Trade* (London: T. Cadell, 1788)

The quality of mercy is not strain'd;
It droppeth, as the gentle rain from heav'n
Upon the place beneath. It is twice bless'd;
It blesseth him that gives, and him that takes.
—Shakespeare[1]

The hollow winds of Night, no more
In wild, unequal cadence pour
On musing Fancy's wakeful ear,
The groan of agony severe
From yon dark vessel, which contains   5
The wretch new bound in hopeless chains;
Whose soul with keener anguish bleeds,
As Afric's less'ning shore recedes—
No more where Ocean's unseen bound
Leaves a drear world of waters round,   10
Between the howling gust, shall rise
The stifled Captive's latest sighs—;
No more shall suffocating death
Seize the pent victim's sinking breath;
The pang of that convulsive hour   15

---

1 Portia, *The Merchant of Venice* (4.1.182-85).

Reproaching Man's insatiate power;
Man! who to Afric's shore has past
Relentless, as the annual blast
That sweeps the Western Isles, and flings
Destruction from its furious wings—   20
And Woman, she, too weak to bear
The galling chain, the tainted air;
Of mind too feeble to sustain
The vast, accumulated pain;
No more, in desperation wild,   25
Shall madly strain her gasping child;
With all the mother at her soul,
With eyes where tears have ceas'd to roll,
Shall catch the livid infant's breath;
Then sink in agonizing death.   30
     Britain! the noble, blest decree
That sooths despair, is fram'd by Thee!
Thy powerful arm has interpos'd,
And *one* dire scene for ever clos'd;
Its horror shall no more belong   35
To that foul drama, deep with wrong.
Oh, first of Europe's polish'd lands,
To ease the Captive's iron bands!
Long as thy glorious annals shine,
This proud distinction shall be thine: 40
Not first alone when Valour leads,
To rush on Danger's noblest deeds;
When Mercy calls thee to explore
A gloomy path, untrod before,
Thy ardent spirit springs to heal,   45
And, greatly gen'rous, dares to feel!—
Valour is like the meteor's light,
Whose partial flash leaves deeper night;
While Mercy, like the lunar ray,
Gilds the thick shade with softer day.   50
     For this, in Fame's immortal shrine,
A double wreathe, O Pitt,[1] is thine!
For this! while distant ages hear
With Admiration's sacred tear,

---

1 William Pitt (1759-1806), prime minister from 1793 to 1801 and from 1804
to 1806, supported William Wilberforce's movement for the abolition of the
slave trade. An Act for the Abolition of the Slave Trade was passed by Parlia-
ment on 25 March 1807.

Of powers, whose energy sublime   55
Disdain'd to borrow force from Time,
With no gradations mark'd their flight,
But rose, at once, to Glory's height;
The deeds of Mercy, that embrace
A distant sphere, an alien-race,   60
Shall Virtue's lips record, and claim
The fairest honors of thy name!
'Tis ever Nature's gen'rous view;
Great minds, should noble ends pursue;
As the clear sun-beam, when most bright,   65
Warms, in proportion to its light.—
And Richmond,[1] he! who, high in birth,
Adds the unfading rays of worth;
Who stoops, from scenes in radiance drest,
To ease the mourner's aching breast;   70
The tale of private woe to hear,
And wipe the friendless orphan's tear!—
His bosom for the Captive bleeds,
He, Guardian of the injur'd! pleads
With all the force that Genius gives,   75
And warmth that but with Virtue lives;
For Virtue, with divine controul,
Collects the various powers of soul;
And lends, from her unsullied source,
The gems of thought their purest force.   80
          Oh blest decree! Whose lustre seems
Like the sweet Morn's reviving beams,
That chase the hideous forms of night,
And promise day more richly bright;
Great deed! that met consenting minds   85
In all, but those whom Av'rice binds;
Who creep in Interest's crooked ways,
Nor ever pass her narrow maze;
Or those, whom hard Indiff'rence steels
To every pang another feels.   90
For *Them* has Fortune, round their bowers,
Twin'd (partial nymph!) her lavish flowers;
For *Them*, from unsunn'd caves, she brings
Her summer ice; for *Them*, she springs

---

1   Charles Lennox, third Duke of Richmond (1735-1806) supported many of
    Pitt's proposals for reform, including abolition of the slave trade.

To climes, where hotter suns produce   95
The richer fruits' delicious juice:
While *They*, whom wasted blessings tire,
Nor leave *one* want, to feed desire;
With cool, insulting ease, demand
Why for yon hopeless, Captive Band,   100
Is ask'd, to mitigate despair,
The mercy of the common air?
The boon of larger space to breathe,
While coop'd that hollow deck beneath?
A lengthen'd plank, on which to throw   105
Their shackled limbs, while fiercely glow
The beams direct, that on each head
The fury of contagion shed?—
And dare presumptuous, guilty man,
Load with offence his fleeting span?   110
Deform Creation with the gloom
Of crimes, that blot its cheerful bloom;
Darken a work so perfect made,
And cast the Universe in shade!—
Alas, to Afric's fetter'd race   115
Creation wears no form of grace!
To Them, Earth's pleasant vales are found
A blasted waste, a sterile bound;
Where the poor wand'rer must sustain
The load of unremitted pain!   120
A region, in whose ample scope
His eye discerns no gleam of hope;
Where Thought no kind asylum knows,
On which its anguish may repose,
But Death, that to the ravag'd breast   125
Comes not in shapes of terror drest,
Points to green hills where Freedom roves,
And minds renew their former loves;
Or, low'ring in the troubled air,
Hangs the fierce spectre of Despair,   130
Whose soul abhors the gift of life,
Who stedfast grasps the reeking knife,
Bids the charg'd heart in torrents bleed,
And smiles in frenzy, at the deed.
So, when rude winds the sailor urge   135
On polar seas, near Earth's last verge;
Long with the blast he struggles hard,
To save his bark, in ice imbarr'd;

But finds at length, o'ercome with pain,
The conflict with his fate is vain;   140
Then heaves no more the useless groan,
But hardens like the wave to stone.
      Ye noble minds! who o'er a sky
Where clouds are roll'd, and tempests fly,
Have bid the lambent lustre play   145
Of *one* pure, lovely, azure ray;
Oh, far diffuse its op'ning bloom,
And the wide hemisphere illume!
Ye, who *one* bitter drop have drain'd
From Slav'ry's cup, with horror stain'd;   150
Oh, let no fatal dregs be found,
But dash her chalice on the ground:
Oh, while she links her impious chain,
And calculates the price of pain;
Weighs Agony in sordid scales,   155
And marks if Death, or Life prevails;
In one short moment, seals the doom
Of years, which anguish shall consume;
Decides how near the mangling scourge
May to the grave its victim urge,   160
Yet for awhile, with prudent care
The half-worn wretch, if useful, spare;
And speculates with skill refin'd,
How deep a wound will stab the mind;
How far the spirit can endure   165
Calamity, that hopes no cure;—
Ye! who can selfish cares forego,
To pity those which others know;
As Light, that from its centre strays,
To glad all Nature with its rays;   170
Oh! ease the pangs ye stoop to share,
And rescue millions from despair!—
For you, while Morn in graces gay,
Wakes the fresh bloom of op'ning Day;
Gilds with her purple light your dome,   175
Renewing all the joys of home;
Of home! dear scene, whose ties can bind
With sacred force the human mind;
That feels each little absence pain,
And lives but to return again;   180
To that lov'd spot, however far,
Points, like the needle to its star;

That native shed which first we knew,
Where first the sweet affections grew;
Alike the willing heart can draw,   185
If fram'd of marble, or of straw;
Whether the voice of pleasure calls,
And gladness echoes thro' its walls;
Or, to its hallow'd roof we fly,
With those we love to pour the sigh;   190
The load of mingled pain to bear,
And soften every pang we share!—
Ah, think how desolate *His* state,
How *He* the chearful light must hate,
Whom, sever'd from his native soil,   195
The Morning wakes to fruitless toil;
To labours, hope shall never chear,
Or fond domestic joy endear;
Poor wretch! on whose despairing eyes
His cherish'd home shall never rise!   200
Condemn'd, severe extreme, to live
When all is fled that life can give!—
And ah! the blessings valued most
By human minds, are blessings lost!
Unlike the objects of the eye,   205
Enlarging, as we bring them nigh,
Our joys, at distance strike the breast,
And seem diminish'd when possest.
    Who, from his far-divided shore,
The half-expiring Captive bore?   210
Those, whom the traffic of their race
Has robb'd of every human grace;
Whose harden'd souls no more retain
Impressions Nature stamp'd in vain;
All that distinguishes their *kind*,   215
For ever blotted from their mind;
As streams, that once the landscape gave
Reflected on the trembling wave,
Their substance change, when lock'd in frost,
And rest, in dead contraction lost;—   220
Who view unmov'd, the look, that tells
The pang that in the bosom dwells;
Heed not the nerves that terror shakes,
The heart convulsive anguish breaks;
The shriek that would their crimes upbraid,   225
But deem despair a part of trade.—

Such only, for detested gain,
The barb'rous commerce would maintain.
The gen'rous sailor, he, who dares
All forms of danger, while he bears   230
The British Flag o'er untrack'd seas,
And spreads it on the polar breeze;
He, who in Glory's high career,
Finds agony, and death are dear;
To whose protecting arm we owe   235
Each blessing that the happy know;
Whatever charms the soften'd heart,
Each cultur'd grace, each finer art,
E'en thine, most lovely of the train!
Sweet Poetry! thy heav'n-taught strain—   240
His breast, where nobler passions burn,
In honest poverty, would spurn
The wealth, Oppression can bestow,
And scorn to wound a fetter'd foe.
True courage in the unconquer'd soul   245
Yields to Compassion's mild controul;
As, the resisting frame of steel
The magnet's secret force can feel.
　　　When borne at length to Western Lands,
Chain'd on the beach the Captive stands,   250
Where Man, dire merchandize! is sold,
And barter'd life is paid for gold;
In mute affliction, see him try
To read his new possessor's eye;
If one blest glance of mercy there,   255
One half-formed tear may check despair!—
Ah, if that eye with sorrow sees
His languid look, his quiv'ring knees,
Those limbs, which scarce their load sustain,
That form, consum'd in wasting pain;   260
Such sorrow melts his ruthless eye
Who sees the lamb, he doom'd to die,
In pining sickness yield his life,
And thus elude the sharpen'd knife.—
Or, if where savage habit steels   265
The vulgar mind, one bosom feels
The sacred claim of helpless woe—
If Pity in that soil can grow;
Pity! Whose tender impulse darts
With keenest force on nobler hearts;   270

As flames that purest essence boast,
Rise highest when they tremble most.—
Yet *why* on one poor chance must rest
The int'rests of a kindred breast?
Humanity's devoted cause   275
Recline on Humour's wayward laws?
To Passion's rules must Justice bend,
And life upon Caprice depend?—
        Ah ye, who one fix'd purpose own,
Whose untir'd aim is *Self* alone;   280
Who think in gold the essence lies
From which extracted bliss shall rise;
To whose dull sense, no charm appears
In social smiles, or social tears;
As mists that o'er the landscape sail,   285
Its beauteous variations veil;
Or, if in some relenting hour,
When Nature re-assumes her power,
Your alms to Penury ye lend,
Or serve, for once, a suff'ring friend;   290
Whom no weak impulse e'er betray'd
To give that friend incautious aid;
Who with exact precision, pause
At that nice point which Int'rest draws;
Your watchful footsteps never found   295
To stray beyond that guarded bound;—
Does fleeting Life proportion bear
To all the wealth ye heap with care?
When soon your days in measur'd flight
Shall sink in Death's terrific night;   300
Then seize the moments in your power,
To Mercy consecrate the hour!
Risque something in her cause at last,
And thus atone for all the past;
Break the hard fetters of the Slave;   305
And learn the luxury to save!—
Does Avarice, your god, delight
With agony to feast his sight?
Does he require that victims slain,
And human blood, his altars stain?   310
Ah, not alone of power possest
To check each *virtue* of the breast;
As when the numbing frosts arise,

The charm of vegetation dies;
His sway the harden'd bosom leads   315
To Cruelty's remorseless deeds;
Like the blue lightning when it springs
With fury on its livid wings,
Darts to its goal with baleful force,
Nor heeds that ruin marks its course.—   320
  Oh Eloquence, prevailing art!
Whose force can chain the list'ning heart;
The throb of Sympathy inspire,
And kindle every great desire;
With magic energy controul   325
And reign the sov'reign of the soul!
That dreams while all its passions swell,
It shares the power it feels so well;
As visual objects seem possest
Of those clear hues by light imprest;   330
Oh, skill'd in every grace to charm,
To soften, to appal, to warm;
Fill with thy noblest rage the breast,
Bid on those lips thy spirit rest,
That shall, in Britain's Senate, trace   335
The wrongs of Afric's Captive Race!—
But Fancy o'er the tale of woe
In vain one heighten'd tint would throw;
For ah, the Truth, is all we guess
Of anguish in its last excess: 340
Fancy may dress in deeper shade
The storm that hangs along the glade,
Spreads o'er the ruffled stream its wing,
And chills awhile the flowers of Spring:
But, where the wintry tempests sweep   345
In madness, o'er the darken'd deep;
Where the wild surge, the raging wave,
Point to the hopeless wretch a grave;
And Death surrounds the threat'ning shore—
Can Fancy add one horror more?   350
  Lov'd Britain! whose protecting hand
Stretch'd o'er the Globe, on Afric's strand
The honour'd base of Freedom lays,
Soon, soon the finish'd fabric raise!
And when surrounding realms would frame,   355
Touch'd with a spark of gen'rous flame,

Some pure, ennobling, great design,
Some lofty act, almost divine;
Which Earth may hail with rapture high,
And Heav'n may view with fav'ring eye;   360
Teach them to make all Nature free,
And shine by emulating Thee!—

Appendix B: Williams's Historical and Literary Sources

[Williams drew upon contemporary histories, particularly William Robertson's popular *History of America* (1777) and Abbé Raynal's *Histoire philosophique et politique* (1770), as well as the more fictionalized *Les Incas* (1777) by Jean-François Marmontel. She did not slavishly rely upon these sources, but they provided her with a philosophical framework that challenged intellectual and political power structures with their revolutionary humanism. Within their pages, Peru became a case study in civilization, empire, commerce, class, and freedom. Williams also read avowedly fictional accounts, including Françoise de Graffigny's wildly popular *Lettres d'une Péruvienne* (1747), translated as *Letters Written by a Peruvian Lady*, a text that parallels *Peru* and "Peruvian Tales" in its philosophical exploration of the concept of the noble savage, bold interrogation of society's treatment of women, stark indictment of imperialism, and complex depictions of Christianity and conversion.]

1. **Joseph Warton, "The Dying Indian" and "The Revenge of America," published in *A Collection of Poems by Several Hands*, ed. Robert Dodsley (London: R. and J. Dodsley, 1755) IV: 208-10**

[Joseph Warton (1722-1800) was an English literary critic, poet, editor, church rector, headmaster of Winchester School, and associate of Samuel Johnson. His best-known book of poetry is *The Enthusiast, or The Lover of Nature* (1744), but he also published several other books, including *Odes on Various Subjects* (1746). His *Essay on the Genius and Writings of Pope* (1756, 1782) was a well-respected volume of criticism. Warton edited the works of Virgil, Pope, and John Dryden. Andrew Kippis introduced Williams to Joseph Warton in 1782 (Kennedy 26), at about the same time that she began composing *Peru*. Warton's "The Revenge of America" and "The Dying Indian" contain representations of the Spaniards as gold-greedy rapists of an Edenic land and depict indigenous people as noble savages on the verge of extinction—elements that would influence Williams's portrayals.]

The Dying Indian

The dart of Izdabel prevails! 'twas dipt
In double poison——I shall soon arrive
At the blest island, where no tigers spring
On heedless hunters; where anana's bloom
Thrice in each moon; where rivers smoothly glide,   5
Nor thundering torrents whirl the light canoe
Down to the sea; where my forefathers feast
Daily on hearts of Spaniards!——O my son,
I feel the venom busy in my breast,
Approach, and bring my crown, deck'd with the teeth   10
Of that bold christian who first dar'd deflour
The virgins of the sun; and, dire to tell!
Robb'd Vitzipultzi's statue[1] of its gems!
I mark'd the spot where they interr'd this traitor,
And once at midnight stole I to his tomb,   15
And tore his carcass from the earth, and left it
A prey to poisonous flies. Preserve this crown
With sacred secrecy: if e'er returns
Thy much-lov'd mother from the desert woods
Where, as I hunted late, I hapless lost her,   20
Cherish her age. Tell her I ne'er have worship'd
With those that eat their God. And when disease
Preys on her languid limbs, then kindly stab her
With thine own hands, nor suffer her to linger,
Like christian cowards, in a life of pain.   25
I go! great Copac beckons me! farewell!

The Revenge of America

When Cortez' furious legions flew
O'er ravag'd fields of rich Peru,
Struck with his bleeding people's woes,
Old India's awful Genius rose.
He sat on Andes' topmost stone,   5
And heard a thousand nations groan;
For grief his feathery crown he tore,
To see huge Plata foam with gore;
He broke his arrows, stampt the ground,
To view his cities smoaking round.   10

---

1   Aztec god of war and also god of the sun; Huitzilopochtli. His temple at
    Tenochtitlán was an architectural marvel, destroyed by the Spanish in 1521,
    along with the rest of the city.

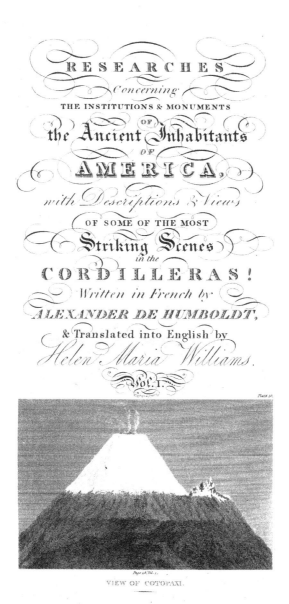

RESEARCHES

Concerning

THE INSTITUTIONS & MONUMENTS

of

the Ancient Inhabitants

of

AMERICA,

with Descriptions & Views

OF SOME OF THE MOST

Striking Scenes

in the

CORDILLERAS!

Written in French by

ALEXANDER DE HUMBOLDT,

& Translated into English by

Helen Maria Williams.

Vol. I.

VIEW OF COTOPAXI.

LONDON:

Published by Longman, Hurst, Rees, Orme & Brown, J. Murray & H. Colburn.

1814.

Title page to Williams's English translation of Humboldt's *Researches Concerning the Institutions & Monuments of the Ancient Inhabitants of America*. Published in London, 1814. Private collection.

What woes, he cry'd, hath lust of gold
O'er my poor country widely roll'd;
Plunderers proceed! my bowels tear,
But ye shall meet destruction there;
From the deep-vaulted mine shall rise   15
Th' insat[i]ate fiend, pale Avarice!
Whose steps shall trembling Justice fly,
Peace, Order, Law, and Amity!
I see all Europe's children curst
With lucre's universal thirst: 20
The rage that sweeps my sons away,
My baneful gold shall well repay.

2. From William Hayley, *An Essay on Epic Poetry; in Five Epistles* (London: J. Dodsley, 1782)

[William Hayley's *An Essay on Epic Poetry* (1782) applauds the success
of classical and modern epics as it asks for English poets to free them-
selves from current literary fads and return to the venerable and
ancient genre of the epic. Williams had met Hayley by 1782. Their
friendship influenced Williams to take on the challenge of writing in
the epic form. Hayley's notes are not included here.]

[From Epistle I]

Perish that critic pride, which oft has hurl'd
    Its empty thunders o'er the Epic world;
Which, eager to extend its mimic reign,
Would bind free Fancy in a servile chain;
With papal rage the eye of Genius blind,   5
And bar the gates of Glory on the mind!
    Such dark decrees have letter'd Bigots penn'd,
Yet seiz'd that honor'd name, the Poet's Friend.
But Learning from her page their laws will blot;
Scorn'd be their arrogance! their name forgot!   10
Th' indignant Bard, abhorring base controul,
Seeks the just Critic of congenial soul.
Say! Mason, Judge and Master of the Lyre!
Harmonious Chief of Britain's living Choir,
Say! wilt Thou listen to his weaker strains,   15
Who pants to range round Fancy's rich domains;
To vindicate her empire, and disown
Proud System, seated on her injur'd throne?
Come! while thy Muse, contented with applause,

Gives to her graceful song a little pause, 20
Enjoying triumphs past; at leisure laid
In thy sweet Garden's variegated shade,
Or fondly hanging on some favorite Oak
That Harp, whose notes the fate of Mona[1] spoke,
Strung by the sacred Druid's social band, 25
And wisely trusted to thy kindred hand!
Come! for thy liberal and ingenuous heart
Can aid a Brother in this magic art;
Let us, and Freedom be our guide, explore
The highest province of poetic lore, 30
Free the young Bard from that oppressive awe,
Which feels Opinion's rule as Reason's law,
And from his spirit bid vain fears depart,
Of weaken'd Nature and exhausted Art!
Phantoms! that literary spleen conceives! 35
Dullness adopts, and Indolence believes!
While with advent'rous step we wind along
Th' expansive regions of Heroic song,
From different sources let our search explain
Why few the Chieftains of this wide domain. 40
Haply, inspiriting poetic youth,
Our verse may prove this animating truth,
That Poesy's sublime, neglected field
May still new laurels to Ambition yield;
Her Epic trumpet, in a modern hand, 45
Still make the spirit glow, the heart expand.
Be such our doctrine! our enlivening aim
The Muse's honor, and our Country's fame!
  Thou first and fairest of the social Arts!
Sovereign of liberal souls, and feeling hearts, 50
If, in devotion to thy heavenly charms,
I clasp'd thy altar with my infant arms,
For thee neglected the wide field of wealth,
The toils of int'rest, and the sports of health,
Enchanting Poesy! that zeal repay 55
With powers to sing thy universal sway!
To trace thy progress from thy distant birth,
Heaven's pure descendant! dear delight of Earth!

---

1 The island of Mona, or Anglesey, was, according to Tacitus (*Annals* 14.30), the site of a massacre of Druids during the Roman conquest of Britain in the first century CE.

Charm of all regions! to no age confin'd!
The prime ennobler of th' aspiring mind!   60
  Nor will thy dignity, sweet Power! disdain
What Fiction utters in her idle strain,
Thy sportive Friend! who, mocking solemn Truth,
Tells her fond tales of thy untutor'd youth.
As wrong'd Latona[1] (so her tale begins)   65
To Delphos travell'd with her youthful twins;
Th' envenom'd Python, with terrific sway,
Cross'd the fair Goddess in her destin'd way·
The heavenly parent, in the wild alarm,
Her little Dian in her anxious arm,   70
High on a stone, which she in terror trod,
Cried to her filial guard, the Archer God,[2]
Bidding with force, that spoke the Mother's heart,
Her young Apollo launch his ready dart;
In measur'd sounds her rapid mandate flow'd,   75
The first foundation of the future Ode!
Thus, at their banquets, fabling Greeks rehearse
The fancied origin of sacred Verse:
And though cold Reason may with scorn assail,
Or turn contemptuous from their simple tale,   80
Yet, Poesy! thy sister Art may stoop
From this weak sketch to paint th' impassion'd group.
Though taste refin'd to modern Verse deny
The hacknied pageants of the Pagan sky,
Their sinking radiance still the Canvass warms,   85
Painting still glories in their graceful forms;
Nor canst thou envy, if the world agree
To grant thy Sister claims denied to thee;
For thee, the happier Art! the elder-born!
Superior rights and dearer charms adorn: 90
Confin'd she catches, with observance keen,
Her single moment of the changeful scene;
But thou, endu'd with energy sublime,

---

1 The Roman goddess Latona was the mother of Apollo and Diana. Juno became angry when Jupiter fell in love with Latona and sent a large snake, Python, to hunt her down and kill her. Neptune gave her sanctuary on the Island of Delos.

2 Apollo was not only the god of poetry, art, music, medicine, and the sun, but also of archery.

Unquestion'd arbiter of space and time!
Canst join the distant, the unknown create, 95
And, while Existence yields thee all her state,
On the astonish'd mind profusely pour
Myriads of forms, that Fancy must adore.
Yet of thy boundless power the dearest part
Is firm possession of the feeling Heart: 100
No progeny of Chance, by Labor taught,
No slow-form'd creature of scholastic thought,
The child of Passion thou! thy lyre she strung,
To her parental notes she tun'd thy tongue;
Gave thee her boldest swell, her softest tone, 105
And made the compass of her voice thy own.
   To Admiration, source of joy refin'd!
Chaste, lovely mover of the simple mind!
To her, though sceptics, in their pride, declaim,
With many an insult, on her injur'd name; 110
To her, sweet Poesy! we owe thy birth,
Thou first encomiast of the fruitful Earth!
By her inspir'd, the earliest mortal found
The ear-delighting charm of measur'd sound;
He hail'd the Maker of a world so fair, 115
And the first accent of his song was prayer.
O, most attractive of those airy Powers,
Who most illuminate Man's chequer'd hours!
Is there an Art, in all the group divine,
Whose dawn of Being must not yield to thine? 120
Religion's self, whose provident controul
Takes from fierce Man his anarchy of soul,
She o'er thy youth with fond affection hung,
And borrow'd music from thy infant tongue.
Law, sterner Law, whose potent voice imprest 125
Severest terror on the human breast,
With thy fresh flow'rs her aweful figure crown'd,
And spoke her mandate in thy softer sound.
E'en cold Philosophy, whom later days
Saw thy mean rival, envious of thy praise; 130
Who clos'd against thee her ungrateful arms,
And urg'd her Plato to defame thy charms;
She from thy childhood gain'd no fruitless aid,
From thee she learnt her talent to persuade.
Gay Nature view'd thee with a smiling glance, 135

The Graces[1] round thee fram'd the frolic dance:
And well might festive Joy thy favor court;
Thy song turn'd strife to peace, and toil to sport.
Exhausted Vigor at thy voice reviv'd,
And Mirth from thee her dearest charm deriv'd.   140
Triumphant Love, in thy alliance blest,
Enlarg'd his empire o'er the gentle breast;
His torch assum'd new lustre from thy breath,
And his clear flame defied the clouds of death.
But of the splendid train, who felt thy sway,   145
Or drew existence from thy vital ray,
Glory, with fondest zeal, proclaim'd thy might,
And hail'd thee victor of oblivious Night.
Her martial trumpet to thy hand she gave,
At once to quicken, and reward the Brave: 150
It sounds—his blood the kindling Hero pays,
A cheap and ready price for thy eternal praise!
Tho' selfish Fear th' immortal strain deride,
And mock the Warrior's wish as frantic pride!
     Ye gallant, hapless Dead of distant time,   155
Whose fame has perish'd unembalm'd in rhyme,
As thro' the desert air your ashes fly,
In Fancy's ear the nameless atoms cry,
"To us, unhappy! cruel Fates refuse
The well-earn'd record of th' applauding Muse."   160
Blest are those Chiefs, who, blazon'd on her roll,
Still waken virtue in each kindred soul;
Their bright existence still on earth prolong,
And shine for ever in the deathless song.
Yet oft Oblivion, in a treacherous shade,   165
Has sunk the tuneful rites to Valor paid;
Her palsied lips refusing to rehearse
The sacred, old, traditionary verse.
     As well the curious eye, with keen desire,
Might hope to catch that spark of vital fire,   170
Which first thro' Chaos shot a sudden light,
And quicken'd Nature in its transient flight;
As the fond ear to catch the fleeting note,
Which on the ravish'd air was heard to float,

---

1   The three graces in Greek mythology were Aglaia, Euphrosyne, and Thalia,
    the goddesses of joy, dance, song, beauty, charm, creativity, and festivity. They
    were associated with Aphrodite, goddess of love.

When first the Muse her Epic strain began,   175
And every list'ning Chief grew more than Man.
    But, as the Ruler of the new-born day
From Chaos rose, in glory's rich array;
So from deep shades, impenetrably strong,
That shroud the darken'd world of antient song,   180
Bright Homer[1] bursts, magnificently clear,
The solar Lord of that poetic sphere;
Before whose blaze, in wide luxuriance spread,
Each Grecian Star hides his diminish'd head;
Whose beams departed yet enchant the sight,   185
In Latium's[2] softer, chaste, reflected light.
    Say ye! whose curious philosophic eye
Searches the depth where Nature's secrets lie;
Ye, who can tell, how her capricious fit
Directs the flow and ebb of human wit,   190
And why, obedient to her quick command,
Spring-tides of Genius now enrich her fav'rite land,
Now sink, by her to different climes assign'd,
And only leave some worthless weeds behind!
Say! why in Greece, unrival'd and alone,   195
The Sovereign Poet grac'd his Epic throne?
Why did the realm that echoed his renown,
Produce no kindred heir to claim his crown?
If, as the liberal mind delights to think,
Fancy's rich flow'rs their vital essence drink   200
From Liberty's pure streams, that largely roll
Their quick'ning virtue thro' the Poet's soul;
Why, in the period when this Friend of Earth
Made Greece the model of heroic worth,
And saw her votaries act, beneath her sway,   205
Scenes more sublime than Fiction can display,
Why did the Epic Muse's silent lyre
Shrink from those feats that summon'd all her fire?
Or if, as courtly Theorists maintain,
The Muses revel in a Monarch's reign;   210
Why, when young Ammon's[3] soul, athirst for fame,

---

1   Homer (fl. eighth or ninth century BCE), presumed author of two epic
    poems, the *Iliad* and the *Odyssey*, which have powerfully influenced Western
    literary traditions.
2   Latium was the ancient region of Italy that included Rome.
3   King of Judah, Ammon was said to have been assassinated sometime around
    641 BCE because of his idolatrous practices.

Call'd every Art to celebrate his name;
When ready Painting, at his sovereign nod,
With aweful thunder arm'd this mimic God;
Why did coy Poesy, tho' fondly woo'd,   215
Refuse that dearer smile for which he sued,
And see him shed, in martial Honor's bloom,
The tear of envy on Achilles'[1] tomb?
    In vain would Reason those nice questions solve,
Which the fine play of mental powers involve: 220
In Bards of ancient time, with genius fraught,
What mind can trace how thought engender'd thought,
How little hints awak'd the large design,
And subtle Fancy spun her variegated line?
Yet sober Critics, of no vulgar note,   225
But such as Learning's sons are proud to quote,
The progress of Homeric verse explain,
As if their souls had lodg'd in Homer's brain.
Laughs not the spirit of poetic frame,
However slightly warm'd by Fancy's flame,   230
When grave Bossu[2] by System's studied laws
The Grecian Bard's ideal picture draws,
And wisely tells us, that his Song arose
As the good Parson's quiet Sermon grows;
Who, while his easy thoughts no pressure find   235
From hosts of images that croud the mind,
First calmly settles on some moral text,
Then creeps—from one division—to the next?
Nor, if poetic minds more slowly drudge
Thro' the cold comments of this Gallic judge,   240
Will their indignant spirit less deride
That subtle Pedant's more presumptive pride,
Whose bloated page, with arrogance replete,
Imputes to Virgil his own dark conceit:
And from the tortur'd Poet dares to draw   245
That latent sense, which Horace never saw;
Which, if on solid proof more strongly built,
Must brand the injur'd Bard with impious guilt.
    While such Dictators their vain efforts waste
In the dark visions of distemper'd Taste,   250

---

1 One of the great warriors of the Trojan War; Homer describes his exploits in
   the *Iliad*.

2 René Le Bossu (1631-80) was a French critic who wrote *Traité du poème
   épique* (1675).

Let us that pleasing, happier light pursue,
Which beams benignant from the milder few;
Who, justly conscious of the doubts that start
In all nice questions on each finer Art,
With modest doubt assign each likely cause,   255
But dare to dictate no decisive laws!
'Tis said by one, who, with this candid claim,
Has gain'd no fading wreath of Critic fame,
Who, fondly list'ning to her various rhyme,
Has mark'd the Muse's step thro' many a clime;   260
That, where the settled Rules of Writing spread,
Where Learning's code of Critic Law is read,
Tho' other treasures deck th' enlighten'd shore,
The germs of Fancy ripen there no more.
Are Critics then, that bold, imperious tribe!   265
The Guards of Genius, who his path prescribe;
Are they like Visirs[1] in an Eastern court,
Who sap the very power they should support?
Whose specious wiles the royal mind unnerve,
And sink the monarch they pretend to serve.   270
No! of their value higher far I deem;
And prize their useful toil with fond esteem.
When Lowth's[2] firm spirit leads him to explore
The hallow'd confines of Hebraic lore,
When his free pages, luminous and bold,   275
The glorious end of Poesy unfold,
Assert her powers, her dignity defend,
And speak her, as she is, fair Freedom's friend;
When thus he shines his mitred Peers above,
I view his warmth with reverential love;   280
Proud, if my verse may catch reflected light
From the rich splendor of a mind so bright.
    Blest be the names, to no vain system tied,
Who render Learning's blaze an useful guide,
A friendly beacon, rais'd on high to teach   285
The wand'ring bark to shun the shallow beach.
But O! ye noble, and aspiring few,
Whose ardent souls poetic fame pursue,
Ye, on whom smiling Heaven, perfection's source,

---

1   In the Middle East and some other Muslim countries, a vizier is a high state
    official or minister, governor, or viceroy (*OED*).
2   Robert Lowth (1710-87), Oxford Professor of Poetry, Anglican Bishop, gram-
    marian, and author of *Lectures on the Sacred Poetry of the Hebrews* (1787).

Seems to bestow unlimitable force,   290
The inborn vigor of your souls defend,
Nor lean too fondly on the firmest friend!
Genius may sink on Criticism's breast,
By weak dependence on her truth opprest,
Sleep on her lap, and stretch his lifeless length,   295
Shorn by her soothing hand of all his strength.

....

'Tis here, O Friendship! here thy glories shine;   415
The hard, th' important talk is only thine;
For thou alone canst all the powers unite,
That justly make it thy peculiar right:
Thine the fixt eye, which at no foible winks;
Thine the warm zeal, which utters all it thinks,   420
In those sweet tones, that hasty Spleen disarm,
That give to painful Truth a winning charm,
And the quick hand of list'ning Genius teach,
To grasp that excellence he burns to reach:
Thou sweet Subduer of all mental strife!   425
Thou Source of vigor! thou Support of life!
Nor Art nor Science could delight or live,
Without that energy thy counsels give:
Genius himself must sink in dumb despair,
Unblest, uncherish'd by thy cheering care.   430
    Nor let the Bard, elate with youthful fire,
When Fancy to his hand presents the lyre,
When her strong plumes his soaring spirit lift,
When Friendship, Heaven's more high and holy gift,
With zeal angelic prompts his daring flight,   435
And round him darts her doubt-dispelling light,
Let him not then, by Vanity betray'd,
Look with unjust contempt on Learning's aid!
But, as th' advent'rous Seaman, to attain
That bright renown which great Discoverers gain,   440
Consults the conduct of each gallant name,
Who fail'd before him in that chace of Fame,
Reviews, with frequent glance, their useful chart,
Marks all their aims, and fathoms all their art,
So let the Poet trace *their* happy course,   445
So bravely emulate *their* mental force,
Whose daring souls, from many a different clime,
Have nobly ventur'd on the sea of Rhyme!

Led by no fear, his swelling sail to slack,
Let him, with eager eyes, pursue the track;   450
Not like a Pirate, with insidious views
To plunder every vessel he pursues,
But with just hope to find yet farther shores,
And pass each rival he almost adores!

[From Epistle III]

If with just love I hold their Genius dear,
Lament their hardships, and their fame revere,   380
O bid thy Epic Muse, with honor due,
Range her departed Champions in my view!
    See, on a party-colour'd steed of fire,
With Humour at his side, his trusty Squire,
Gay Chaucer[1] leads—in form a Knight of old,   385
And his strong armour is of steel and gold;
But o'er it age a cruel rust has spread,
And made the brilliant metals dark as lead.
    Now gentle Spenser,[2] Fancy's fav'rite Bard,
Awakes my wonder and my fond regard;   390
Encircling Fairies bear, in sportive dance,
His adamantine shield and magic lance;
While Allegory, drest with mystic art,
Appears his Guide; but, promising to dart
A lambent glory round her list'ning Son,   395
She hides him in the web herself has spun.
    Ingenuous Cowley,[3] the fond dupe of Wit,
Seems like a vapour o'er the field to flit;
In David's praise he strikes some Epic notes,
But soon down Lethe's stream their dying murmur floats.   400

---

1   Geoffrey Chaucer (c. 1340-1400), English poet most famous for writing *The
    Canterbury Tales*, a humorous and sometimes bawdy series of stories told by
    pilgrims.
2   Edmund Spenser (c. 1552-99), author of *The Faerie Queene*.
3   Abraham Cowley (1618-67), royalist English poet known for his wit, political
    satires, love poems, Pindaric odes, and for an unfinished biblical epic about
    the early life of King David, the *Davideis*. His work was influential in the
    seventeenth century, but by the mid-eighteenth century it had fallen out of
    favor.

While Cowley vanish'd in an amorous riddle,
Up rose the frolic Bard of Bear and Fiddle:[1]
His smile exhilarates the sullen earth,
Adorning Satire in the mask of Mirth:
Taught by his Song, Fanatics cease their jars,   405
And wise Astrologers renounce the Stars.
Unrivall'd Butler! blest with happy skill
To heal by comic verse each serious ill,
By Wit's strong flashes Reason's light dispense,
And laugh a frantic nation into sense!   410
     Apart, and on a sacred hill retir'd,
Beyond all mortal inspiration fir'd,
The mighty Milton sits—an host around
Of list'ning Angels guard the holy ground;
Amaz'd they see a human form aspire   415
To grasp with daring hand a Seraph's lyre,
Inly irradiate with celestial beams,
Attempt those high, those soul-subduing themes,
(Which humbler Denizens of Heaven decline)
And celebrate, with sanctity divine,   420
The starry field from warring Angels won,
And God triumphant in his Victor Son.
Nor less the wonder, and the sweet delight,
His milder scenes and softer notes excite,
When at his bidding Eden's blooming grove   425
Breathes the rich sweets of Innocence and Love.
With such pure joy as our Forefather knew
When Raphael, heavenly guest, first met his view,
And our glad Sire, within his blissful bower,
Drank the pure converse of th' aetherial Power,   430
Round the blest Bard his raptur'd audience throng,
And feel their souls imparadis'd in song.
     Of humbler mien, but not of mortal race,
Ill-fated Dryden,[2] with Imperial grace,
Gives to th' obedient lyre his rapid laws;   435
Tones yet unheard, with touch divine, he draws,

---

1   Samuel Butler (c. 1613-80), author of *Hudibras* (1663-64, 1678), a mock
    heroic epic about a knight errant and his squire, described in the argument to
    Canto I as "Th' adventure of the Bear and Fiddle."

2   John Dryden (1631-1700), English poet, dramatist, and critic whose works
    are often satirical. He became poet laureate in 1668, only to lose that title
    twenty years later after the abdication of the Catholic James II, with whom
    Dryden was aligned politically and religiously.

The melting fall, the rising swell sublime,
And all the magic of melodious rhyme.
See with proud joy Imagination spread
A wreath of honor round his aged head!   440
But two base Spectres, tho' of different hue,
The Bard unhappy in his march pursue;
Two vile disgraceful Fiends, of race accurst,
Conceiv'd by Spleen, by meagre Famine nurst,
Malignant Satire, mercenary Praise,   445
Shed their dark spots on his immortal bays.

[From Epistle IV]

Say, generous Power, benignant Nature, say,
Who temp'rest with thy touch our human clay,
Warming the fields of Thought with genial care,
The various fruits of mental growth to bear;
Shall not thy vot'ries glow with just disdain,   5
When Sloth or Spleen thy bounteous hand arraign?
Art thou the Niggard they pretend thou art,
A grudging Parent with a Stepdame's heart;
And dost thou shed, with rare, reluctant toil,
Bright Fancy's germins[1] in the mental soil?   10
Is Genius, thy sweet Plant of richest power,
Whose dearly priz'd and long-expected flower
More tardy than the Aloe's[2] bloom appears,
Ordain'd to blow[3] but in a thousand years?
Perish the sickly thought—let those who hold   15
Thy quick'ning influence so coy, so cold,
Calmly the habitable earth survey,
From time's first æra to the passing day;
In what rude clime, beneath what angry skies,
Have plants Poetic never dar'd to rise?   20
In torrid regions, where 'tis toil to think,
Where souls in stupid ease supinely sink;
And where the native of the desert drear

---

1 Literally, that which germinates, but figuratively meaning poetry. In this
  metaphor, the mind is a garden; Fancy brings about the germination of poetic
  thought.
2 *Agave americana*, sometimes called the "century plant" or "American aloe,"
  although it is not in the genus Aloe. It was mistakenly believed to bloom only
  once in a hundred years.
3 Blossom or bloom.

Yields to blank darkness half his icy year;
In these unfriendly scenes, where each extreme   25
Of heat and cold forbids the mind to teem,
Poetic blossoms into Being start,
Spontaneous produce of the feeling heart.
  Can we then deem that in those happier lands,
Where every vital energy expands;   30
Where Thought, the golden harvest of the mind,
Springs into rich luxuriance, unconfin'd;
That in such soils, with mental weeds o'ergrown,
The Seeds of Poesy were thinly sown?
  Shall we deny the labor of the swain,   35
Who to the cultur'd earth confides the grain,
If all the vagrant harpies of the air
From its new bed the pregnant treasure tear;
If, when scarce rising, with a stem infirm,
It dies the victim of the mining worm;   40
If mildew, riding in the eastern gust,
Turns all its ripening gold to sable dust?
  These foes combin'd (and with them who may cope?)
Are not more hostile to the Farmer's hope,
Than Life's keen passions to that lighter grain   45
Of Fancy, scatter'd o'er the infant brain.
Pleasure, the rambling Bird! the painted Jay!
May snatch the richest seeds of Verse away;
Or Indolence, the worm that winds with art
Thro' the close texture of the cleanest heart,   50
May, if they haply have begun to shoot,
With partial mischief wound the sick'ning root;
Or Avarice, the mildew of the soul,
May sweep the mental field and blight the whole;
Nay, the meek errors of the modest mind,   55
To its own vigor diffidently blind,
And that cold spleen, which falsely has declar'd
The powers of Nature and of Art impair'd,
The gate that Genius has unclos'd may guard,
And rivet to the earth the rising Bard: 60
For who will quit, tho' from mean aims exempt,
The cares that summon, and the joys that tempt,
In many a lonely studious hour to try
Where latent springs of Poesy may lie;
Who will from social ease his mind divorce,   65
To prove in Art's wide field its secret force,

If, blind to Nature's frank parental love,
He deems that Verse, descended from above,
Like Heaven's more sacred signs, whose time is o'er,
A gift miraculous, conferr'd no more?   70
   O Prejudice! thou bane of Arts, thou pest,
Whose ruffian powers the free-born soul arrest;
Thou who, dethroning Reason, dar'st to frame
And issue thy proud laws beneath her name;
Thou Coaster on the intellectual deep,   75
Ordering each timid bark thy course to keep;
Who, lest some daring mind beyond thee steer,
Hast rais'd, to vouch thy vanity and fear,
Herculean pillars where thy sail was furl'd,
And nam'd thy bounds the Limits of the World.   80
Thou braggart, Prejudice, how oft thy breath
Has doom'd young Genius to the shades of death!
How often has thy voice, with brutal fire
Forbidding Female hands to touch the lyre,
Deny'd to Woman, Nature's fav'rite child,   85
The right to enter Fancy's opening wild!
Blest be this smiling hour, when Britain sees
Her Fair-ones cancel such absurd decrees,
In one harmonious group, with graceful scorn,
Spring o'er the Pedant's fence of wither'd thorn,   90
And reach Parnassian[1] heights, where, laurel-crown'd,
This softer Quire the notes of triumph sound;
Where Seward, leader of the lovely train,
Pours o'er heroic tombs her potent strain;
Potent to sooth the honor'd dead, and dart   95
Congenial virtue thro' each panting heart;
Potent thro' spirits masculine to spread
Poetic jealousy and envious dread;
If Love and Envy could in union rest,
And rule with blended sway a Poet's breast;   100
The Bards of Britain, with unjaundic'd eyes,
Will glory to behold such rivals rise.
Proceed, ye Sisters of the tuneful Shell,
Without a scruple, in that Art excel,
Which reigns, by virtuous Pleasure's soft controul,   105
In sweet accordance with the Female soul;

---

1 In Greek mythology, Mount Parnassus was the home of the Muses and was
    sacred to Apollo, god of the sun, poetry, light, and learning.

Pure as yourselves, and like your charms design'd
To bless the earth, and humanize mankind.
   Where'er that Parent of engaging thought,
Warm Sensibility, like light, has taught   110
The bright'ning mirror of the mind to shew
Nature's reflected forms in all their glow;
Where in full tides the fine affections roll,
And the warm heart invigorates the soul;
In that rich spot, where winds propitious blow,   115
Culture may teach poetic Fame to grow.
Refin'd Invention and harmonious Rhyme,
Are the slow gifts of Study and of Time;
But to the Bard whom all the Muses court,
His Sports are study, and his Studies sport.   120
E'en at this period, when all tongues declare
Poetic talents are a gift most rare,
Unnumber'd Spirits, in our generous isle,
Are ripening now beneath kind Nature's smile,
Whom happy care might lead to lasting fame,   125
And art ennoble with a Poet's name.

...

   For me, who feel, whene'er I touch the lyre,
My talents sink below my proud desire;
Who often doubt, and sometimes credit give,   415
When Friends assure me that my Verse will live;
Whom health too tender for the bustling throng
Led into pensive shade and soothing song;
Whatever fortune my unpolish'd rhymes
May meet, in present or in future times,   420
Let the blest Art my grateful thoughts employ,
Which sooths my sorrow and augments my joy;
Whence lonely Peace and social Pleasure springs,
And Friendship, dearer than the smile of Kings!
While keener Poets, querulously proud,   425
Lament the Ills of Poesy aloud,
And magnify, with Irritation's zeal,
Those common evils we too strongly feel,
The envious Comment and the subtle Style
Of specious Slander, stabbing with a smile;   430
Frankly I wish to make her Blessings known,
And think those Blessings for her Ills atone:

Nor wou'd my honest pride that praise forego,
Which makes Malignity yet more my foe.

[From Epistle V]

For, if the Epic Muse still wish to tower
Above plain Nature's firm and graceful power,
Tho' Critics think her vital powers are lost   265
In cold Philosophy's petrific frost;
That Magic cannot her sunk charms restore,
That Heaven and Hell can yield her nothing more;
Yet may she dive to many a secret source
And copious spring of visionary force: 270
India yet holds a Mythologic mine,
Her strength may open, and her art refine:
Tho' Asian spoils the realms of Europe fill,
Those Eastern riches are unrifled still;
Genius may there his course of honor run,   275
And spotless Laurels in that field be won.

3. From Alonso de Ercilla, *La Araucana*, translated by William Hayley and published in the notes to *An Essay on Epic Poetry* (London: J. Dodsley, 1782) 214-24

[Alonso de Ercilla (1533-94) was a Spanish soldier and poet. He fought against the Araucanians, but the heroism and bravery of these natives of Chile inspired him to write *La Araucana*, an epic poem of 37 cantos, published in three parts within the span of two decades. Ercilla appears as himself in the poem and champions the Araucanians, attempting to see the battles and suffering from their perspective. Hayley writes of his translation: "the English reader will be enabled to judge, and to enjoy an author, who, considering his subject and its execution, may be said to stand single and unparalleled in the host of Poets" (*An Essay on Epic Poetry* 211).]

[From Canto I]

I sing not love of ladies, nor of sights
Devised for gentle dames by courteous knights,
Nor feasts, nor tourneys, nor that tender care
Which prompts the Gallant to regale the Fair;
But the bold deeds of Valor's fav'rite train,
Those undegenerate sons of warlike Spain,

Who made Arauco their stern laws embrace,
And bent beneath their yoke her untam'd race.
Of tribes distinguish'd in the field I sing;
Of nations who disdain the name of King;
Courage, that danger only taught to grow,
And challenge honour from a generous foe;
And persevering toils of purest fame,
And feats that aggrandize the Spanish name:
For the brave actions of the vanquish'd spread
The brightest glory round the victor's head.

[From Canto II]

Many there are who, in this mortal strife,
Have reach'd the slippery heights of splendid life:
For Fortune's ready hand its succour lent;   ˋ
Smiling she rais'd them up the steep ascent,
To hurl them headlong from that lofty seat
To which she led their unsuspecting feet;
E'en at the moment when all fears disperse,
And their proud fancy sees no sad reverse.
Little they think, beguil'd by fair success,
That Joy is but the herald of Distress:
The hasty wing of time escapes their sight,
And those dark evils that attend his flight:
Vainly they dream, with gay presumption warm,
Fortune for them will take a steadier form;
She, unconcern'd at what her victims feel,
Turns with her wonted haste her fatal wheel.

...

The Indians first, by novelty dismay'd,
As Gods rever'd us, and as Gods obey'd;
But when they found we were of woman born,
Their homage turn'd to enmity and scorn:
Their childish error, when our weakness show'd,
They blush'd at what their ignorance bestow'd;
Fiercely they burnt, with anger and with shame,
To see their masters but of mortal frame.
Disdaining cold and cowardly delay,
They seek atonement, on no distant day:
Prompt and resolv'd, in quick debate they join,
To form of deep revenge their dire design.

Impatient that their bold decree should spread,
And shake the world around with sudden dread,
Th' assembling Chieftains led so large a train,
Their ready host o'erspread th' extensive plain.
No summons now the soldier's heart requires;
The thirst of battle every breast inspires;
No pay, no promise of reward, they ask,
Keen to accomplish their spontaneous task;
And, by the force of one avenging blow,
Crush and annihilate their foreign foe.
Of some brave Chiefs, who to this council came,
Well may'st thou, Memory, preserve the name;
Tho' rude and savage, yet of noble soul,
Justly they claim their place on Glory's roll,
Who robbing Spain of many a gallant son,
In so confin'd a space such victories won;
Whose fame some living Spaniards yet may spread,
Too well attested by our warlike dead.

...

Assembled Chiefs! ye guardians of the land!
Think not I mourn from thirst of lost command,
To find your rival spirits thus pursue
A post of honour which I deem my due.
These marks of age, you see, such thoughts disown
In me, departing for the world unknown;
But my warm love, which ye have long possest,
Now prompts that counsel which you'll find the best.
Why should we now for marks of glory jar?
Why wish to spread our martial name afar?
Crush'd as we are by Fortune's cruel stroke,
And bent beneath an ignominious yoke,
Ill can our minds such noble pride maintain,
While the fierce Spaniard holds our galling chain.
Your generous fury here ye vainly shew;
Ah! rather pour it on th' embattled foe!
What frenzy has your souls of sense bereav'd?
Ye rush to self-perdition, unperceiv'd.
'Gainst your own vitals would ye lift those hands,
Whose vigor ought to burst oppression's bands?
    If a desire of death this rage create,
O die not yet in this disgraceful state!
Turn your keen arms, and this indignant flame,

Against the breast of those who sink your fame,
Who made the world a witness of your shame.
Haste ye to cast these hated bonds away,
In this the vigor of your souls display;
Nor blindly lavish, from your country's veins,
Blood that may yet redeem her from her chains.
    E'en while I thus lament, I still admire
The fervor of your souls; they give me fire:
But, justly trembling at their fatal bent,
I dread some dire calamitous event;
Lest in your rage Dissention's frantic hand
Should cut the sinews of our native land.
If such its doom, my thread of being burst,
And let your old compeer expire the first!
Shall this shrunk frame, thus bow'd by age's weight,
Live the weak witness of a nation's fate?
No: let some friendly sword, with kind relief,
Forbid its sinking in that scene of grief.
Happy whose eyes in timely darkness close,
Sav'd from that worst of sights, his country's woes!
Yet, while I can, I make your weal my care,
And for the public good my thoughts declare.
    Equal ye are in courage and in worth;
Heaven has assign'd to all an equal birth:
In wealth, in power, and majesty of soul,
Each Chief seems worthy of the world's controul.
These gracious gifts, not gratefully beheld,
To this dire strife your daring minds impell'd.
    But on your generous valor I depend,
That all our country's woes will swiftly end.
A Leader still our present state demands,
To guide to vengeance our impatient bands;
Fit for this hardy task that Chief I deem,
Who longest may sustain a massive beam:
Your rank is equal, let your force be try'd,
And for the strongest let his strength decide.

[From Canto III]

O Cureless malady! Oh fatal pest!
Embrac'd with ardor and with pride carest;
Thou common vice, thou most contagious ill,
Bane of the mind, and frenzy of the will!

Thou foe to private and to public health;
Thou dropsy of the soul, that thirsts for wealth,
Insatiate Avarice!—'tis from thee we trace
The various misery of our mortal race.

...

The steady pikemen of the savage band,
Waiting our hasty charge, in order stand;
But when th' advancing Spaniard aim'd his stroke,
Their ranks, to form a hollow square, they broke;
An easy passage to our troop they leave,
And deep within their lines their foes receive;
Their files resuming then the ground they gave,
Bury the Christians in that closing grave.
    As the keen Crocodile, who loves to lay
His silent ambush for his finny prey,
Hearing the scaly tribe with sportive sound
Advance, and cast a muddy darkness round,
Opens his mighty mouth, with caution, wide,
And, when th' unwary fish within it glide,
Closing with eager haste his hollow jaw,
Thus satiates with their lives his rav'nous maw:
So, in their toils, without one warning thought,
The murd'rous foe our little squadron caught
With quick destruction, in a fatal strife,
From whence no Christian soldier 'scap'd with life.

...

The hostile sword, now deeply dy'd in blood,
Drench'd the wide field with many a sanguine flood;
Courage still grows to form the fierce attack,
But wasted vigor makes the combat slack:
No pause they seek, to gain exhausted breath,
No rest, except the final rest of death:
The wariest combatants now only try
To snatch the sweets of vengeance ere they die.
    The fierce disdain of death, and scorn of flight,
Give to our scanty troop such wond'rous might,
The Araucanian host begin to yield;
They quit with loss and shame the long-fought field:
They fly; and their pursuers shake the plain

With joyous shouts of Victory and Spain.
But dire mischance, and Fate's resistless sway,
Gave a strange issue to the dreadful day.
    An Indian Youth, a noble Chieftain's son,
Who as our friend his martial feats begun,
Our Leader's Page, by him to battle train'd,
Who now beside him the hard fight sustain'd,
As he beheld his kindred Chiefs retire,
Felt an indignant flash of patriot fire;
And thus incited to a glorious stand
The flying champions of his native land:
    Misguided Country, by vain fear possest,
Ah whither dost thou turn thy timid breast?
Ye brave compatriots, shall your ancient fame
Be vilely buried in this field of shame?
Those laws, those rights, ye gloried to defend,
All perish, all by this ignoble end?
From Chiefs of dreaded power, and honor'd worth,
Ye sink to abject slaves, the scorn of earth!
To the pure founders of your boasted race
Ye give the cureless wound of deep disgrace!
Behold the wasted vigor of your foe!
See, bath'd in sweat and blood, their coursers blow!
Lose not your mental force, your martial fires,
Our best inheritance from generous sires;
Sink not the noble Araucanian name,
From glory's summit to the depths of shame;
Fly, fly the servitude your souls detest!
To the keen sword oppose the dauntless breast.
Why shew ye frames endued with manly power,
Yet shrink from danger in the trying hour?
Fix in your minds the friendly truth I speak;
Vain are your fears, your terror blind and weak:
Now make your names immortal; now restore
Freedom's lost blessings to your native shore:
Now turn, while Fame and Victory invite,
While prosp'rous Fortune calls you to the fight;
Or yet a moment cease, O cease to fly,
And for our country learn of me to die!
    As thus he speaks, his eager steps advance,
And 'gainst the Spanish Chief he points his lance;
To lead his kindred fugitives from flight,
Singly he dares to tempt th' unequal fight:

Against our circling arms, that round him shine,
Eager he darts amidst the thickest line,
Keen as, when chas'd by summer's fiery beam,
The young Stag plunges in the cooling stream.

...

Say, of these famous Chiefs can one exceed
Or match this young Barbarian's noble deed?
Vict'ry for them, her purpose unexplor'd,
Tempted by equal chance their happy sword:
What risk, what peril did they boldly meet,
Save where Ambition urg'd the splendid feat;
Or mightier Int'rest fir'd the daring mind,
Which makes a Hero of the fearful Hind?
Many there are who with a brave disdain
Face all the perils of the deathful plain,
Who, fir'd by hopes of glory, nobly dare,
Yet fail the stroke of adverse chance to bear;
With animated fire their spirit shines,
Till the short splendor of their day declines;
But all their valor, all their strength expires,
When fickle Fortune from their side retires.
This youthful Hero, when the die was cast,
War's dire decree against his country past,
Made the stern Power the finish'd cause resume,
And finally reverse the cruel doom:
He, by his efforts in the dread debate,
Forc'd the determin'd will of adverse Fate;
From shouting Triumph rush'd the palm to tear,
And fix'd it on the brow of faint Despair.

4. **From Françoise de Graffigny, "Historical Introduction,"**
   Lettres d'une Péruvienne **or** *Letters from a Peruvian*
   Woman **(1752), translated by David Kornacker (New York:**
   Modern Language Association, 1993)

[Françoise de Graffigny (1695-1758) was one of the most influential literary figures in France during the mid-eighteenth century. Her epistolary novel, *Lettres d'une Péruvienne* (1747), was exceedingly popular. She included the "Historical Introduction" excerpted below in her revised and expanded 1752 edition entitled, *Lettres d'une Péruvienne, Nouvelle édition, augmentée de plusieurs lettres, et d'une introduction à l'histoire.*]

There is no other people whose knowledge of their origins and antiquity is as limited as that of the Peruvians. Their annals barely contain the history of four centuries.

Mancocapac, according to these people's traditions, was their law giver and first Inca. The Sun (which they called their father and viewed as their God), moved by the barbarism in which they had long been living, sent them from Heaven two of his children, a son and a daughter, to give them laws and to urge them, by establishing cities and tending the earth, to become rational men.

Thus, it is to *Mancocapac* and his wife *Coya Mama-Oello-Huaco* that the Peruvians owe the principles, customs, and arts that had made of them a happy people when avarice, coming from the heart of a world whose very existence they never suspected, cast upon their lands tyrants whose barbarity became the shame of humanity and the crime of their century. (7)

Thus were the Peruvians made the sad victims of a greedy people who at first showed them only good faith and even friendship. Ignorance of our vices and the naive nature of their customs flung them into the arms of their venal enemies. For naught had vast spaces separated the cities of the Sun from our world: they became its prey and most precious dominion.... In general those peoples were open and humane; their attachment to their religion made them strict observers of laws they viewed as the work of *Mancocapac*, son of the Sun they worshipped.

Although that star was the lone God to whom they had built temples, they recognized a God of creation above him whom they called *Pachacamac*. For them, this was the *great name*. The word Pachacamac was uttered but rarely, and with signs of the utmost admiration....

A belief in the immortality of the soul was well established among the Peruvians. They believed, as do the majority of Indians, that the soul journeys to places unknown where it is rewarded or punished as it deserves. (10-11)

The obedience and respect of the Peruvians for their kings was based on their belief that the Sun was the father of those kings. But the fondness and love they felt for them was the fruit of their own virtues, and of the Incas' fairness.

Young people were brought up with all the care required by the happy simplicity of their moral beliefs. Subordination in no way frightened their minds because its necessity was demonstrated to them early on and because neither tyranny nor vainglory had any part in it.

Modesty and mutual consideration were the cornerstones of their child rearing. Those who were assigned this task were careful to correct their charges' first failings and to halt the progress of any budding passions, or to divert them to the benefit of society. There are certain virtues that imply many others. To give some idea of the Peruvians', suffice it to say that before the landing of the Spaniards, it was taken for granted that no Peruvian had ever lied. (12-13)

5. From Françoise de Graffigny, *Letters Written by a Peruvian Lady* (Dublin: S. Powell, 1748)

[From "Letter I"]

Aza! My dear *Aza!* the cries of thy tender *Zilia*, like a morning vapour, exhale and are dissipated before they arrive in thy presence; in vain I call thee to my succour; in vain I expect thy love to come, and break the chains of my slavery: alas! perhaps the misfortunes I am ignorant of are the most terrible! perhaps thy woes surpass even mine. The city of the sun, delivered to the fury of a barbarous nation, should make my eyes o'erflow with tears: but my grief, my fears, my despair, are for thee alone. (7)

[T]hese impious savages bore me away from the worship of the Sun, from myself, from thy love; retained in strait captivity, deprived of all communication, ignorant of the language of these fierce men, I experience only the effects of misfortune, without being able to discover the cause of it.... my ravishers are not touch'd even with my tears; equally deaf to my language, and to the cries of my despair. (8)

The pavement of the temple stained with blood; the image of the Sun trodden under foot; our affrighted virgins flying before a troop of furious soldiers, who massacred all that opposed their passage; our *Mamas*[1] expiring under their wounds, their garments still burning with the fire of the thunder. (9)

[T]he effects of their cruelty abated at the sight of the precious ornaments that overspread the temple; that they seized those whose lustre struck them most feelingly; and that they even plucked off the plates of gold that lined the walls. I judged that theft was the motive of their barbarity ... (10)

---

1 A kind of Gorvernantes [rulers] over the virgins of the sun [1748 footnote].

Instead of the flowers which should have been strewed under my feet, I saw the ways covered with blood and carnage: instead of the honours of the throne, which I was to have been partaker of with thee, a slave under the laws of tyranny, shut up in an obscure prison ... (10)

[From "Letter II"]

Thou [Aza] wilt be more a king in reigning over my soul, than in doubting of the affection of a people without number: my submission to thy will shall cause thee to enjoy, without tyranny, the undisputed right of commanding. While I obey thee, I will make thy empire resound with my joyous songs; thy diadem shall be always the work of my hands, and thou shalt lose nothing of royalty but the cares and fatigues. (13)

[From "Letter IV"]

Two of these savages seldom quit the sides of my bed: one, which I guess to be the *Cacique*[1] by his air of Grandeur, seems to shew me, in his way, a great deal of respect: the other gives me part of the assistance which my malady requires; but his goodness is severe, his succours are cruel, and his familiarity imperious. (21)

[From "Letter V"]

One moment destroys the opinion which another had given me of their character: for if I am sway'd by the frequent opposition of their wills to mine, I cannot doubt but they believe me their slave, and that their power is tyrannical.... On the other side, if I reflect on the extreme concern they have shewn for the preservation of my days, and the respect with which the services they render me are accompanied; I am tempted to believe that they take me for a species superior to human kind. Not one of them appears before me without bending his body more or less, as we used to do in worshipping the Sun. The *Cacique* seems to attempt to imitate the ceremonial of the *Incas* on the days of *Raymi*:[2] he kneels down very nigh my bed-side, and continues

---

1 *Cacique* is a kind of Governor of a Province [1748 footnote].

2 The *Raymi* was the principal feast of the Sun, when the *Incas* and Priests adored him on their knees [1748 footnote].

a considerable time in that painful posture: sometimes he keeps silent, and, with his eyes cast down, seems to think profoundly: I see in his countenance that respectful confusion which the great name[1] inspires us with when spoken aloud. If he finds an opportunity of taking hold of my hand, he puts his mouth to it with the same veneration that we have for the sacred diadem.[2] Sometimes he utters a great number of words, which are not at all like the ordinary language of his nation: the sound of them is more soft, more distinct, and more harmonious. He joins to this that air of concern which is the forerunner of tears, those sighs which express the necessities of the soul, the most plaintive action, and all that usually accompanies the desire of obtaining favours! Alas! my dear *Aza*, if he knew me well, if he was not in some error with regard to my being, what prayer could he have to address to me? (23-24)

[From "Letter IX"]

I know that the name of the *Cacique* is *Deterville*; that of our floating house, a *Ship*; and that of the Country we are going to, *France*. (30)

As soon as I have repeated after him, *oui, je vous aime, (yes, I love you)* or else, *je promets d'être à vous, (I promise to be yours)* joy expands over his countenance, he kisses my hands with transport, and with an air of gaiety quite contrary to that gravity which accompanies divine adoration. (31)

[From "Letter XI"]

To judge of their minds by the vivacity of their gestures, I am sure that our measur'd expressions, the sublime comparisons which so naturally convey our tender sentiments and affectionate thoughts, would to them appear insipid. They would take our serious and modest air for stupidity, and the gravity of our gait for mere stiffness. Would'st thou believe it, my dear *Aza*? (36)

---

1   The great name was *Pachacamac*, which they spoke but seldom, and always with great signs of adoration [1748 footnote].
2   They kissed the diadem of *Mancocapac* in the same manner as the Roman Catholicks kiss the relicks of their saints [1748 footnote].

[From "Letter XII"]

I confess, my dear *Aza*, that, notwithstanding my tender inquietudes, I have tasted pleasures, during this journey, that were before unknown to me. Shut up in the temple from my most tender infancy, I was unacquainted with the beauties of the universe, and every thing that I see ravishes and enchants me. (39)

[From "Letter XIII"]

Their house is almost as magnificent as that of the Sun: the furniture and some parts of the walls are of gold, and the rest is adorned with a various mixture of the finest colours, which prettily enough represent the beauties of nature. (41)

[From "Letter XV"]

The simple manners, the native goodness, and the modest gaiety of *Celina*, would make one think she had been bred up among our virgins. The honest sweetness, the serious tenderness of her brother, would easily persuade me that he was born of the Blood of the *Incas*. They both treat me with as much humanity as we should shew them, if like misfortunes had brought them among us. (46-47)

[From "Letter XVI"]

[Zilia watches a play and asks,] Could one think, my dear *Aza*, that a whole people, whose outside is so humane, should be pleased at the representation of those misfortunes or crimes, which either overwhelmed or degraded creatures like themselves? But perhaps they have occasion here for the horror of vice to conduct them to virtue. This thought starts upon me unsought, and if it were true, how should I pity such a nation? Ours, more favour'd by nature, cherishes goodness for its own charms: we want only models of virtue to make us virtuous; as nothing is requisite but to love thee in order to become amiable. (50-51)

[From "Letter XVIII"]

How fatal, alas, has the knowledge of the language I now use been to me! How deceitful was the hope that prevail'd on me to learn it!

Scarce had I got acquainted with it but a new universe opened to my eyes; objects took another form, and every light I gain'd discover'd to me a new misfortune. My mind, my heart, my eyes, the Sun himself has deceived me. (54)

[From "Letter XX"]

The government of this empire, quite opposite to that of thine, must needs be defective. Whereas the *Capa-Inca* is oblig'd to provide for the subsistence of his people, in *Europe* the sovereigns subsist only on the labours of their subjects: whence it is that most of the crimes and misfortunes proceed here from unsatisfied necessities. The misfortunes of the nobles in general arise from the difficulties they are under to reconcile their apparent magnificence with their real misery. The common people support their condition by what is called commerce or industry, the least evil arising from which is insincerity. Part of the people, in order to live, are obliged to depend on the humanity of others; and that is so bounded, that scarce have those wretches sufficient to keep them alive. Without gold, it is impossible to acquire any part of that land which nature has given in common to all men. Without possessing what they call wealth, it is impossible to have gold; and by a false consequence, repugnant to reason and natural light, this senseless people, thinking it a shame to receive from any other than the sovereign the means of life, and the support of dignity, give that sovereign an opportunity of showering down his liberalities on so small a number of his subjects, in comparison with those that are miserable, that there would be as much folly in pretending to any share in them, as there would be ignominy in obtaining deliverance by death from the impossibility of living without shame. The knowledge of these woful truths excited in my heart at first only pity for the miserable wretches, and indignation against the laws. But alas! how many cruel reflections does the contemptuous manner, in which I hear them speak of those that are not rich, cause me to make on myself! I have neither gold, nor land, nor address, and yet I necessarily make a part of the citizens of this place. O heaven! in what class must I rank myself? Though I am a stranger to all sentiment of shame, which does not arise from a fault committed; though I perceive how foolish it is to blush for causes independent of my power and my will, I cannot help suffering from the idea which others have of me. (58-59)

Their virtues, my dear *Aza*, have no more reality than their riches. The moveables, which I thought were of gold, have only a thin superficies of that metal, their true substance being wood. (59)

[From "Letter XXI"]

With regard to the origin and principles of this religion, they did not appear to me either more incredible, or more incompatible with good sense, than the history of *Manco-capac* and the lake *Titicaca*: I should therefore have been ready to embrace it, if the *Cusipata* had not indignantly despised the worship which we render to the Sun. Partiality of any kind destroys confidence. I might have applied to his arguments what he opposed to mine: but if the laws of humanity forbid to strike another, because it is doing him an injury, there is more reason why one should not hurt the soul of another by a contempt of his opinions. (61)

The learned man informed me also how chance had conducted the *Spaniards* to thy unfortunate empire, and that the thirst of gold was the sole cause of their cruelty. (62)

[From "Letter XXVI"]

A small part of thy treasures would amaze and confound the pride of the magnificent indigents of this kingdom: thy virtues and thy sentiments will be cherish'd by me only. (78)

[From "Letter XXVIII"]

The diversions of this country appear to me as affected and unnatural as the manners: They consist of a violent gaiety, express'd by loud laughter, in which the soul seems to take no part; of insipid games, in which money makes all the pleasure; or else in conversations so frivolous, in which the same things are continually repeated, that they resemble rather the chattering of birds than the discourse of thinking beings. (84)

[From "Letter XXX"]

Naturally susceptible of virtuous sentiments, I never saw one of them that was not melted at the history, which they oblige me often to give them, of the rectitude of our hearts, the candour of our sentiments, and the simplicity of our manners. If they lived amongst us, they would become virtuous: but example and custom are the tyrants by which they are sway'd. (91)

Happy the nation which has nature only for its guide, truth for its mover, and virtue for its principle! (92)

[From "Letter XXXI"]

Among the great number of those [shocking contradictions] which strike me every day, I do not see any one that more dishonours their understanding than their manner of thinking with regard to women. They respect them, my dear *Aza*, and at the same time despise them with equal excess. The first law of their politeness or virtue (I do not know that they have any other) regards the women. A man of the highest rank owes the utmost complaisance to a woman of the most vile condition, and would blush for Shame, and think himself ridiculous in the highest degree, if he offered her any personal insult. And yet a man of the least consideration and credit may deceive and betray a woman of merit, and blacken her reputation without fear of either blame or punishment. (92)

Docile to the notions of nature, our genius proceeds no farther: we have found that the strength and courage of one sex indicates that it ought to be the support and defence of the other, and our laws are conformable to this discovery.[1] Here, far from compassionating the weakness of women, those of the common people, tied down to labour, have no relief either from the laws or their husbands. Those of more elevated rank, the prey either of the seduction or malice of men, have no recompence for their perfidies, except a shew of merely imaginary outside respect, which is continually followed by the most biting satire. I perfectly well perceived, when I first conversed in the world here, that the habitual censure of the nation falls principally upon the women, and that the men do not despise one another without some caution or reserve. (93)

... the men, naturally cowards, without shame, and without remorse, are afraid only of corporal punishments. And if the women were authorized to punish the outrages offered them in the same manner, as the men are oblig'd to revenge the slightest insult offered to one

---

1 The *Peruvian* laws dispence the women from all hard bodily labour [1748 footnote].

another, such persons as we see now well received in society, would not be so any longer. (93-94)

Impudence and effrontery are the first sentiments that the men are inspired with: timidity, gentleness, and patience are the sole virtues that are cultivated in the women: How then are these to avoid being the victims of impunity? ... Let us not forget, though, the obligation thou art under to be my example, my guide, and my support in the path of virtue; I, the duty that lies on me to preserve thy esteem and thy love, by imitating my model, even by surpassing it if possible, and meriting a respect founded on virtue, and not on a frivolous custom. (94)

[From "Letter XXXV"]

I learned from the *Spaniards* to know misfortunes: but the last is the most sensible of all their strokes. It is they that have robbed me of *Aza's* heart; it is their cruel religion that renders me odious in his eyes. That religion approves, it ordains infidelity, perfidy, ingratitude: but it forbids the love of one's near relations. If I was a stranger, unknown, *Aza* might love me: but, being united to him by the ties of blood, he must abandon me, he must take away my life without shame, without regret, without remorse. Alas! contradictory as this religion is, if nothing had been necessary but to embrace it, in order to recover the good it had deprived me of, I could have submitted my mind to its illusions, without corrupting my heart by its principles. (105)

[From "Letter XXXVIII"]

The pleasure of being: that forgotten, unknown pleasure to so many mortals; this thought so sweet, this happiness so pure, *I am, I live, I exist*: is alone enough to convey bliss, if we remember it, if we enjoy it, if we know the value of it. (112)

6. **From Abbé Raynal,** *A Philosophical and Political History of the Settlements and Trade of the Europeans in the East and West Indies*, **translated by J. Justamond. 2 vols. 3rd London edition (London: Thomas Cadell, 1777)**

[Originally published in 1770 as *L'Histoire philosophique et politique des établissements et du commerce des Européens dans les deux Indes*, Raynal's book ultimately saw thirty-eight editions in French, eighteen in English, and five in other languages. Williams drew her quotations of

Raynal from Justamond's English translation. Abolitionist and democratic, the work was deeply critical of the Catholic Church and of imperialism, advocating for revolution against all forms of tyranny. The book was banned in France in 1779 and burned in public displays. Williams drew heavily upon Raynal's natural and cultural histories, as well as upon his descriptions of the Peruvian countryside and natural events. She sympathized both with Raynal's philosophical ideals of freedom and revolution and with his idealization of the Peruvian people, children of nature whose nobility is crushed by the fanaticism and greed of "civilized" Europe.]

Volume 2

Conquest of Peru by the Spaniards. Changes that have happened in this Empire since that revolution.

Nothing but the allurement of immediate gain could excite men to enterprises so hazardous as were those for which this age was distinguished. Gold alone attracted them to the continent of America, and made them brave dangers, diseases, and death ... and by a terrible but just vengeance, the cruelty of the Europeans and their lust of gold exhausted at once the two hemispheres of their inhabitants, and destruction raged equally among those who were the plunderers and assassins, as among the plundered people. Among the number of villains who ravaged, depopulated, and destroyed, these unhappy coasts of a world which was no sooner discovered than it was exterminated, there was one man [Balboa] who had naturally an agreeable aspect, a robust constitution, an intrepid courage, and a popular eloquence, and who had imbibed some principles from a liberal education. (467-68)

[Pizarro's] avarice and ambition inspired him with inconceivable activity.... The use he had hitherto made of his natural and acquired abilities, persuaded him that nothing was above his talents; and he formed the plan of exerting them against Peru. To these designs he associated Diego de Almagro, whose birth was equivocal, but whose courage was proved. (471)

Pizarro was to command the troops, Almagro conduct the succours, and Luques prepare the means. This plan of ambition, avarice, and ferociousness, was completed by fanaticism. Luques publicly consecrated a host; part of which he ate, and divided the rest between his two associates; all three swearing, by the blood of their God, that, to enrich themselves, they would not spare the blood of man. The expedition, commenced under these horrible auspices, was not fortunate; the measures being continually interrupted by famine, sickness, and misunderstanding, by a profound ignorance of the theory of the winds and currents, and by the arms of the Indians; the adventurers found themselves reduced to the necessity of returning without having effected any establishment, or done any thing worthy of being transmitted to posterity. (472)

Peru had been an extensive and civilized empire for four centuries. It had been founded by Manco-Capac, and by his wife Mama-Ocello-Huaco. (473)

... [I]t has been said, that it was a tradition generally diffused throughout Peru, and handed down from age to age, that there would one day arrive by sea men with beards, and of such superiority in arms, that nothing could resist them. (474)

This young prince [Atabalipa], after the death of his father, demanded the inheritance of his mother. His elder brother Huascar refusing to give it up to him, immediate recourse was had to arms.... These troubles, which for the first time had agitated Peru, were not entirely appeased when the Spaniards landed in the empire. (475-76)

Atabalipa came without suspicion to the place appointed. He was attended by about fifteen thousand men. He was carried on a throne of gold, and gold glittered in the arms of his troops. He turned to the principal officers, and said to them: *These strangers are the messengers of the Gods; be careful of offending them.* The procession was now pretty near the palace, which was occupied by Pizarro, when a dominican, named Vincent de Valverdo, with a crucifix in one hand, and his breviary in the other, came up to the emperor. He stopped him in his march, and, by his interpreter, made him a long speech, in which he expounded to him the christian religion, pressed him to embrace that form of worship, and proposed to him to submit to the king of Spain, to whom the pope had given Peru.

The emperor, who heard him with a great deal of patience, replied, *I am very willing to be the friend of the king of Spain, but not his vassal; the pope must surely be a very extraordinary man, to give so liberally what does not belong to him. I shall not change my religion for another; and if the christians adore a God who died upon a cross, I worship the sun, who never dies.* He then asked Vincent where he had learned all that he had said of God and the creation. *In this Book*, replied the monk, presenting at the same time his breviary to the emperor. Atabalipa took the book, examined it on all sides, fell a laughing, and, throwing away the breviary, added, *This book tells me nothing of all this.* Vincent then turned towards the Spaniards, crying out with all his might, *Vengeance, my friends, vengeance. Christians, do you not see how he despises the gospel? Kill these dogs, who trample under foot the law of God.*

The Spaniards, who probably had with difficulty restrained that fury, and that thirst of blood, which the sight of the gold and of the infidels had inspired them with, instantly obeyed the dominican.... A dreadful massacre was made of them. Pizarro himself advanced towards the emperor, made his infantry put to the sword all that surrounded his throne, took the monarch prisoner, and pursued all the rest of the day those who had escaped the sword of his soldiers. A multitude of princes of the race of the Incas, the ministers, the flower of the nobility, all that composed the court of Atabalipa, were massacred. Even the crowd of women, old men, and children, who were come from all parts to see their emperor and the Spaniards, were not spared. Whilst this carnage continued, Vincent ceased not to animate the assassins who were tired with slaughter, exhorting them to use not the edge but the point of their swords, to inflict deeper wounds. When the Spaniards returned from this infamous massacre, they passed the night in drunkenness, dancing, and all the excesses of debauchery. (477-78)

There was in the train of the Spanish general an Indian, who had embraced the christian faith. His name was Philipillo, and he was employed as interpreter. He was fixed upon to frame an accusation against the emperor, for having designed to excite his subjects to rebel against the tyrants. On this sole deposition, Atabalipa was condemned to death. The Spaniards had the effrontery to bring him to a formal trial; and this atrocious farce was followed with those horrid consequences that must necessarily be expected from it. After this judiciary assassination, Pizarro penetrated into the inland parts of the empire. Cusco opened to him its gates, and offered him more treasures than there were perhaps in all Europe before the discovery of the new world. These treasures became the spoil of two hundred Spaniards, who, though in possession of such immense riches, still desired more; impelled by that thirst of gold which increases in proportion as it is gratified. Temples and private houses were stripped from one end of the kingdom to the other. The Peruvians were oppressed in all parts, and rapes committed every where on their wives and daughters. The people driven to desperation took up arms, and laid siege at once to Cusco and Lima: but these unfortunate men in several engagements were not able to destroy more than six hundred of their enemies; who, continually receiving fresh supplies, were at last universally victorious.... The Peruvians were under a necessity of submitting to the yoke, such as the tyrants chose to impose on them. (479-80)

Manco Capac, who collected together the savages of Peru that were scattered among the forests, styled himself the offspring of the sun, who was sent by his father to teach men to be good and happy. He persuaded a great number of savages to follow him; and he founded the city of Cusco. He taught his new subjects to cultivate the ground, to sow corn and pulse, to wear cloaths, and to build houses. His wife taught the Indian women to spin, to smooth cotton and wool; and instructed them in all the occupations suitable to their sex, and in all the arts of domestic economy. He told them they must adore the sun; he built temples to this luminary, and abolished human sacrifices, and even those of animals. His descendents were the only priests of his nation. (481)

The Peruvians were enjoined to love one another, and every circumstance induced them to it. Those common labours, which were always enlivened by agreeable songs; the object itself of these labours, which was to assist every one who had occasion for succour; that apparel that was made by young women devoted to the worship of the sun, and distributed by the emperor's officers to the poor, to the aged, and to orphans; that union which must necessarily reign in the decuries,[1] where every one was mutually inspired with respect for the laws, and with the love of virtue, because the punishments, that were inflicted for the faults of one individual, fell on the whole body; that custom of regarding each other as members of one single family, which was the empire; all these circumstances united, maintained among the Peruvians concord, benevolence, patriotism, and a certain public spirit; and contributed as much as possible to substitute the most sublime and amiable virtues, in lieu of personal interest, of the spirit of property, and of the usual incentives employed by other legislators. (482-83)

The laws were severe, but this severity was attended only with good effects. The Peruvians were strangers to crimes. All their laws were reputed to come to them from the sun, which threw light upon their actions. Thus the violation of a law became a sacrilege. They even went

---

1   "The whole state was distributed into decuries, with an officer that was appointed to superintend ten families that were intrusted to him. A superior officer had the same inspection over fifty families; others over a hundred, five hundred, and a thousand." (484)

of their own accord to reveal their most secret faults, and to solicit permission to expiate them. (484)

The emperor levied no tribute; and exacted nothing from his subjects, but that they should cultivate his lands; the whole produce of which, being deposited in public magazines, was sufficient to defray all the expences of the empire.... With regard to the lands that were in the possession of individuals, they were neither hereditary, nor even estates for life: the division of them was continually varying, and was regulated with strict equity according to the number of persons which composed every family. There was no other wealth, but what arose from the produce of the fields, the temporary enjoyment of which was all that was granted by the state. (485)

Thus was the despotism of the Incas founded on a mutual confidence between the sovereign and the people; a confidence, which resulted from the beneficence of the prince, from the constant protection he granted to all his subjects, and from the evident interest they had to continue in obedience to him. (488-89)

The first testimonies, and those even were contradictory, have been invalidated by succeeding accounts, and at last totally destroyed, when men of enlightened understandings had visited this celebrated part of the new hemisphere. (490)

But whatever were the arts which the Spaniards found in the country of the Incas, they could not prevent the empire from submitting to its conquerors. A moment of resistance longer, and perhaps the Peruvians had been free. The conquerors [Pizarro and Almagro] had differences to settle among themselves, which did not admit of a division of their forces.... [J]ealousy and hatred prevailed among them. (495)

Almagro and his adherents had passed the sea for no other purpose than to enrich themselves with the gold of the country. They had acquired less than their opponents [Pizarro and his men], and therefore wanted to wrest it from them by the sword. (496)

The soul of young Almagro seems to have been formed for tyranny.... [Those who expressed uneasiness with] undertakings which filled them with horror.... were either put to death in private, or perished on a scaffold. (498)

We must judge of those revolutions which are produced by civil wars by the causes from which they spring. When an abhorrence of tyranny and the natural love of liberty stimulate a brave people to take up arms, if the goodness of their cause is crowned with success, the tranquility that follows this transitory calamity is an aera of the greatest happiness.... But when civil wars proceed from a corrupt source; when slaves fight about the choice of a tyrant; when the ambitious contend in order to oppress, and robbers quarrel for the sake of spoil; the peace which terminates these horrors is scarcely preferable to the war which gave them birth.... Avarice seeks to grow rich without any trouble, vengeance to gratify its resentments without fear, licentiousness to throw off every restraint, and discontent to occasion a total subversion of affairs. The phrenzy of carnage is succeeded by that of debauchery. The sacred bed of innocence or of marriage is polluted with blood, adultery, and brutal violence. The fury of the multitude rejoices in destroying every thing it cannot enjoy; and thus in a few hours perish the monuments of many centuries. (500-01)

[After 1750] The liberty of the Indians underwent the same fate as their property. Those who were the slaves of government, and were employed in the labours indispensably necessary for new establishments, were ill-fed and ill-cloathed. (515)

If the court of Madrid pretends that it has prevented these flagrant enormities, by giving the Peruvians a Spanish protector, who is obliged to defend them, and a cacique of the country, who is charged with the management of their affairs, it is deceived.... The protector sells the Indians to any that will purchase them; and the cacique is too much debased to be able to oppose this oppression. (518)

The collections of the monks are real military executions. They are a species of plunder committed by authority, and almost always accompanied with violence. This conduct could not fail to render christianity odious to the Indians. These people go to church as they do to the labours imposed upon them, execrating those foreign barbarians who overwhelm both their bodies and their souls with intolerable yokes and burdens. (519)

The traveller, who was led by accident or curiosity into these desolate plains, could not forbear abhorring the barbarous and bloody authors of these devastations, while he reflected that it was not owing even to the cruel illusions of glory and to the fanaticism of conquest, but to the stupid and abject desire of gold, that they had sacrificed so much more real treasure, and so numerous a population. This insatiable thirst of gold, which neither attended to subsistence, safety, nor policy, was the only motive for establishing new settlements, some of which have been kept up, while several have decayed, and others have been formed in their stead. The fate of them all has corresponded with the discovery, progress, or declension of the mines to which they were subordinate. (526)

The mine of Guança Velica generally affects those, who work in it, with convulsions: this and the other mines, which are not less unhealthy, are all worked by the Peruvians. These unfortunate victims of an insatiable avarice are crowded all together and plunged naked into these abysses, the greatest part of which are deep, and all excessively cold. (542)

7. From William Robertson, *The History of America* (London: W. Strahan, T. Cadell; Edinburgh: J. Balfour, 1777)

[Less well known than fellow Scottish Enlightenment historians Edward Gibbon and David Hume, William Robertson (1721-93) was highly influential in the late eighteenth century, and his *History of America* was considered the standard work on the subject. Williams relied heavily on his account of the conquest of Peru. Like Raynal and Humboldt, Robertson aimed at a study of culture, science, and the arts in order to illuminate the progress of human history. His character-driven history is told primarily from the "civilized" perspective of the Spanish conquistadors, but his take on the Spanish is far from flattering.]

Alexander VI, a pontiff infamous for every crime that disgraces humanity, filled the papal throne at that time.... By an act of liberality which cost him nothing, and that served to establish the jurisdiction and pretensions of the papal see, he bestowed on Ferdinand and Isabella all the countries inhabited by Infidels, which they had discovered, or should discover; and in virtue of that power which he derived from Jesus Christ, he vested in the crown of Castile a right to vast regions, to the possession of which he himself was so far from having any title, that he was unacquainted with their situation, and even with their existence.... Zeal for propagating the Christian faith was the consideration employed by Ferdinand in soliciting this bull, and is mentioned by Alexander as his chief motive for issuing it. (I: 113-14)

The violent operations of Albuquerque, the new distributor of Indians, revived the zeal of the Dominicans against the *repartimientos*, and called forth an advocate for that oppressed people, who possessed all the courage, the talents, and activity requisite in supporting such a desperate cause. This was Bartholomew de las Casas, a native of Seville, and one of the clergymen sent out with Columbus in his second voyage to Hispaniola, in order to settle in that island. He early adopted the opinion prevalent among ecclesiastics, with respect to the unlawfulness of reducing natives to servitude; and that he might demonstrate the sincerity of his conviction, he relinquished all the Indians who had fallen to his own share in the division of the inhabitants among their conquerors, declaring that he should ever bewail his own misfortune and guilt, in having exercised for a moment this impious dominion over his fellow creatures. From that time, he was the avowed patron of the Indians; and by his bold interpositions in their behalf, as well as by the respect due to his abilities and character, he had often the merit of setting some bounds to the excesses of his countrymen. He did not fail to remonstrate warmly against the proceedings of Albuquerque, and, though he soon found that attention to his own interest rendered him deaf to admonition, he did not abandon the wretched people whose cause he had espoused. He instantly set out for Spain, with the most sanguine hopes of opening the eyes and softening the heart of Ferdinand, by that striking picture of the oppression of his new subjects, which he would exhibit to his view.... [Las Casas returned] with the title of Protector of the Indians. (I: 218-20)

Upon their arrival [Las Casas and others], the first act of their authority was to set at liberty all the Indians who had been granted to the Spanish courtiers, or to any person not residing in America. This ... spread a general alarm. (I: 221)

[Rather than use the indigenous people as slaves,] Las Casas proposed to purchase a sufficient number of negroes from the Portuguese settlements on the coast of Africa, and to transport them to America, in order that they might be employed as slaves in working the mines and cultivating the ground.... While he contended earnestly for the liberty of the people born in one quarter of the globe, he laboured to enslave the inhabitants of another region; and in the warmth of his zeal to save the Americans from the yoke, pronounced it to be lawful and expedient to impose one still heavier upon the Africans. Unfortunately for the latter, Las Casas's plan was adopted. (I: 225-26)

[Las Casas] engaged, in the space of two years, to civilize ten thousand of the natives, and to instruct them so thoroughly in the arts of social life, that, from the fruits of their industry, an annual revenue of fifteen thousand ducats should arise to the king. (I: 228)

While the negro on the coast of Africa is scorched with unremitting heat, the inhabitant of Peru breathes an air equally mild and temperate, and is perpetually shaded under a canopy of grey clouds, which intercepts the fierce beams of the sun, without obstructing his friendly influence. (I: 253)

Not only the incapacity, but the prejudices of the Spaniards, render their accounts of the people of America extremely defective. Soon after they planted colonies in their new conquests, a difference in opinion arose with respect to the treatment of the natives. One party, solicitous to render their servitude perpetual, represented them as a brutish, obstinate race, incapable either of acquiring religious knowledge, or of being trained to the functions of social life. The other, full of pious concern for their conversion, contended that, though rude and ignorant, they were gentle, affectionate, docile, and by proper instructions and regulations might be formed gradually into good Christians and useful citizens. (I: 285-86)

[Francisco] Pizarro was the natural son of a gentleman of an honourable family by a very low woman, and, according to the cruel fate which often attends the offspring of unlawful love, had been so totally neglected in his youth by the author of his birth, that he seems to have destined him never to rise beyond the condition of his mother. In consequence of this ungenerous idea, he set him, when bordering on manhood, to keep hogs. But the aspiring mind of young Pizarro disdaining that ignoble occupation, he abruptly abandoned his charge, enlisted as a soldier, and after serving some years in Italy, embarked for America, which, by opening such a boundless range to active talents, allured every adventurer whose fortune was not equal to his ambitious thoughts. There, Pizarro early distinguished himself. With a temper of mind no less daring than the constitution of his body was robust, he was foremost in every danger, patient under the greatest hardships, and unsubdued by any fatigue. Though so illiterate that he could not even read, he was soon considered as a man formed to command....

[Diego de] Almagro had as little to boast of his descent as Pizarro. The one was a bastard, the other a foundling. Bred, like his companion, in the camp, he yielded not to him in any of the soldierly qualities of intrepid valour, indefatigable activity, or insurmountable constancy in enduring the hardships inseparable from military service in the New World. But in Almagro these virtues were accompanied with the openness, generosity, and candour natural to men whose profession is arms; in Pizarro, they were united with the address, the craft, and the dissimulation of a politician, with the art of concealing his own purposes, and with sagacity to penetrate into those of other men. (II: 148-50)

By his [the Inca ruler, Manco-Cápac's,] institutions ... the various relations in private life were established, and the duties resulting from them prescribed with such propriety, as gradually formed a barbarous people to decency of manners. In public administration, the functions of persons in authority were so precisely defined, and the subordination of those under their jurisdiction maintained with such a steady hand, that the society in which he presided, soon assumed the aspect of a regular and well-governed state.... But, among the Peruvians, this unbounded power of their monarchs is said to have been uniformly accompanied with attention to the good of their subjects. It was not the rage of conquest, if we may believe the accounts of their countrymen, that prompted the Incas to extend their dominions, but the desire of diffusing the blessings of civilization, and the knowledge of the arts which they possessed, among the barbarous people whom they reduced. During a succession of twelve monarchs, it is said that not one deviated from this beneficent character. (II: 165-66)

[T]he ambition of two young men, [Huascar and Atahualpa], the tide of the one founded on ancient usage, and that of the other asserted by the veteran troops, involved Peru in civil war, a calamity, to which, under a succession of virtuous princes, it had hitherto been a stranger. In such a contest, the issue was obvious. The force of arms triumphed over the authority of laws. Atahualpa remained victorious, and made a cruel use of his victory. Conscious of the defect in his own title to the crown, he attempted to exterminate the royal race, by putting to death all the children of the Sun descended from Manco Capac, whom he could seize either by force or stratagem. From a political motive, the life of his unfortunate rival Huascar, who had been taken prisoner in the battle which decided the fate of the empire, was saved for some time, that, by issuing orders in his name, the usurper might more easily establish his own authority.

When Pizarro landed in the bay of St. Matthew, this civil war raged between the two brothers in its greatest fury. (II: 167-68)

Pizarro, according to the usual artifice of his countrymen in America, pretended to come as the ambassador of a very powerful monarch, and declared that he was now advancing with an intention to offer

Atahualpa his aid against those enemies who disputed his title to the throne.

As the object of the Spaniards in entering their country was altogether incomprehensible to the Peruvians, they had formed various conjectures concerning it, without being able to decide whether they should consider their new guests as beings of a superior nature, who had visited them from some beneficent motive, or as formidable avengers of their crimes, and enemies to their repose and liberty. The continual professions of the Spaniards, that they came to enlighten them with the knowledge of truth, and lead them in the way of happiness, favoured the former opinion; the outrages which they committed, their rapaciousness and cruelty, were awful confirmations of the latter. While in this state of uncertainty, Pizarro's declaration of his pacific intentions so far removed all the Inca's fears, that he determined to give him a friendly reception. (II: 170)

[Pizarro's reception by Atahualpa in Caxamalca:] The decent deportment of the Peruvian monarch, the order of his court, and the reverence with which his subjects approached his person and obeyed his commands, astonished those Spaniards, who had never met in America with any thing more dignified than the petty cazique of a barbarous tribe. But their eyes were still more powerfully attracted by the vast profusion of wealth which they observed in the Inca's camp. The rich ornaments worn by him and his attendants, the vessels of gold and silver in which the repast offered to them was served up, the multitude of utensils of every kind formed of those precious metals, opened prospects far exceeding any idea of opulence that a European of the sixteenth century could form. (II: 171-72)

[Valverde asks Atahaulpa to give up his land, worship the Christian God, and subject himself to the Pope and the king of Castile. Valverde's] strange harangue, unfolding deep mysteries ... of which no power of eloquence could have conveyed at once a distinct idea to an American, was so lamely translated by an unskilful interpreter ... that its general tenor was altogether incomprehensible to Atahualpa. Some parts in it, of more obvious meaning, filled him with astonishment and indignation. His reply, however, was temperate. He began with observing, that he was lord of the dominions over which he reigned by hereditary succession; and added, that he could not conceive how a foreign priest should pretend to dispose of territories which did not belong to him; that if such a preposterous grant had been made, he, who was the rightful possessor, refused to confirm it; that he had no inclination to renounce the religious institutions established by his ancestors; nor would he forsake the service of the Sun, the immortal divinity whom he and his people revered, in order to worship the God of the Spaniards, who was subject to death; that with respect to other matters contained in his discourse, as he had never heard of them before, and did not now understand their meaning, he desired to know where he had learned things so extraordinary. "In this book," answered Valverde, reaching out to him his breviary. The Inca opened it eagerly, and turning over the leaves, lifted it to his ear: "This," says he, "is silent; it tells me nothing;" and threw it with disdain to the ground. The enraged monk, running towards his countrymen, cried out, "To arms, Christians, to arms; the word of God is insulted; avenge this profanation on those impious dogs."

Pizarro, who, during this long conference, had with difficulty restrained his soldiers, eager to seize the rich spoils of which they had now so near a view, immediately gave the signal of assault.... The Peruvians, astonished at the suddenness of an attack which they did not expect, and dismayed with the destructive effects of the fire-arms, and the irresistible impression of the cavalry, fled with universal consternation on every side.... Pizarro seizing the Inca [Atahualpa] by the arm, dragged him to the ground, and carried him as a prisoner to his quarters.... Not a single Spaniard fell, nor was one wounded but Pizarro himself, whose hand was slightly hurt by one of his own soldiers, while struggling eagerly to lay hold on the Inca. (II: 174-76)

[The judges, Pizarro, Almagro, and two assistants,] pronounced Atahualpa guilty, and condemned him to be burnt alive. Friar Valverde prostituted the authority of his sacred function to confirm this sentence, and by his signature warranted it to be just. Astonished at his fate, Atahualpa endeavoured to avert it by tears, by promises, and by entreaties, that he might be sent to Spain, where a monarch would be the arbiter of his lot. But pity never touched the unfeeling heart of Pizarro. He ordered him to be led instantly to execution; and what added to the bitterness of his last moments, the same monk who had just ratified his doom, offered to console, and attempted to convert him. The most powerful argument Valverde employed to prevail with him to embrace the Christian faith, was a promise of a mitigation in his punishment. The dread of a cruel death extorted from the trembling victim a desire of receiving baptism. The ceremony was performed; and Atahualpa, instead of being burnt, was strangled at the stake. (II: 184-85)

In consequence of what had been agreed with Pizarro, Almagro began his march towards Chili.... [I]nstead of advancing along the level country on the coast, [Almagro] chose to march across the mountains by a route that was shorter indeed, but almost impracticable. In this attempt his troops were exposed to every calamity which men can suffer, from fatigue, from famine, and from the rigour of the climate in those elevated regions of the torrid zone, where the degree of cold is hardly inferior to what is felt within the polar circle. Many of them perished; and the survivors, when they descended into the fertile plains of Chili, had new difficulties to encounter. They found there a race of men very different from the people of Peru, intrepid, hardy, independent, and in their bodily constitution, as well as vigour of spirit, nearly resembling the warlike tribes in North America.... The Spaniards, however, continued to penetrate into the country, and collected some considerable quantities of gold; but were so far from thinking of making any settlement amidst such formidable neighbours, that, in spite of all the experience and valour of their leader, the final issue of the expedition still remained extremely dubious, when they were recalled from it by an unexpected revolution in Peru. (II: 194-96)

The Pizarros advanced without any obstruction, but what arose from the nature of the desert and horrid regions through which they marched. As soon as they reached the plain, both factions were equally impatient to bring this long-protracted contest to an issue. Though countrymen and friends, the subjects of the same sovereign, and each with the royal standard displayed; and though they beheld the mountains that surrounded the plain in which they were drawn up, covered with a vast multitude of Indians, assembled to enjoy the spectacle of their mutual carnage, and prepared to attack whatever party remained master of the field.... The conflict was fierce, and maintained by each party with equal courage. On the side of Almagro, were more veteran soldiers, and a larger proportion of cavalry, but these were counterbalanced by Pizarro's superiority in numbers, and by two companies of well-disciplined musketeers, which, on receiving an account of the insurrection of the Indians, the emperor had sent from Spain.... [T]he rout became general. The barbarity of the conquerors stained the glory which they acquired by this complete victory. The violence of civil rage hurried on some to slaughter their countrymen with indiscriminate cruelty; the meanness of private revenge instigated others to single out individuals as the objects of their vengeance....

The Indians, instead of executing the resolution which they had formed, retired quietly after the battle was over; and in the history of the New World, there is not a more striking instance of the wonderful ascendant which the Spaniards had acquired over its inhabitants, than that after seeing one of the contending parties ruined and dispersed, and the other weakened and fatigued, they had not courage to fall upon their enemies, when fortune presented an opportunity of attacking them with such advantage. (II: 205-07)

The governor [Pizarro], considering himself, upon the death of Almagro, as the unrivalled possessor of that vast empire, proceeded to parcel out its territories among the conquerors.... But Pizarro conducted this transaction not with the equity and candour of a judge attentive to discover and to reward merit, but with the illiberal spirit of a party leader. Large districts, in parts of the country most cultivated and populous, were set apart as his own property, or granted to his brothers, his adherents and favourites. To others, lots less valuable and inviting were assigned. The followers of Almagro, amongst whom were many of the original adventurers to whose valour and perseverance Pizarro was indebted for his success, were totally excluded from any portion in those lands, towards the acquisition of which they had contributed so largely.... The partisans of Almagro murmured in secret, and meditated revenge. (II: 211-12)

[To make peace in Peru, the] Spanish ministers fixed with unanimity of choice, upon Pedro de la Gasca, a priest in no higher station than that of counsellor to the inquisition. Though in no public office, he had been occasionally employed by government in affairs of trust and consequence, and had conducted them with no less skill than success; displaying a gentle and insinuating temper, accompanied with much firmness; probity, superior to any feeling of private interest; and a cautious circumspection in concerting measures, followed by such vigour in executing them, as is rarely found in alliance with the other.... Gasca, notwithstanding his advanced age and feeble constitution, and though, from the apprehensions natural to a man, who, during the course of his life, had never been out of his own country, he dreaded the effects of a long voyage, and of an unhealthy climate, did not hesitate a moment about complying with the will of his sovereign. In order to shew that it was from this principle alone that he acted, he refused a bishopric which was offered to him, in order that he might bear a more dignified character; he would accept of no higher title than that of president of the court of audience in Lima; and declared that he would receive no salary on account of his discharging the duties of that office. All he required was, that the expence of supporting his family should be defrayed by the public, and as he was to go like a minister of peace with his gown and breviary, and without any retinue but a few domestics, this would not load the revenue with any enormous burden.

But while he discovered such disinterested moderation with respect to whatever related personally to himself, he demanded his official powers in a very different tone. He insisted, as he was to be employed in a country so remote from the seat of government, where he could not have recourse to his sovereign for new instructions on every emergence; and as the whole success of his negociations must depend upon the confidence which the people with whom he had to treat could place in the extent of his powers, that he ought to be invested with unlimited authority, that his jurisdiction must reach to all persons and to all causes; that he must be empowered to pardon, to punish, or to reward, as circumstances and the behaviour of different men might require; that, in case of resistance from the malcontents, he might be authorised to reduce them to obedience by force of arms, to levy troops for that purpose, and to call for assistance from the governors of all the Spanish settlements in America.... Gasca hastened his departure, and without either money or troops, set out to quell a formidable rebellion.... Gasca appeared in such pacific guise, with a train so little formidable, and with a title of no such dignity as to excite terror, that he was received with much respect. (II: 247-49)

The *repartimientos*, or allotments of lands and Indians which fell to be distributed, in consequence of the death or forfeiture of the former possessors, exceeded two millions of pesos of yearly rent. Gasca, when now absolute master of this immense property, retained the same disinterested sentiments which he had originally professed, and refused to reserve the smallest portion of it for himself. But the number of claimants was great; and whilst the vanity or avarice of every individual fixed the value of his own services, and estimated the recompence which he thought due to him, the pretensions of each were so extravagant, that it was impossible to satisfy all. Gasca listened to them one by one, with the most patient attention, and that he might have leisure to weigh the comparative merit of their several claims with accuracy....

The indignation excited by publishing the decree of partition was not less than Gasca had expected. Vanity, avarice, emulation, envy, shame, rage, and all the other passions that most vehemently agitate the minds of men when both their honour and their interest are deeply affected, conspired in adding to its violence. It broke out with all the fury of military insolence. Calumny, threats, and curses were poured out openly upon the president. He was accused of ingratitude, of partiality, and of injustice.... Gasca, however, perceiving that the flame was suppressed rather than extinguished, laboured with the utmost assiduity to soothe the malcontents, by bestowing large gratuities on some, by promising *repartimientos*, when they fell vacant, to others, and by caressing and flattering all.... He introduced order and simplicity into the mode of collecting the royal revenue. He issued regulations concerning the treatment of the Indians, well calculated to protect them from oppression, and to provide for their instruction in the principles of religion, without depriving the Spaniards of the benefit accruing from their labour. Having now accomplished every object of his mission, Gasca, longing to return again to a private station, committed the government of Peru to the court of audience, and set out for Spain.... He was received in his native country with universal admiration of his abilities, and of his virtue. (II: 262-64)

The Spaniards, as they pretend, conscious of their own inability to occupy the vast regions which they had discovered, and foreseeing the impossibility of maintaining their authority over a people infinitely superior to themselves in number, in order to preserve America, resolved to exterminate the inhabitants, and by converting it into a desart, endeavoured to secure their own dominion over it. (II: 348)

8. **From Jean-François Marmontel, _The Incas: or, The Destruction of the Empire of Peru_. 2 vols. (Dublin: A. Stewart, 1797)**

[Jean-François Marmontel's historical novel, _Les Incas, ou la destruction de l'empire du Pérou_, was originally published in 1777; immensely popular, it was translated into English the same year it appeared in France and was read throughout Europe. Like Raynal and Robertson, Marmontel embodies zealous religious intolerance in the character of the priest, Valverde, and idealizes the Peruvian Indians and their society. But, unlike them, he prominently features female characters, who often share the same strength of will, passion, nobility, and even arms, as the men. From _Les Incas_, Williams may have borrowed the characters of Cora, Zorai, and Aciloe, and both works place the historical figure Las Casas in Peru, a country he never actually visited.]

... Peru was still in vigour, but one of its monarchs had made a death-bed division of it between his two sons.... The haughty Huascar, who was left king of Cusco, had been cruelly hurt by a disposition, which had robbed him, as he thought, of the fairest of his provinces; nor could he help looking on Atabalipa as an usurper. (I: 1)

Of all the climates of the globe, there is no one that is visited by that luminary with so temperate and benign an influence: in return, there is not any one from whose inhabitants he receives so solemn and devout an homage. (I: 2)

The second law addressed itself to the sovereign.... It recommended to him to maintain a generous affection, a holy respect for truth, the guide and counselor of justice; and to look with an eye of horror and contempt upon fals[e]hood, the accomplice of iniquity. It exhorted him to subdue and reign over men's hearts by the power of beneficence.... The same law addressed itself next to the royal family of the Incas. It enjoined them to set an example of obedience and zeal, to make a modest use of the privileges of their rank, to shun superciliousness and sloth.... The third law exacted from the people the most inviolable respect for the family of the Sun, an unbounded deference to the commands of that person.... (I: 9-10)

Of three equal portions of land in culture, one was to belong to the Sun, another to the Inca, another to the people: each family had its allotment.... By birth, every person became entitled to a provision out of the common stock: his only riches were the produce of his own labor, and at his death his property reverted to the fund from which it came.... Not that the law itself laid them under any restriction; but, according to their pious and moderate way of thinking, any thing of parade or ostentation would but turn to their disgrace; they placed their whole dignity in innocence and virtue.... The respective lots of the orphans, the widows, and the infirm, were cultivated by the people. (I: 11-12)

The burthen of the public works sat light, in consequence of the equality and impartiality with which it was distributed. None were exempted from it: every one set his shoulders to it with equal zeal. (I: 13)

[In a prayer by a priest to the Sun:] The rich harvests ripened by thy warmth, the fruits coloured by thy rays, the flocks nourished by the juices of thy herbs and flowers, are treasures but to us: to diffuse them all around is to imitate thee. (I: 20)

[When three virgins of the Sun come into the temple to become Spouses of the Sun and to be separated from society:] the most beautiful of the three, in a face that bespoke the same innocent simplicity, betrayed evident symptoms of melancholy and dejection. Cora (that was the name of the reluctant maid) before the vow that was to detach her from mankind had passed her lips, seized her father's hand, and imprinting on it an ardent kiss, suffered no more to escape ... than a timid and half-stifled sigh. (I: 22)

The North of America was laid waste already, and destruction began to extend itself to the South. In vain had that pious churchman, that resolute and tender friend of the unhappy Indias, Bartholemew de Las Casas, in vain had he conveyed the cries of a suffering nation to the hearts of Kings; an unavailing pity, a faint wish to apply a remedy to such a mass of evils was all he could obtain. (I: 90)

To effect the ruin of the New World, it was necessary that Nature should have formed a man endowed with such a degree of resolution and intrepidity, as fitted him to stand the worst of evils: a man inured to labour, to distress, to suffering; who could support himself under the most pressing wants, could steel himself against the most fearful dangers, could rise superior to every obstacle, and stand firm against the stroke of the most severe adversity. This wonderful man was Pizarro. Nor was this unconquerable vigour of mind his only virtue. Foe to every thing that favoured of luxury and ostentation; plain and yet commanding in his address; dignified and yet popular; severe when severity was necessary; indulgent where indulgence was practicable; moderating by the engaging frankness of his manners, the rigour of his discipline and the weight of his authority; lavish of his own blood, frugal of that of the soldier; liberal, generous, and not unfeeling; he stood untainted by that lust of wealth by which others in the same station had been disgraced. (I: 91-92)

Shocked at this barbarity [natives forced to row a boat to the point of exhaustion], Las-Casas felt an emotion like what a father would have felt, had the sufferers been his children. "Cease," he cried, "ye cruel men! cease torturing these poor creatures, exhausted as you see they are by their efforts in your service. Would you see them die outright? Consider; for shame, consider: they are your brethren; they are men; they are children of the same God that you are." Then turning to one of the rowers who seemed to be the youngest and the weakest of them: "Friend," says he, "you may take breath a little—go—I'll take up the oar instead of you." This generous humanity kindled the latent sparks of shame in the breasts of the young Spaniards. They now took up the oars with one accord, vying with each other in their alacrity to relieve the Indians. The poor creatures held up their hands to the good man who had got them this indulgence, poured on him benedictions without number, and called on him by that tender name of Father, which he had so well deserved. (I: 97-98)

At the name of Las-Casas, at the name of that champion of Religion and Humanity, whom Spain had honored with the title of Protector of the Indies, Pizarro felt himself penetrated with a respectful awe.... "Is it you then," says he, "my venerable father! is it you who are come to share and bring a blessing on our labours! What an earnest is this of the favour of Providence! how flattering a presage of success!" (I: 102)

"Come," says he [Luquez, the "sacrilegious Priest"], "Pizarro, and you Almagro, come and seal with the blood of our God, our holy and illustrious alliance." Then, breaking the Host into three parts, he reserved one to himself: and giving the other two parts, one to each of his mute and trembling associates, "Thus," says he, "be the spoils of the Indians divided." Such was their mutual oath: such was the sacrilegious compact dictated by rapacity. Las-Casas shuddered at the sight.... But Las-Casas, who saw, that according to this plan the Indians were to be vassals, or more properly slaves to the Spaniards, and doomed to the severest drudgeries, could not dissemble his concern. (I: 103-04)

[Las Casas, addressing Fernando Luquez:] "Keep you then to that law which he has given to all mankind: *love me, and love your neighbour as yourself*: this is his law, Fernando. Do you find here your chains, your tortures, and your fires? The cruelties which the Indians have practiced one upon another, are certainly by no means to be justified: but were they still more inexcusable, is it for you to imitate them? It is their misfortune, alas! to believe in Gods whom they suppose to delight in blood. If instead of the tiger they saw upon their altars the lamb without spot, like the lamb they would be gentle.... Let us lament, then, instead of condemning those victims of prejudice, these slaves of custom.... [A]nd what it was that the people of Hispaniola and Cuba had done amiss. What, I pray, could be more quiet, more meek, more innocent than those people? Their whole lives were as harmless as the infancy of other men: they had not so much as an arrow to shoot birds with. Did those poor creatures find any protection in their innocence? 'Tis in those countries that I have seen ruffians without a motive, and without remorse, massacring young children, assassinating old men, ripping up women with child, and tearing their fruit out of their wombs.... O Holy Religion! are these thy ministers! O God of nature, are these then thy avengers! To immure whole nations alive in gloomy caverns, there to perish with hunger and fatigue; all this only to heap up riches upon riches, to fill your coffers with, and to disseminate thro' the world all those vices that are the offspring of laziness, luxury and pride! ... Yes, you do serve a God; but it is the God of avarice. 'Tis he who, through your mouth, has now been offering insults to human nature; seeking to render Heaven an instrument of his fury, and an accomplice in his guilt." (I: 109-11)

[Valverde,] the blackest dissembler that for the misfortune of the New World Spain had ever produced, harboured in his heart all kinds of villainy: but he kept them close: and the mask of hypocrisy, which he never quitted, was such as imposed on every eye. (I: 111)

[Las Casas on slavery:] No, my friends, there is no middle way: we must either renounce the name of men, abjure the name of Christians, or debar ourselves for ever of the right of making slaves. That shameful state of degradation in which the stronger holds the weaker, is shocking to humanity; but, above all things, most abominable in the eyes of religion. *Brother, thou art my slave*, is an absurdity in the mouth of any man; but it is perjury and blasphemy in that of a Christian. (I: 117-18)

[Alonzo, upon seeing the magnificence of a city of the temple of the Sun:] "Ah!" says he, with a sigh, "if ever European avarice should discover these treasures, with what greedy fury would it haste to devour them!" (II: 42)

[Ataliba's army conquers Cusco and subjects Huascar to his rule, but his son Zoraï dies in the battle:] The Prince, the son of their King, Zoraï was no more. O unhappy father! how wilt thou lament thy conquest! When the standard was attacked, Zoraï advanced at the head of his men and animated them by his own example. Emotions were excited in every heart by his youth, beauty, and courage. The enemy, seeing him expose himself to their strokes, admired and pitied him; forgetting to fear him, they dared not to strike him. One only ... seized the standard.... The flint, with which it was barbed, penetrated his breast. He tottered, and his Indians pressed around to support him, but alas! in vain. His eyes lost their fire, and the flower of beauty faded on his cheek, a mortal chillness began to spread thro' all his limbs. As a young cedar on the edge of a forest, torn from its roots by a storm, inclines on the surrounding trees, which hold it up from falling, and appears to be still alive, though its drooping branches and withering leaves discover that the earth, which nourished it, supports it no longer; so appeared the young Inca, mortally wounded and leaning on his soldiers. "O my father!" cries he, with a faltering voice, "how great will be thy grief! Tell him my friends, that my blood hath at least gained him the victory. Wrap me in the standard which hath cost me my life, to conceal from the eyes of my father, too painful a sight, and console him with the thought, that I died worthy of him." The united exclamations of grief and revenge resounded around him. "No," says he, "it is enough to have conquered; I wish not for vengeance. I am an Inca, and I forgive." (II: 97-98)

"Riches," said Pizarro [to the Emperor], with an air of mortification and disdain, "my sailors and my soldiers will bring back in abundance. Glory is the object of my aim. Every other consideration is beneath my regard. If I am unworthy to govern, I am not worthy to conquer." (II: 163)

Vincent de Valverde ... a furious and fanatical priest, was enraged to discover in the language of Pizarro, the sentiments of Las-Casas; and knitting his atrocious brows: "They shall bend," said he, within himself, "they shall bend beneath the yoke of the faith, or be destroyed." (II: 188)

[Valverde says of God:] know, there is but one: and it is he whom I serve. All tremble before him; and he hath committed into my hands his power. My spirit is his; my voice is his organ; I speak, and it is he who is heard; it is his will that I declare; and his will changes when, and how, I please: for he hears me; and my prayer either provokes, or appeases him, according to my pleasure. (II: 207-08)

[T]he dearest of [Ataliba's] wives, the lovely and tender Aciloe, ... [whose] eyes were yet streaming with tears, called forth by the memory of her son.... Cora, by whose misfortunes the Princess had been sensibly touched, and who had been received at her court, accompanied her to the feast. She met again her Alonzo with transport, proud to display the effects of their mutual passion. (II: 215)

[Ataliba questions the doctrine of Valverde:] The Peruvian Monarch[,] astonished at a doctrine so strange, mildly inquired of the propounder, from whence he had collected these positions. "From this book," replied Valverde, in an arrogant tone, "from this sacred book, dictated by the Holy Ghost himself." The Inca, without emotion, receiving the book, and looking upon it, said: "Every thing that Pizarro hath told me, I can conceive, and, without difficulty, believe. But what I hear from you appears to be unintelligible; and this book is silent, it tells me nothing." He added, it is said, some offensive expressions concerning the man, who arrogated to himself the right of commanding Kings, and disposing of Empires; and either through contempt or negligence, in returning the book to Valverde, let it fall. This was enough. The fanatical monk[,] transported with rage, ran towards the Spaniards and began to cry out for vengeance in the name of Religion, which this barbarian had trampled under foot. Instantly, a vigorous and destructive fire succeeded.... The battalion opened; and from the centre issued forth thunder and death. At the discharge of these brazen volcanos, from whence proceeded flames and a stupendous report, at the unexpected massacre and the invisible strokes that fell before the throne, the King was confounded; he beheld at his feet, his guard astonished and trembling, crowd together for their general safety, and perish before his eyes, like a fearful flock, amongst which the destructive blaze of lightening had descended. The Inca, having forbidden them to commit any kind of hostility, they strictly observed his prohibition. Alonzo, enraged, incited them to follow him, and charge in despair this troop of assassins. "Avenge yourselves, avenge me of the traitors that dishonour my country. Defend, save your King." The brave youth, at these words, felt himself wounded, and fell. The Inca, at the sight of his fall, broke forth in exclamations of sorrow. (II: 237-39).

Of Ataliba's guard six thousand were already massacred, and the same fate awaits the rest.... [T]he dying fall on the dead, whose places they supplied. Pizarro, who had thrown himself before his soldiers to stop their ruthless fury, not being able to make them obey, or even hear him, saw but one means of preserving the life of the Inca. He put himself at the head of these murderers, preceded them, entered the camp, arrived at the throne, with one hand diverting the sword that was raised against Ataliba, himself received the stroke, while with the other he seized the Prince, dragged him from his seat, threw him at his feet, and cried out while he guarded him, "Let us take him alive for the sake of his treasure." This speech suspended their rage. Pale, terrified, distracted, the King fell, and beheld himself weltering in Indian gore. He discovered the bodies of his friends torn, mutilated, and hacked, and embraced them with such cries of distress, that even the hearts of their executioners were moved. Amongst the rest he perceived Alonzo. "Dear and ill-fated friend! thou hast undone me," cried he; "but they deceived thee: it was thy misfortune to possess an Indian soul." At these words, observing that Alonzo still breathed: "Ah! cruel man," said he to Pizarro, "at least save him who delivered me to thee." (II: 240-41)

[On the field of battle] There, Valverde, in the midst of slaughter, with a crucifix in his hand, while his mouth was foaming with rage, exclaimed: "Friends, Christians, go on, go on. The destroying angel is your guide. Strike only with the point, that ye break not your swords; plunge them, dye them in blood." "Begone, execrable monster," said Pizarro, "retire, or I will make thee yield up thine atrocious soul." (II: 241-42)

The Spaniards, [were] fatigued with murder, and burdened with the valuable spoils they had amassed in the Indian camp. (II: 244)

"You [Ataliba] suppose me treacherous and perjured," said Pizarro; "but behold this hand, wounded and bleeding, which warded off from you a mortal blow. Is this the hand of an enemy? I drew you from the throne, where twenty swords were aiming to pierce your heart; I have imprisoned you to protect you from the fury of those whom I was unable to disarm, or restrain. Ask these warriors if, during this horrible massacre, I did not exert my utmost efforts to suppress it.... But, of this, unhappy Prince, be assured, I will protect your life at the hazard of my own." (II: 247)

... [T]hese desolated fields ... were still reeking with the blood that had been spilt. The companion of Aciloe, Cora, wept not: a deadly paleness was spread over her face; and the gloomy and devouring fire which glimmered in her eyes, had dried up the source of her tears. Her looks, sometimes fixt, at others, wild, sought on these plains of slaughter the wandering shade of her husband. "Where is he? in what spot reposes my dear Alonzo?" said she: "Where, in this horrid carnage, fell those who guarded our King?" An Indian replied to her: "This is the place. Here was the throne of the Inca; there fell all his friends around him; there they are buried. Alonzo was at their head; and this small eminence that you see, is his tomb." At these words, which pierced the heart of the tender wife of Alonzo, she with a shriek that expressed her anguish, threw herself headlong, and fell on the damp earth, as yet uncovered by turf, embraced it with the same ardor as tho' it had been the body of her husband, resisted every effort to draw her from the grave; and when they would remove her by force, it seemed from the groans that she uttered, as tho' they were rending her heart-strings. (II: 275)

[The Peruvians pay the captured Ataliba's ransom, but the Spaniards do not release him.] Valverde then went on. "Do you not desire to worship the God of the Christians?"—"Certainly," answered the unhappy Prince, "if this God, as he is declared to be, is beneficent, powerful, and just, if nature is his work, and the Sun himself one of his gifts, I join, with all nature, to adore him. How ungrateful, how irrational must he be, who should refuse him his love?"—"And do you desire to be instructed," still asked this perfidious monk, "in the sacred truths that he hath revealed to us, to become acquainted with his worship and follow his law?"—"I earnestly desire it," replied the Inca, "as I have told you, and am impatient to open my eyes to the light, that they may be enlightened and I may believe."—"Heaven be praised," replied Valverde, "he is disposed as I wished him to be. Implore then on your knees this God of goodness and of clemency; and receive the salutary water that regenerates his children." The Inca, with an humble mind and a docile disposition, bowed, and received, on his knees, the holy water of baptism. "Heaven is opened," said Valverde, "and the moments are precious." At the same instant he gave the signal to his two attendants; and the fatal cord suppressed the Inca's last sighs. It was from the lamentable cries of his children and their mothers that the news of his death was spread, at the return of morning. Some of the Spaniards were stricken with horror; but the greatest part applauded the audacity of the assassins; and it was thought they had been sufficiently merciful in not extending the fate of this unhappy Prince to his wives and children, who, from this moment, were abandoned to the compassion of the Indians. Pizarro, indignant, shocked and weary of contending against wickedness, after having imprecated curses on these execrable assassins and their fanatical partisans, retired to the city of the Kings, which then was beginning to be built in the vale of Rimac. Licentiousness, plunder, rapacity, murder, and desolation, without restraint, every where prevailed; the face of this continent presented nothing to the view but tribes of Indians, falling, as they fled, into the snares, or beneath the swords, of the Spaniards. (II: 284-86)

[*The Incas* concludes with the following words:] Cusco, sacked and deserted, saw the carcases of its tyrants scattered on its plains. The waves of the Amazon were red with the blood of those it had beheld spreading desolation on its banks; and fanaticism, surrounded by massacres and devastation, sitting on heaps of slain, extended her looks over immense ruins, applauded herself at the sight, and praised Heaven for crowning her labours. (288)

Appendix C: Poetic Responses to Helen Maria Williams

[Most poets who responded to *Peru* in verse did so to express their admiration, including Anna Seward, who praised Williams's daring and called her art "divine." Even Richard Polewhele, disdainful of so many women poets, treats Williams less harshly than others. William Wordsworth's "Sonnet, on seeing Miss Helen Maria Williams Weep at a Tale of Distress" originally appeared in *The European Magazine* in March of 1787, shortly after the publication of Williams's volume *Poems* (1786), which contained *Peru*, as well as other works such as "To Sensibility" and "Part of an Irregular Fragment." Wordsworth could only imagine Williams's emotional responsiveness—as well as the sensibility she would ignite in him—because he was not to meet her until 1820.]

1. **Anna Seward, "Sonnet to Miss Williams on her Epic Poem, *Peru*." *The Gentleman's Magazine* 54 (August 1784): 613**

[Anna Seward (1742-1809) was a widely respected poet and woman of letters who helped to revive the sonnet in English. Her *Elegy on Captain Cook* (1780) won applause from Samuel Johnson. Williams praises Seward in *An Ode on the Peace* (65-72), which appeared the year before Seward published this sonnet. Walter Scott would later edit Seward's *Poetical Works* (1810).]

Poetic sister, who with daring hand,
Ere thy fourth lustre's last soft year is flown,
Hath seiz'd the epic lyre—with art divine
Wak'd on its golden strings each spirit bland,
Or bade its deep sonorous tones expand:
Shalt thou the claim to glory's meed resign,
Call other strains, less silver sweet than thine,
To hymn the fate of a disastrous land?
See! at that call, Peru's wild genius flies
To Thespian bowers: there, as Urania[1] strays,   10
Grasps her bright robe, and thus impatient cries,
With bending knee and supplicating gaze:

---

1   In Greek mythology, goddess of music, song and dance; one of the nine
    Muses.

"Be mine alone thy lovely female bard,
O from obtrusive lyres my well-sung story guard!"
                                        Lichfield, May 3 [1784]

2. Eliza, "To Miss Helen Maria Williams: On her Poem of *Peru.*" *The Gentleman's Magazine* 54 (July 1784): 532

[Probably Eliza Gilding of Woolwich, Kent, author of *The Breathings of Genius* (1776), who later married Rev. Daniel Turner. Deborah Kennedy suggests another possibility. Eliza Knipe Cobbold (1767-1824), author of *Poems on Various Subjects* (1783) (Kennedy 220, n. 47). That this sonnet does not appear in Laetitia Jermyn's 1825 edition, *Poems by Mrs. Elizabeth Cobbold with a Memoir of the Author,* argues against Cobbold's authorship, although not definitively. However, the reference to "breathings rude and wild / T' attempt to praise such heavenly strains as thine" (ll. 3-4) suggests an affinity with Gilding's mode of thought and expression.]

Accept, fair Helen, from a grateful heart,
    The willing praise which sympathy bestows;
And let my feeble pen those thanks impart,
    With which delighted fancy warmly glows.

While others waste their smiling youthful hours   5
    In dissipation's light fantastic maze,
You in a bright display of mental powers
    Burst on our reason, and command our praise.

Your polish'd verse with ev'ry beauty shines
    Which just design and harmony can give;   10
While brilliant fancy decorates your lines,
    And in your sentiment doth feeling live.

A country ravag'd yields a theme of woe
    For all that can affect the human soul,
Where each fond tie must force the tear to flow,   15
    And griefs to rise, which cannot bear controul.

Your hoary sires our veneration claim;
    Your youthful heroes with their ardor charm;
Your nymphs on virtue build a lasting name;
    Your matrons with the tenderest feelings warm!   20

When soft description at your call draws nigh,
    For love you can command what dress you please;
While ardent hope, and ev'ry trembling sigh,
    Aided by you, full on our passions seize.

And when Alzira mourns a father slain,   25
    Or frantic gazes on a slaughter'd lord,
With her we feel each agonising pain,
    With her we snatch the ready reeking sword.

Or when the priest before the altar falls,
    And pity in a child's despair would plead;   30
How loud the impious deed for vengeance calls,
    And Zilia's misery makes our bosom's bleed!

But as a mother when thy Cora mourns,
    When on her breast the languid babe reclines,
What various passions seize the heart by turns!   35
    What tender sympathy the soul refines!

You, who so well sharp misery can paint;
    You who so sweetly can the passions lead;
May all your hours be kept from keen complaint,
    And from love's griefs your gentle breast be freed!   40

But should misfortune, that intrusive guest,
    E'er cloud so fair, so bright a morning sun;
Should you with sad affliction be opprest,
    Ere yet you finish life, so well begun;

May some Las Casas, child of heaven, be near,   45
    To sooth with piety thy soul refin'd;
To blend with thine the sympathetic tear,
    And pour soft consolation o'er thy mind!
                    Woolwich, June 25 [1784]

3. E., "Sonnet to Miss Helen Maria Williams, on her Poem of Peru." *The Gentleman's Magazine* 56 (June 1786): 513

["E" is, most likely, "Eliza." When *The Gentleman's Magazine* published "To Miss Helen Maria Williams: on her Poem of Peru" in July 1784, the editor affixed the following note: "The other valuable Poem to Miss W. is unluckily mislaid. May we beg another copy?" Frequently editors of periodicals assigned pseudonyms to those authors who did not wish to use their full names, and editors were not always consistent.]

Daughter of Verse—soft Pity's sweetest child—
Meek virgin-priestess of the tuneful Nine!
Wilt thou admit of breathings rude and wild
T' attempt to praise such heavenly strains as thine?

All unoontroul'd to thy enchanting song   5
I gave my feeling, nor the gift could rue;
For every note they sound, while led along,
To nature faithful, and to passion true.

What though no longer now thy numbers roll
Peru's sad story on my list'ning ear,   10
Still, sunk their charming tenour in my soul,
I think I hear them, and could ever hear;
While, like the thanks some blest oration draws,
I can but murmur thus my hoarse applause.

4. W. Upton, "To Miss Helen Maria Williams. Authoress of *Peru*, a Poem." *Public Advertiser* (24 March 1786): 2

["William Upton" or "W. Upton" were pseudonyms for William Strange of Upton (1766-1836), singer, dramatist, poet, and songwriter for Astley's Amphitheatre in London. He reprinted this poem in his 239-page volume, *Poems on Several Occasions, Dedicated with Permission, to Her Grace, the Duchess of Devonshire* signed "W. Upton" (London: John Strahan, 1788; 2nd edition, 1791) and *The Words of the Most Favourite Songs, Duets, &c., Sung at the Royal Amphitheatre, Westminster Bridge and the Royalty Theatre, Well-Close Square. Dedicated to Mrs. Astley* (1802). He also wrote a popular play, *The Black Castle*, as well as *Fair Rosamond*. His lyrics appeared regularly in London periodicals, and Lord Byron refers to him in a ballad (letter of 11 April 1818 to John Murray).]

Peru's rich mines by captive slaves explor'd,
Where Plutus reigns supreme, by all ador'd,
'Tis not his treasures, Williams' pen impart,
Her subject's nature, glowing from the heart;
To her the Muse, the daring task consign,   5
Expanded thought, gave energy divine,

Unfolded nature's secrets to her view,
And form'd the line her conduct should pursue;
And well the maid's perform'd the mighty task,
The deed was great—no more the Muse could ask.   10
Peru unbosoms, all the Nine foretold
Where nature forms the universal mould,
Whose true impressions, proves superior skill,
Subdues the heart, and conquers e'en the will.
So sweet Maria pleads a parent's cause,   15
That echo vibrates back its Muse, applause;
So lively paints the lovers ardent flame,
That doubts will rise, but Williams feels the same,
Each scene she tints, such beaming truth displays,
That envy's self unwilling gives her praise.   20
In vain to trace o'er Peru's vast domain,
Her boundless fancy boundless praises claim.
Peruvia's woes, when time shall bear no date,
Will stand recorded in the page of fate;
And while Zamor's and Aciloe's fates are read,   25
Shall Helen's fame be rescu'd from the dead.

                                            Strand, March 17.

5. J. B———o, "Sonnet. To Miss Helena-Maria Williams."
The European Magazine, and London Review 12 (August
1787): 152

Enchanting Muse, whose clear melodious lay
(Like the sweet incense of a fragrant flower)
Steals on the sense with fascinating power,
Inrob'd in Pity's mild, benignant ray,
Pure simple nature unadorn'd by art,   5
With native beauty in thy song we trace;
(Where beaming Fancy with poetic grace,
Pourtrays the softer feelings of the Heart.)
While More and Seward, fav'rites of the Nine,
Each in their varied happy strains excel,   10
And tune the lyre to notes of highest swell;
Equal with them thy name shall splendid shine.
O then encourage still the glorious flame;
And let not Fear thy Muse's flight restrain:
Resume the pen—and may thy labours gain   15
A well-earn'd plaudit from the voice of fame.

6. [William Wordsworth] Axiologus, "Sonnet, on Seeing Miss Helen Maria Williams Weep at a Tale of Distress." *The European Magazine, and London Review* 11 (March 1787): 202

[Wordsworth seems to have taken inspiration not only from *Peru* but from other Williams poems, such as "To Sensibility" and "Part of an Irregular Fragment." In 1787, Wordsworth could only imagine Williams's emotional responsiveness—as well as the sensibility she would ignite in him—because he would not meet her until October 1820 (Kennedy 199).]

She wept.—Life's purple tide began to flow
In languid streams through every thrilling vein;
Dim were my swimming eyes—my pulse beat slow,
And my full heart was swell'd to dear delicious pain.
Life left my loaded heart, and closing eye;   5
A sigh recall'd the wanderer to my breast;
Dear was the pause of life, and dear the sigh
That call'd the wanderer home, and home to rest.
That tear proclaims—in thee each virtue dwells,
And bright will shine in misery's midnight hour;   10
As the soft star of dewy evening tells
What radiant fires were drown'd by day's malignant pow'r,
That only wait the darkness of the night
To chear the wand'ring wretch with hospitable light.

7. From Richard Polewhele, *The Unsex'd Females: A Poem* (London: Cadell and Davies, 1798)

And Helen, fir'd by Freedom, bade adieu
To all the broken visions of Peru; (ll. 97-98)

[Polewhele appended the following note to these lines:

Miss Helen Williams is, doubtless, a true poet. But is it not extraordinary, that such a genius, a female and so young, should have become a politician—that the fair Helen, whose notes of love have charmed the moonlight vallies, should stand forward, an intemperate advocate for Gallic licentiousness—that such a·woman should import with her, a blast more pestilential than that of Avernus, though she has so often delighted us with melodies, soft as the sighs of the Zephyr, delicious as the airs of Paradise?—(See her "Letters from France.")]

Appendix D: Contemporary Critical Reviews of Peru and of "Peruvian Tales"

[When *Peru* first came out in 1784, reviews in leading contemporary journals were generally positive and praised Williams for her skill in tackling the difficult subject matter. By 1786, when *Peru* was republished in the two-volume collection of Williams's *Poems*, reviews were more critical; although still willing to admire the effort, reviewers were quick to point out what they saw as faults, even given the thoughtful and imaginative revisions to the epic. In 1823, Williams reshaped *Peru* from an epic into six poetic "Peruvian Tales," including them in the collection *Poems on Various Subjects*. By this time, Williams's reputation had suffered, and reviewers compared the poems in this volume unfavorably against her early output; "Peruvian Tales" was met with little regard.]

Peru (London: T. Cadell, 1784)

1. From *The New Annual Register ... for the Year 1784* 5.3 (1785): 268-69

Miss Helen Williams's "Peru" is the production of a truly poetic genius, and it will appear the more extraordinary when it is considered that it is written by a very young person, who has had no peculiar advantages of literary education, and that the completion of the poem, as we have reason to believe, took up but a small portion of time. To write on such a subject was rather a bold undertaking; but our poetess apologizes for it, by declaring, that she has not had the presumption even to attempt a full, historical narration of the fall of the Peruvian empire. To describe, she says, that important event with precision, and to display with just force the various causes which combined to produce it, would require all the energy of genius, all the strong colouring of the most glowing imagination. Conscious, she adds, of her utter inability to execute such a design, she hath only aimed at giving a simple detail of a few incidents in that affecting and romantic history; where the unparalleled sufferings of an innocent and amiable people afford the finest subjects for true pathos, while their climate, entirely dissimilar to our own, furnishes new and ample materials for poetic description. Miss Williams has performed more than her promise. Her descriptions are admirably picturesque, the incidents very affecting, and her versification eminently beautiful. It is in pathos

P E R U,

A

P O E M.

IN SIX CANTOS,

BY

HELEN MARIA WILLIAMS.

LONDON:

PRINTED FOR T. CADELL, IN THE STRAND.

MDCCLXXXIV.

[PRICE FOUR SHILLINGS SEWED.]

Title page to *Peru* (1784). This first edition of *Peru* was published as a quarto volume. Private collection.

that she greatly excels; pathos is her fort[e]; to the pathetic she recurs on every occasion. The fine imagination of Miss Williams perpetually supplies her with images and expressions, perhaps too richly luxuriant. To point out the striking parts of the poem before us, would carry us too far; and, therefore, we shall only observe, that we were much pleased with the episode of Zamor and Aciloe. He must be a fastidious critic indeed, who will not, upon the whole, give his verdict to the great merit of the present work. It must be acknowledged that the fair author has redundancies to correct; and we doubt not but that they will be corrected by maturer years and judgment. It is the fault of some modern poetry that it affects too splendid a dress, and that it is loaded with epithets not sufficiently precise, appropriated, and expressive. The chaste and beautiful reserve of the ancient classics in this respect would be a proper object of imitation. We must not forget to mention, that Miss Williams has dedicated her Peru to Mrs. Montagu, in a copy of verses wherein simplicity and elegance are happily united.

2. From *The Critical Review* 57 (May 1784): 376-80

It is an excellent rule, prescribed by Horace,[1] that a poet should not raise the reader's expectation by ostentatious promises. A pompous exordium resembles a fire of straw, which blazes for a little time, but is soon extinguished. The author of this poem, in conformity to the foregoing precept, has chosen a title which is simple and unaffected; and has modestly acknowledged, that she had not the presumption even to attempt a full historical narration of the fall of the Peruvian empire....

[Quotes what became I: 137-76.]

There is great propriety and beauty in this passage. The Spaniards are said to have arrived on the coast of Peru at midnight. The profound tranquility of the scene is happily contrasted with the horrors and agonies of Peruvia, on the approach of a cruel and malignant enemy; and renders her ejaculations on that occasion more pathetic and affecting....

Our ingenious author, as those who have read Edwin and Eltruda[2] may recollect, has a peculiar talent in describing despair and madness....

Though this poem proceeds in historical order, and consists of detached episodes, without any proper unity of action, it is a work of superior merit. Some passages in it are exquisitely pathetic; and others are animated with that warmth of imagination, that harmony of numbers, and that energy of expression, which distinguish the genuine poet from the mere coupler of rhymes.

---

1 Quintus Horatius Flaccus (65-8 BCE), the leading Roman lyric poet and satirist during the time of the Emperor Augustus.

2 *Edwin and Eltruda, a Legendary Tale* (1782) was Williams's first published volume of poetry. The War of the Roses forms the backdrop to this account of a woman who loses her lover and her father to a pointless war.

3. From *The English Review* 4 (July 1784): 28-31

It is impossible to discover a theme for poetical composition, more fertile and interesting, than the proceedings of the Spaniards in the new world: in which, as the fair author remarks, "the unparalleled sufferings of an amiable and innocent people, afford the finest subjects for true pathos; while their climate, entirely dissimilar to our own, furnishes new and ample materials for poetic description." It is also pleasing to observe, that, after so many venal muses have employed their art in celebrating and adorning the Spanish achievements, a true born daughter of freedom has at last arisen, who, proceeding in a path diametrically the reverse of theirs, has made it her business to place in their proper light the virtues of the Peruvians, and to brand with merited infamy the avarice and cruelty of their conquerors.

Such were the prejudices we felt, when we opened the performance before us. Nor were our expectations disappointed. Miss Williams was born a poet. She does not, like some of her contemporaries, labour with the muse, and "strain from hard-bound brains eight lines a year."[1] Her style is rich, flowing, and unaffected, and proves her composition to be the child of nature; not the sickly and artificial produce of cultivation. She is every where glowing, animated, and metaphorical. Nor does she seek after the figurative, and adopt it because it is proper for poetry. No, it is in this kind of composition she is most at home; her tropes flow spontaneously from her pen; and before the magic of her imagination every object of nature becomes informed with a soul, and the whole prospect is decorated with the colours of the rainbow. A few extracts will probably convince our readers of the justice of these observations. The following, in which the mutual passion of Atabalipa (or, as he is here called for the sake of harmony, Ataliba) and Alzira is announced, conveys a strong idea of the vigour and rapidity of conception with which it was written ... [Quotes what became I: 63-108.]

It is impossible to conceive of a more picturesque and luxuriant imagination than that which dictated the following lines ... [Quotes what became IV: 1-14.]

Such are the claims Miss Williams has to our applause. It is not, however, to be pretended, that she is without her faults. She has indeed all the faults, that can be expected to spring from an inexhaustible fancy, untutored by learning, and unpruned by the severity of criticism and the tardy hand of experience. It may be observed, that of all modes of composition, a style highly figurative is most inimical

---

1 Alexander Pope, "Epistle to Dr. Arbuthnot," l. 182.

to the pathetic. When the affections are to be excited, the language must be perfectly simple and natural. We ought to lose sight of the poet, and to appear to be touched only by incident and situation. *Si vis me flere, dolendum est primum ipsi tibi.*[1] The moment the art of the poet appears, we are convinced that his mind is disengaged and at ease, we forget the distress of his personages, and attend only to the skill and ingenuity of the description. What kind of sensations, for example, are excited by such verses as these? ... [Quotes what became V: 97-122.]

We do not mean, however, to insinuate, that the fair author has always failed even in her attempts upon the pathetic. The following lines are in our opinion a strong instance to the contrary. They treat the most obvious of all appearances in an original manner, they give novelty to a threadbare idea, and carry it home to the heart in a way not less irresistible than unexpected.... [Quotes what became V: 141-46.]

In the mean time, the unbounded profusion of images of which we have complained, is not confined to those parts in which pathos ought to have predominated. It pervades the whole poem. And the disadvantage is increased in the present instance, by the plan of the performance. Miss Williams has not, as she observes in the preface, "attempted a full, historical narration of the fall of the Peruvian empire: she has only aimed at detailing a few incidents in that romantic story." In pursuance of this idea, she has selected three or four independent stories for the subject of her work. No one of them is sufficiently dilated to make a strong impression upon the reader, and far from combining their effect, we are scarcely able to perceive by what chain of connexion they have been brought together. Upon the whole, we may say of the metaphors of this poem, without an improper compliment to the author, that, like the stars in the galaxy, each of them separately would attract our admiration; but united, they present an object too confused and indistinct, to be able to excite the highest degree of pleasure.

4. From *The Monthly Review* 71 (July 1784): 12-20; reprinted in *The London Magazine* n.s. 3 (December 1784): 474-76

Reviewers may be considered as a kind of circumnavigators on the ocean of letters. The perils they undergo, and the difficulties they must contend with, are many and perplexing. Frequently are they driven upon inhospitable shores, where the natives are as malignant as the soil

---

1 "If you would have me weep, you must first feel grief yourself," Horace, *Ars Poetica, or the Epistle to the Pisones*, v. 102 (Loeb translation).

is barren. But as in most pursuits of life a diversity of fortune prevails, so it is in theirs. Among the various regions to which their voyage of discovery conducts them, though there are some doomed to perpetual sterility, or involved in impenetrable fogs, others are clothed in unfading beauty and inexhaustible fertility. It is not to be wondered at, if, when arriving at regions like these, they are sometimes willing to stay longer than the nature of their engagements may admit. Their conduct, however, is not without an excuse: the rest and refreshment they thus occasionally meet with enables them to bear up against the mortifications they must encounter in less favourable climes, and to continue the remainder of their voyage with spirit and alacrity. This consideration must be their apology for the stay they intend making where they now are. Indeed, the richness and beauty of the scenery before them are too captivating to be passed by inattentively even by the most careless observer. They are, in short, just going to land in "Peru," a newly discovered country in the poetical hemisphere; a country which, from the glimpse they have had of it, promises them every gratification. Their farther progress will, no doubt, confirm the ideas with which a first view has impressed them. But enough of allegory; let us now enter on the business of this article—the present poem is a production of the same elegant pen to which the public is indebted for the Legendary Tale, entitled, Edwin and Eltruda. The author, judiciously confining herself to the leading and most pathetic incidents in the history of the fall of the Peruvian empire, has not attempted to give a full narrative of all the interesting circumstances which lead to that memorable event.

The poem commences with a general description of the country, and the character of its inhabitants. After painting the external beauties of this favoured region, which, perhaps, may boast the prodigality of nature in preference to any other portion of the globe, the ingenious Author exhibits its moral portrait, previous to its invasion by the Spaniards, in colours at once glowing and just. The following intellectual group will convey an idea of the spirit and delicacy of her pencil:

[Quotes what became I: 41-54.]

In the same expressive style has she sketched out the consequences that flowed from the plunder of Peru:

[Quotes what became I: 179-82.]

The first appearance of Pizarro is in the second Canto, which concludes with the murder of Ataliba, and Alzira's consequent madness. In the next, the savage fanaticism of Valverde, a Spanish priest, and the benevolence of the amiable Las Casas, are admirably described. The fourth Canto is occupied by Almagro's expedition to Chili, and the events that took place at Cuzco during his absence....

The fifth Canto is in a great measure episodical, though not, indeed, unconnected with the principal story. It contains the loves of Zamor and Aciloe.

[Quotes what became V: 1-54.]

In the conflict which immediately succeeds, Alphonso, who has the command of the Spanish troops, is victorious. Aciloe hears that Zamor is slain, and her father, the Cazique, taken prisoner. Going to supplicate his release, Alphonso, smitten with her beauty, conceives a violent passion for her.

[Quotes what became V: 125-220.] ...

To add any commendations of this masterly poem, after the liberal extracts that have been given of it, would be unnecessary. If there be any thing to which we would object (and what is there that has nothing to be objected to?) it is the soliloquy of Alzira, who is driven to distraction by the murder of her husband Ataliba. The poetess has, we think, extended it to too great a length; had it been more compressed, its effect might possibly have been more forcible. In the structure of her verse we observe she frequently introduces the Trochaic:[1]

> But more the hollow sound the *wild winds* form,
> Its *white foam* trembling on the darken'd deep.

Occasionally introduced, it is not without its beauty: a too liberal use of it is all we would have guarded against.

5. From *Town and Country Magazine* 16 (July 1784): 380

This modest title veils an excellent poem; but as some more essential testimonial may be expected, than our bare *ipse dixit*,[2] we shall submit the following quotation from the first Canto.

[Quotes what became I: 137-76.]

---

1 A poetic meter consisting of a two-beat foot with a stressed syllable followed by an unstressed syllable. William Blake's "The Tyger" is one of the most famous examples of a poem written in trochaic tetrameter.

2 Asserted but not proven.

"Peru" in *Poems*, 2 vols. (London: T. Cadell, 1786)

6. From *The English Review* 8 (October 1786): 300-05

The writer of this article has already, on a former occasion,[1] had an opportunity of delivering his sentiments upon the talents and genius of Miss Williams, so far as they had then been displayed to the world. He imagined he, at that time, discovered in her an ability extremely superior to that which had been so much vaunted in some of her contemporary writers. He readily believed of this lady, that she was of too generous a turn of mind to wish to build her fame upon the ruins of another. But, inattentive to this circumstance, and preferring the information of the public to the gratification of the individual, he indulged that liberty which will ever be found to be the characteristic of honest criticism. He set Miss Seward and Miss Williams in contiguous pages; and he intended, by his manly censure of the one, and his sincere applause of the other, to place the respective merits of both in a more striking light....When we pronounced upon the poem of Peru, we could go no farther than we were authorized by the performance before us. We have too often found a merit, which we considered as rising and expansive, sinking afterwards into humble mediocrity. We saw defects in the cantos of Peru of no small magnitude; and we dared not unhesitatingly to predict that these would ultimately vanish; and that of consequence the amiable author would rise to first-rate perfection. What was at that time refused by the severity of criticism, is now most eagerly and most willingly bestowed by the warmth of admiration. Miss Williams, particularly from "The irregular Fragment found in a dark Passage of the Tower," is intitled to rank with the first votaries of imagination, and the most favoured children of the muses....

Having thus pointed out those beauties, in this exquisite *morceau,* that rise above the rest, and ... delight the imagination, we beg leave to pronounce of the whole of it that it deserves to be classed with those poems in the style of ode that do such distinguished honour to the English language—The Alexander's Feast, The Progress of Poesy, and The Bard.[2] While such performances are calculated to disgust the fastidious eye of anatomical criticism, and the austere mind that can bear nothing but literal truth, they will for ever be immeasurably dear to the true lovers of sublime and romantic melancholy.

---

1 See *The English Review,* Vol. IV. p. 28 [author's original note].

2 "Alexander's Feast, or the Power of Music" (1697), an ode by John Dryden; "The Progress of Poesy. A Pindaric Ode" (1754) and "The Bard. A Pindaric Ode" (1757) by Thomas Gray.

... [Miss Williams] is not cultivated in the school of elegance and refinement. She can never become, and we wish we could persuade her to believe it, an agreeable trifler. The Epistle to Dr. Moore, in which this style is attempted, will never add to her reputation, and serves only uselessly, we had almost said dishonourably, to blot twenty pages of her publication. Even the more delicate touches of the serious muse are not congenial to Miss Williams. Those finer touches, those strokes of unaffected nature, which distinguished a Shenstone and a Goldsmith,[1] she may aspire to, but she will never reach. The Edwin and Eltruda, destitute of these merits, is spiritless, undigested, desultory, and tedious. And why should she envy the writers we have named? Her's is a higher and a nobler province. She cannot mix, indeed, with a Theocritus[2] and a Gesner; but impartial posterity will associate her with a Spencer and a Gray.[3] The field of imagination is all her own. Here she may expatiate unrestrained. She may cull the choicest flowers of metaphor, and paint the beauteous offspring of her mind, in all the hues of the rainbow. She is dignified, elevated, and sublime. In this respect, she stands intirely secluded from the literary characters of her sex. The fictitious merits of a Seward, and the real excellence of a Sappho or a Barbauld,[4] would never have enabled them to describe the

> 'One big drop of deeper dye,
> The sanguine drop which wakes his woe.'[5]

In fine, it is the boast of the present age to have produced a Burney[6] and a Williams; ladies, who, labouring under a thousand disadvan-

---

1 William Shenstone (1714-63), English poet, and Oliver Goldsmith (1728?-74), Anglo-Irish poet, best known for *The Deserted Village* (1770).
2 Theocritus (c. 300-260 BCE), a Greek poet known for his idylls—brief pastoral poems that influenced Virgil and Milton.
3 Johann Matthias Gesner (1691-1761), friend of Johann Sebastian Bach and Professor of Poetry and Eloquence at the University of Göttingen; Edmund Spenser (c. 1553-99), author of *The Faerie Queene* (1590, 1596); Thomas Gray (1716-71), author of "Elegy Written in a Country Church Yard."
4 Anna Seward (1742-1809), English poet and sonneteer; Anna Letitia Barbauld (née Aikin) (1743-1825), English poet, children's author, and essay writer, author of *Eighteen Hundred and Eleven* (1812).
5 Imperfectly quoting "On one big drop of deeper dye," and "That sanguine drop which wakes his woe—" from Williams's "An Irregular Fragment, Found in a Dark Passage in the Tower" in volume II of *Poems* (1786), p. 40.
6 Frances (Fanny) Burney (later d'Arblay) (1752-1840), English author of *Evelina, or, A Young Lady's Entrance into the World* (1778), *Cecilia, or, Memoirs of an Heiress* (1782), and other novels.

tages, have equalled the happiest efforts of the prouder sex. Miss Burney, in comparative retirement, and full of modest reserve, has been enabled, by a kind of magic, to present us with the widest and most various canvas of men, manners, and character. Miss Williams ... has surpassed every thing that education could have done for her, and soared aloft, upon the wings of imagination, into the most elevated regions of sublimity.

7. From *The European Magazine, and London Review* 10 (August and September 1786): 89-93 and 177-80

When the age of this young Poetess, and, what she with great modesty and candour acknowledges, "the disadvantages of a confined education," are duly considered, he must be a surly and illiberal critic indeed, who would hesitate to pronounce these two little volumes a most agreeable acquisition to our youthful poetry; and that Miss Williams is by no means the least elegant and pleasing of the constellation of females who have lately illumined the British Parnassus.[1] Nay, we are almost tempted to declare, that in true elegant simplicity of poetic expression and colouring, and in the natural easy flow of her versification, she is unrivalled by any of her sisters. Except in some few instances, and those mostly in her *epic poem* Peru, the graceful ease and simplicity of her style is very different from that of a certain celebrated Poetess,[2] who is so continually straining at ornament, at boldness and novelty of phrase, and splendour of epithet heaped on epithet....

But high as our ideas are of the sweetness and natural elegance of Miss Williams's versification, we do not mean to say that her poetry is faultless. That would be doing her no service indeed; and we trust she has too much modesty and good sense, to refuse to avail herself of whatever blemishes may be pointed out in the following remarks on her Poems....

Of all this Lady's works, *Peru* has afforded the most scope to critics of different ranks. It has been called an *Epic Poem*, and highly extolled. That the versification and many of the parts deserve high praise, we readily allow. But in what its title to the name of *Epic Poem* consists, we cannot discover. *Epic* is derived, as every school-boy knows, from the Greek word for *discourse*, and thus far the most inconsistent jumble ever given in a fanatic sermon or political dispute at

---

1 In Greek mythology, Mount Parnassus was the home of the Muses; poetry, music and learning dwelt there, and it was associated with Apollo.

2 Possibly Anna Seward or Charlotte Smith, whose *Elegiac Sonnets* took the literary world by storm in 1784.

the *Goose* and *Gridiron*,[1] may be called *Epic*. But when the word *Poem* is added to the epithet, it has by the canons of criticism, from time immemorial, always been applied and understood to belong only to such poems as narrate some one principal event in its progress and catastrophe, elucidated by episodes connected with the event and its catastrophe, as the branches are with the tree. But such is not the conduct of Miss Williams's *Peru*. It is not even a Tale; for every tale, to be such, has an unity of one event in view.... [Quotes the "Argument" for each canto.]

From the above, the total want of connection is evident. Peru, as said before, is even not a *Tale*;—and General *Howe*'s American Gazettes[2] strung together only want rhyme to be equally entitled to the name of an *Epic Poem*. But justice must here own that it is not herself, but some more zealous than wise, of her admirers, who have given the title of *Epic Poem* to Miss Williams's *Peru*. She herself thus modestly professes that "*she has only aimed at a simple detail of some few incidents that make a part of that romantic story, where the unparalleled sufferings of an innocent and amiable people form the most affecting subjects of true pathos, while their climate, totally unlike our own, furnishes new and ample materials for poetic description.*"

The versification of Peru, and her other poems, has great natural ease, elegance and harmony. It is only when she does not trust to herself, but is straining after the manner of others, that she is faulty on that head. On other views she discovers inexperience, and mistaken ideas of pathos and poetry; it is not an eternal talking of *love*, and *woe*, and *delicious tears*. But whatever ample materials for poetic description the climate of Peru may furnish, our authoress has availed herself little of them. We can trace nothing appropriated in her landscapes. The hackneyed strain of all our flowery eastern tales, and visions, is adopted....

... [N]ot a trace of Miss Williams's *Ataliba*, and his happy reign, is to be found in history. The empire of Peru was yet reeking with the blood of its natives shed in the civil wars between Atabalipa and his elder brother Huescar, when the Spaniards arrived. Huescar was in prison, where he was murdered by order of Atabalipa, a few days before that Prince's own murder by the Spaniards; and the number of his concubines was one of the crimes alledged against him by the

---

1 A famous ale house in St. Paul's Churchyard in London.
2 During the American Revolution, British General William Howe (1729-1814), later 5th Viscount Howe, and his troops occupied the John Street Theatre in New York, where they produced plays. *The Royal American Gazette* referred to them as "Howe's strolling company" (Harvey 150 & n.).

Spaniards in his mock trial. We should not be surprised were we to find some *pathetic* German poetess celebrating our Henry the Eighth for his wonderful and unshaken love and constancy to Anne Bulleine and Jean Seymour [misspellings intentional]. Had Miss Williams confined her stories of love, all ardour and purity, to names wholly fictitious; as her Zamor and Aciloe; her Zilia, &c. &c. they might have passed very well; but where we have no character delineated before us by a train of conduct, as in the Iliad, and in every good Tragedy, the concise assertions of the poet, as in Miss Williams's *Ataliba*, ought not to outrage the facts of well-known history. When the poet falls into this error, the reader, who knows the history, is as much dissatisfied as he would be with a serious elegy on the conjugal tenderness and constancy of our Eighth Henry.

From the arguments of the six Cantos of Peru it appears that the author's design was to aim at tenderness, and to excite pity and the finer feelings. Love and the happy deaths of lovers, some self-murdered and some dying of pure grief, are the chief business of every Canto; and one half of such stories might either be left out, or twenty more added, without the least injury to the connection of the poem; if it be allowable to talk of the connection of a poem which in reality has none.

To those who admire the flowery strain and romantic and wild tenderness of eastern tales (not often quite natural) we recommend the Fifth Canto of Peru. It is, indeed, a master-piece of the kind, and, detached from the rest, is one complete tale, where the interest arising from *unity* is pleasingly felt by the reader. It is, without doubt, in every respect the best part of Peru, which, on the whole, as we have already said, contains, in particular parts, great and genuine poetic merit.

We have much exceeded our usual bounds in these remarks on the Poems of Miss Williams. Our good opinion of her happy genius led us into it, and we were sorry to see a young lady capable of all the natural ornaments and elegant simplicity of classical diction, too often led astray from the bent of her own genius, in search of that tawdry tinsel richness of strained expression, which is too much the characteristic of a great part of the present *fashionable* poetry; and we flatter ourselves that she will profit by the consideration of the blemishes we have pointed out.

8. From *The Monthly Review* 75 (July 1786): 44-49

Miss Williams is already known to the Public, as the writer of the *Legendary Tale of Edwin and Eltruda*, *An Ode on the Peace*, and an historical poem, entitled, *Peru*; pieces which have very justly obtained her no inconsiderable share of reputation. These poems are now republished, after a careful revisal, with corrections and improvements; and to these the Author has added several others, of at least equal merit....

9. From *The New Review* 9 (1786): 337-38

To the few who have not already these Poems, (for there are fifteen hundred subscribers, and most of them the most respectable that ever graced any list); to the many who feel for the worth of private character, rendered still more respectable by a train of misfortunes, I beg leave to recommend the following Sonnets, and to say that there are many of the little pieces equally good throughout; and many stanzas in the larger ones equal to them. [Quotes in full "Sonnet, to Mrs. Bates" and "Sonnet, to Twilight."]

10. From *The New Annual Register* 7.3 (1786): 278

The Poetical History of the year, were we to mention every publication in verse, or rhyme, with which the press hath teemed, would comprehend a vast variety of articles. But we shall only give an account, in our usual compressed form, of such of them as have superior claims to our commendation or notice. In this number are the "Poems by Helen Maria Williams, in two vols." This work consists, partly, of a republication, with corrections and improvements, of some pieces which had obtained for our poetess a considerable share of reputation; and, partly, of some new pieces, which entitle her to rank among the most favoured children of the Muses.

11. From *The English Lyceum* 2 (1787): 45

But the only poem which has lately appeared, professedly founded on the epic plan, is Miss Williams's Peru, which is pleasing and elegant, and such an epic poem as we might expect from the more weak, but not less polished, mind of a female. Miss Williams is indeed a charming poet, and though inferior for splendour of fancy to Miss Seward, can boast more nature, and consequently greater power over the heart.

"Peruvian Tales" in *Poems on Various Subjects* (London: Whittaker, 1823)

12. From *The European Magazine, and London Review* 83 (April 1823): 355-56

It is pleasurable to see the name of this lady again in print, as it recalls to our imagination the older times, when her talents were a passport for her into the society of Johnson, Goldsmith, and the literary host of that memorable period; who does not recollect Boswell's anecdote of the Doctor's complimentary reception of this lady after the appearance of her Ode to Liberty? Her merit won the esteem even of that prejudiced critic, although her fine principles of liberty were, of all others, calculated to inflame his passions and excite his animosity.... If there be any difference of opinion as to the merit of the poems, nobody can hesitate to acknowledge that beauty which this lady's compositions in prose derive from the dignity and consistency of her sentiments, and from the animation and vivacity of her manner.... Miss Williams's sentiments upon public liberty have been justly praised by most eminent writers, but in her enmity to Napoleon, for sacrificing the cause of freedom to his military mania and personal ambition, she appears to us to do too little homage to the surprising talents of that stupendous character, nor does she give a just consideration of the extraordinary circumstances in which he was placed. Miss Williams gives a few tokens of her poetic taste, having been a little affected by her long residence in France.... On the whole, we have seldom read thirty more amusing pages than the introduction to this volume.

The poems are very numerous, and the greater part of a lighter description. Many of them have before appeared in print, and we have no doubt that several of them will be recognised by her readers. The Ode to Peace is remarkably fine, and replete with the rapture and nobleness of thought, which characterise this species of poem. Some of the sonnets are ingenious and elegant, that to Hope is new in its ideas. The sonnet to Burns' Mountain Daisy is forcible, whilst those to Twilight and to the Moon are elegant and tinged with a shade of melancholy, to express which the sonnet is peculiarly adapted. The highest species of composition in the volume are the Peruvian Tales, occupying about sixty pages. These contain passages of fire and of pathos, and may be read with pleasure and improvement. We think the volume a very acceptable offering to the public; and it will be valued by many as a reminiscence of a lady whose name was once so familiar to our studies, but whose pen has latterly kept no pace with the promise of her earlier productions.

13. From *The Literary Gazette* 7 (8 February 1823): 82-83

The celebrity of this lady's name induced us to give an early perusal to her book. Had she lived as long and as lately in England as she has done in France, she would hardly have inflicted such a penance upon us; for she would have known that scores of better works, both in prose and verse, are almost monthly consigned to oblivion. Indeed nothing but that doting affection which we feel for our youthful performances could have led to this publication; and we are sorry the able translator of Humboldt should have afforded so unadvised an example of that frailty. Miss Williams seems to think that if her quondam old friends were still in office at the head of our critical journals, she would have stood a good chance of their favourable report: we cannot tell how that matter stands, but we can inform her that the wide diffusion of knowledge which has taken place since she went to reside in Paris, has rendered partial criticism a very ticklish thing among the present generation, and that the public acumen is so highly cultivated (we do not say public opinion is so jealous) that the recommendation of a bad book only d—ns the panegyrist without serving the author. All that is now in the power of a Reviewer (beyond perhaps two or three experiments the other way) is to promote the success of valuable productions by making their merits known. On these grounds, we trust Miss W. will pardon us for not responding to her appeal to the *moderns* in the tone of praise which our respect for her talents and our admiration for her sex would have rendered so pleasing to us....

... [W]hat an argument against Revolution under the semblance of Reform! After these confessions, one might think the writer was no advocate for changes; but the worthy old lady appears to be just as anxious for revolutions, new rulers, and new disappointments, as ever she was. We beg our readers to consider this as philosophy, not politics—we seldom offend, but such consummate folly is provoking.

The poetry is hardly worth the name: little of it would in our day be admitted into the poorest magazine. There are some very mediocre Peruvian tales, ballad tales still worse, and odes and sonnets, &c. on all the hacknied common-place subjects.

14. From *The Monthly Review* 102 (September 1823): 20-31

The name of Miss Williams has been so long and so frequently before the public, and her literary character, from its outset, has been so connected with some of the deepest and most pathetic feelings of human nature during revolutionary periods, that it cannot have been easily dismissed from general recollection. Her labors in the vast field of modern literature and research have, indeed, been equally various and persevering, occupying the whole of the present together with the latter part of the past century: her opinions have given rise to some discussion; and her political as well as literary views have subjected her to much periodical animadversion. The disputed points and questions, however, leading to this mixed controversy, having been for some time set at rest, it would here be worse th[a]n tedious and useless to revive them; and we shall pass on without farther comment on her former productions in the shape of Letters, Novels, Travels, and Poems, excepting as they are recalled to us by the compositions in the work before us.

It is fairly stated by the writer that some of the contents of this volume are not now for the first time laid before her readers, having been published many years since in two small volumes, which have been "long out of print:" others have been scattered in different works; and those which now first make their appearance are rather of a slighter texture, and form by no means the most interesting portion of the whole. Such, we think, as bear reference to public events, and most of which have already been published, are far superior to the rest; for they have more spirit and poetry, because dictated perhaps by those liberal and patriotic feelings, for which the muse of Miss W. has long been celebrated. Of this character are the "Peruvian Tales in Verse," (formerly given to the public under the title of "Peru,") "A Poem on the Bill passed for regulating the Slave-Trade," and two odes, "On the taking of the Bastille," and on "The Peace signed between the French and English" at Amiens in the year 1801....

Not meaning to undervalue the merits of Miss W.'s poetry, which is always above mediocrity though wanting in some of the higher characteristics of genius, we must be allowed to express a far higher opinion of her prose-writings.... Indeed, the value of the present work, in our estimation, is considerably enhanced by the force and elegance of its prefatory remarks, the spirit and good feeling which they display, and the correct information which they furnish relative to the existing state of science and literature in France....

Perhaps, the poetic character of Miss W. is already too well known to receive much elucidation, or addition, from the accompanying specimens afforded by her later effusions; which, whatever positive degree of merit they may possess, would suffer from a comparison with some of her earlier pieces. This, however, is a sort of parallel on which we feel the same reluctance to enter that we should experience in instituting an inquiry into the changes, varieties, and apparent inconsistencies of political opinion, in which this lady is said, of late years, to have involved herself. On this head, it will be enough to admit that, from the very singular and unexpected course of events in France, as great a diversity and opposition of sentiments must arise; and Miss W. may have had reason at different times to express different views and expectations, by which she became undeservedly exposed to a certain degree of obloquy or suspicion. For ourselves, we can readily account for her enmity towards Bonaparte, without accusing her of tergiversation:—we can even forgive her for hailing the restoration, with the constitutional charter of *Louis le Désiré*,[1] as a prospect of better things, until he proved a deceiver and an oppressor:—but we cannot so easily account for, or reconcile to her known love of liberty, all her subsequent devotion to the Bourbon family.[2] There is certainly something in the tone and character of "A Narrative of Events, from the Landing of Bonaparte to the Restoration of Louis XVIII," which we do not quite approve:—we find not in it the same clearness, earnestness, and decision, or the same degree of honorable political avowal and sincerity, which distinguish some of her earlier writings.

---

1 King Louis XVIII (1755-1824), who, after the defeat of Napoleon, ruled France until 1824 as a constitutional monarchy.

2 The French royal family. The House of Bourbon ruled France from 1589 until the French revolutionaries overthrew them in 1792. They regained power in 1815, after Napoleon's defeat at Waterloo.

Select Bibliography

B———o, J. "Sonnet. To Miss Helena-Maria Williams." *The European Magazine, and London Review* 12 (1787): 152.

Burke, Edmund and William Burke. *An Account of the European Settlements in America*. In Six Parts. Fifth edition, 2 vols. London: J. Dodsley, 1770.

Castro, Daniel. *Another Face of Empire: Bartolomé de Las Casas, Indigenous Rights, and Ecclesiastical Imperialism*. Durham: Duke UP, 2007.

The Catholic Encyclopedia. New York: Robert Appleton, 1913.

Clayden, Peter William. *The Early Life of Samuel Rogers*. Boston: Roberts Brothers, 1888.

Combe, William. *The First of April: Or, the Triumphs of Folly: a Poem*. London: J. Bew, 1777.

Cowley, Abraham. *Poems*. London: Humphrey Moseley, 1656.

Damián, Jessica. "Helen Maria Williams's Personal Narrative of Travels from *Peru* (1784) to *Peruvian Tales* (1823)." *Nineteenth-Century Gender Studies* 3.2 (Summer 2007): 1-27.

Darvill, Timothy. "Cuzco." *The Concise Oxford Dictionary of Archaeology*. Oxford: Oxford UP, 2002. 120.

"Domestic Literature." *The New Annual Register* (1785): 210-76.

E., "Sonnet to Miss Helen Maria Williams, on her Poem of *Peru*." *The Gentleman's Magazine* 56 (June 1786): 513.

Eliza. "To Miss Helen Maria Williams: On her Poem of *Peru*." *The Gentleman's Magazine* 54 (July 1784): 532.

Godwin, William. *Memoirs of the Author of* A Vindication of the Rights of Woman. Ed. Pamela Clemit and Gina Luria Walker. Peterborough, ON: Broadview P, 2001.

Graffigny, Françoise de. *Letters Written by a Peruvian Lady*. Dublin: S. Powell, 1748.

———. *Letters from a Peruvian Woman*. Trans. David Kornacker. New York: Modern Language Association, 1993.

———. *Lettres d'une Péruvienne, nouvelle édition, augmentée de plusieurs lettres, et d'une introduction à l'histoire*. 1747. 2nd ed. 2 vols. Paris: Chez Duchesne, 1752.

Gravil, Richard. *Wordsworth and Helen Maria Williams*. Penrith: Humanities-Ebooks, 2010.

Gray, Thomas. "The Progress of Poesy. A Pindaric Ode." *Odes by Mr. Gray*. London: R. and J. Dodsley, 1757.

Griffin, Dustin. "Milton and the Decline of Epic in the Eighteenth Century." *New Literary History* 14.1 (1982): 143-54.

Hargraves, Neil. "The 'Progress of Ambition': Character, Narrative, and Philosophy in the Works of William Robertson." *Journal of the History of Ideas* 63.2 (April 2002): 261-82.

Harvey, Douglas S. *Theater and Empire*. Ann Arbor: UMI, 2008.

Hayley, William. *An Essay on Epic Poetry; In Five Epistles to the Rev. Mr. Mason*. London: J. Dodsley, 1782.

Hemming, John. *The Conquest of the Incas*. New York: Harcourt, Brace, Jovanovich, 1970.

Homer. *Iliad*. Trans. Stanley Lombardo. Indianapolis: Hackett, 1997.

Irvine, Dallas D. "Abbé Raynal and British Humanitarianism." *The Journal of Modern History* 3.4 (December 1931): 564-77.

Jarrells, Anthony. "Provincializing Enlightenment: Edinburgh Historicism and the Blackwoodian Regional Tale." *Studies in Romanticism* 48.2 (2009): 257-77.

Kennedy, Deborah. *Helen Maria Williams and the Age of Revolution*. Lewisburg: Bucknell UP, 2002.

Klarén, Peter Flindell. *Peru: Society and Nationhood in the Andes*. New York: Oxford UP, 2000.

Knight, Alice. *Las Casas*. New York: Neal, 1917.

Leask, Nigel. "Salons, Alps and Cordilleras: Helen Maria Williams, Alexander von Humboldt, and the Discourse of Romantic Travel." *Women, Writing and the Public Sphere 1700-1830*. Ed. Elizabeth Eger, Charlotte Grant, Clíona Ó Gallchoir, and Penny Warburton. Cambridge: Cambridge UP, 2001. 217-38.

Lockhart, James. *The Men of Cajamarca: A Social and Biographical Study of the First Conquerors of Peru*. Austin: U of Texas P, 1972.

———. *Spanish Peru, 1532-1560: A Social History*. 1968. 2nd ed. Madison: U of Wisconsin P, 1994.

MacQuarrie, Kim. *The Last Days of the Incas*. New York: Simon and Schuster, 2007.

Marmontel, Jean-François. *Les Incas*. 1777. Translated into English as *The Incas: or, The Destruction of the Empire of Peru*. 2 vols. Dublin: A. Stewart, 1797.

Milton, John. *Paradise Lost, A Poem in Twelve Books*. 2 vols. London: R. Bladen, T. Lawes, S. Crowder, C. Ware, and T. Payne, 1784.

Mitchell, Robert Edward. "'The soul that dreams it shares the power it feels so well': The Politics of Sympathy in the Abolitionist Verse of Williams and Yearsley." *Romanticism on the Net* 29-30 (February-May 2003). Web. <www.erudit.org/revue/ron/2003/v/n29/oo7719ar.html>.

Piozzi, Hester Lynch. *The Piozzi Letters: Correspondence of Hester Lynch Piozzi, 1784-1821*. Ed. Edward A. and Lillian D. Bloom. Newark: U of Delaware P, 1989.

Plumwood, Val. *Feminism and the Mastery of Nature.* New York: Routledge, 1993.

Polewhele, Richard. *The Unsex'd Females: A Poem.* London: Cadell and Davies, 1798.

Racine, Karen. *Francisco de Miranda: A Transatlantic Life in the Age of Revolution.* Wilmington, DE: Scholarly Resources, 2003.

Raynal, Abbé. *A Philosophical and Political History of the Settlements and Trade of the Europeans in the East and West Indies,* 3rd ed. (2 vols.) revised and corrected. Trans. J. Justamond. London: Thomas Cadell, 1777.

Reviews of *Peru:*
  The New Annual Register ... for the Year 1784 5.3 (1785): 268-69.
  The Critical Review 57 (May 1784): 376-80.
  The English Review 4 (July 1784): 28-31 and 8 (October 1786): 300-05.
  The London Magazine n.s. 3 (1784) 474-76.
  Town and Country Magazine 16 (July 1784): 380.
  The European Magazine, and London Review 10 (1786): 89-93 and 177-80.
  The Monthly Review 71 (July 1784): 12-20 and 75 (July 1786): 44-49.
  The New Review 9 (1786): 337-38.
  The New Annual Register 7.3 (1786): 278.
  The English Lyceum 2 (1787): 45.

Reviews of "Peruvian Tales":
  The Literary Gazette 7 (8 February 1823): 82-83.
  The European Magazine, and London Review 83 (April 1823): 355-56.
  The Monthly Review 102 (September 1823): 20-31.

Richardson, Alan. "Epic Ambivalence: Imperial Politics and Romantic Deflection in Williams' *Peru* and Landor's *Gebir.*" *Romanticism, Race, and Imperial Culture, 1780-1834.* Ed. Alan Richardson and Sonia Hofkosh. Bloomington: Indiana UP, 1990. 265-82.

Robertson, William. *The History of America.* London: W. Strahan; T. Cadell; Edinburgh: J. Balfour, 1777.

Robertson, William Spence. *The Life of Miranda.* 2 vols. Chapel Hill: U of North Carolina P, 1929.

Robinson, Jeffrey C. *Unfettering Poetry: Fancy in British Romanticism.* New York: Palgrave, 2006.

Seward, Anna. "Sonnet to Miss Williams on her Epic Poem *Peru.*" *The Gentleman's Magazine* 54 (August 1784): 613.

Shields, David. *Oracles of Empire: Poetry, Politics, and Commerce in British America, 1690-1750.* Chicago: U of Chicago P, 1990.

Starn, Orin, Carlos Iván Degregori, and Robin Kirk, eds. *The Peru Reader: History, Culture, Politics*. Durham: Duke UP, 1995.

Stirling, Stuart. *Pizarro: Conqueror of the Inca*. Stroud: Sutton P, 2005.

Thorning, Joseph Francis. *Miranda: World Citizen*. Gainesville: U of Florida P, 1952.

Tucker, Herbert F. *Epic: Britain's Heroic Muse, 1790-1910*. Oxford: Oxford UP, 2008.

Upton, W. "To Miss Helen Maria Williams. Authoress of *Peru*, a Poem." *Public Advertiser* (31 March 1786): 2.

Virgil. *The Aeneid of Virgil*. Trans. Rolfe Humphries. Ed. Brian Wilkie. Englewood Cliffs, NJ: Prentice Hall, 1987.

Voltaire. *Alzire, ou les Américains, tragédie de M. de Voltaire, représentée à Paris pour la première fois le 27 janvier 1736*. Paris: Bauche, 1736.

Walls, Laura Dassow. *The Passage to Cosmos: Alexander von Humboldt and the Shaping of America*. Chicago: U of Chicago P, 2009.

Warton, Joseph. "The Dying Indian." In *A Collection of Poems by Several Hands*. Ed. Robert Dodsley. Vol. 4. London: R. and J. Dodsley, 1755. 209-10.

——. "The Revenge of America." In *A Collection of Poems by Several Hands*. Ed. Robert Dodsley. Vol. 4. London: R. and J. Dodsley, 1755. 208-09.

Williams, Helen Maria. *Letters Written in France*. Ed. Neil Fraistat and Susan S. Lanser. Peterborough, ON: Broadview P, 2001.

——. *An Ode on the Peace*. London: T. Cadell, 1783.

——, [trans.]. Bernardin de Saint-Pierre, Jacques-Henri. *Paul and Virginia*. Paris: [John Hurford Stone?], 1795.

——. *Peru, A Poem*. London: Thomas Cadell, 1784.

——. "Peruvian Tales." *Poems on Various Subjects*. London: Whittaker, 1823.

——. *A Poem on the Bill Lately Passed for Regulating the Slave Trade*. London: T. Cadell, 1788.

——. *Poems*. 2 vols. London: Thomas Cadell, 1786.

Wollstonecraft, Mary. *Collected Letters of Mary Wollstonecraft*. Ed. Ralph M. Wardle. Ithaca: Cornell UP, 1979.

Womack, William. "Guillaume Raynal and the Eighteenth-Century Cult of the Noble Savage." *The Bulletin of the Rocky Mountain Modern Language Association* 26.3 (1972): 98-107.

Wordsworth, William. *Early Poems and Fragments, 1785-1797*. Ed. Carol Landon and Jared Curtis. Ithaca: Cornell UP, 1997.

[Wordsworth, William.] Axiologus. "Sonnet, on Seeing Miss Helen Maria Williams Weep at a Tale of Distress." *The European Magazine, and London Review* 11 (March 1787): 202.

Wu, Duncan. *Wordsworth's Reading 1770-1799*. Cambridge: Cambridge UP, 1993.

Yeğenoğlu, Meyda. *Colonial Fantasies: Towards a Feminist Reading of Orientalism*. Cambridge: Cambridge UP, 1998.

from the publisher

A name never says it all, but the word "broadview" expresses a good deal of the philosophy behind our company. We are open to a broad range of academic approaches and political viewpoints. We pay attention to the broad impact book publishing and book printing has in the wider world; we began using recycled stock more than a decade ago, and for some years now we have used 100% recycled paper for most titles. As a Canadian-based company we naturally publish a number of titles with a Canadian emphasis, but our publishing program overall is internationally oriented and broad-ranging. Our individual titles often appeal to a broad readership too; many are of interest as much to general readers as to academics and students.

Founded in 1985, Broadview remains a fully independent company owned by its shareholders—not an imprint or subsidiary of a larger multinational.

If you would like to find out more about Broadview and about the books we publish, please visit us at **www.broadviewpress.com**. And if you'd like to place an order through the site, we'd like to show our appreciation by extending a special discount to you: by entering the code below you will receive a 20% discount on purchases made through the Broadview website.

Discount code: **broadview20%**

Thank you for choosing Broadview.

Please note: this offer applies only to sales of
bound books within the United States or Canada.

The interior of this book is printed on 100% recycled paper.